Manufacturing the Future

Strategic resonance for
enlightened manufacturing

STEVE BROWN

FINANCIAL TIMES
Prentice Hall

an imprint of Pearson Education

London • New York • San Francisco • Toronto • Sydney • Tokyo • Singapore • Hong Kong

Cape Town • Madrid • Paris • Milan • Munich • Amsterdam

PEARSON EDUCATION LIMITED

Head Office:
Edinburgh Gate
Harlow CM20 2JE
Tel: +44 (0)1279 623623
Fax: +44 (0)1279 431059

London Office:
128 Long Acre
London WC2E 9AN
Tel: +44 (0)20 7447 2000
Fax: +44 (0)20 7240 5771
Website: www.business-minds.com

First published in Great Britain in 2000

The right of Steve Brown to be identified as author
of this work has been asserted by him in accordance
with the Copyright, Designs and Patents Act 1988.

ISBN 0 273 64322 3

British Library Cataloguing in Publication Data
A CIP catalogue record for this book can be obtained from the British Library

10 9 8 7 6 5 4 3 2 1

Typeset by M Rules
Printed and bound in Great Britain by Biddles Ltd., Guildford & King's Lynn

The Publishers' policy is to use paper manufactured from sustainable forests.

Contents

Acknowledgements

I have many people to thank for this book. I am fortunate to be surrounded by excellent colleagues at the University of Bath's School of Management – in particular those in the Operations Management Group: Kate Blackmon; Harvey Maylor; Paul Cousins; as well as Richard Lamming, the Director of the Centre for Research in Strategic Purchasing and Supply (CRISPS). Thanks to Kate Blackmon, Felicia Fai and Sarah Crampin who read various chapters at different stages of completion. My thanks also go to Professor Brian Bayliss, the Director of the University of Bath's School of Management, for his support. I am visiting professor at Baruch College, City University, New York, and I am indebted to colleagues there who have commented on, and supported, the research and work – in particular T.K. Das, George Schneller and Al Booke.

I have very good friends at the University of Brighton, including Colin Harris (who made useful comments of draft chapters), Sue Ridley and Alison Bone.

My thanks go to Pradeep Jethi, who signed the book, and to Richard Stagg and other staff at Pearson Education who continued with the initial momentum, enthusiasm and commitment to it.

I owe a great deal of gratitude to those plants that provided data for the book. Thank you for your involvement, as well as for your honesty and commitment to this research. Without you there would be no book.

Most of all my thanks go to Violaine who not only puts up with my locking myself away in my office at home for hours on end so that I can write but also makes it all worthwhile!

Introduction

Whenever I go into a manufacturing plant I do not tend to see an average plant. Rather, I see a plant that is going in one of two directions. The plant is either equipping itself to compete successfully in a very dynamic, exciting, but challenging business environment, or I see a plant that is going in the opposite direction and is failing to equip itself in a range of necessary operations capabilities. There are many reasons why plants go in either direction, and the change from a traditional to an enlightened approach – whereby the plant changes direction and equips itself in order to compete – does not come about by chance. It comes about on a strategic level. Often the change does not come because a CEO wakes up one day and decides that it would be a good thing to do. Instead, change often comes about because the plant – and the firm within which the plant operates – recognizes that it must change. This recognition will come either from customer feedback or from awareness of the expertise of a competitive plant, or sometimes both. But many firms and plants struggle to change. They struggle because they are limited by their senior managers who are often too busy measuring the wrong things. For example, as you will see in later chapters I am very wary of using accounting ratios as a means of determining how well a plant is doing because it is not until you walk around the plant that you see how it is really performing. In other words, the accounting numbers are important, but they are not sufficient. What does make the difference in becoming an enlightened plant are the following:

- excellent layouts
- customer-focused operations
- excellent – but not excessive – process technology
- commitment to innovation
- superb process and product quality
- expert inventory systems aligned with strategic partnerships with suppliers
- trained, dedicated men and women in the plant who actually care about what they are doing.

I have had the honour of working with plants and firms that have transformed themselves from traditional to enlightened. As a result, these plants are out-performing their competitors, and more to the point they are delighting their customers. This book is not about trying to score points over other publications that have made, and continue to make, important contributions to improving capabilities within plants. However, what I have seen time and time again are plants struggling to achieve lean or world-class capabilities because they fail to understand the underpinning strategic factors that shape their plants. I have often spoken with senior-level strategic-decision makers within firms who know very little about the plants' operational capabilities and who then make strategic decisions that are almost designed to fail. As a result, a plant attempts to become lean, agile or world class (assuming that it knows what these terms really mean in the first place) but does not realize that the firm's strategy process is fatally flawed and will prevent the plant from achieving these operations capabilities. The world has changed since Richard Schonberger wrote his influential book, *World Class Manufacturing*. Then the term 'world class' meant being better than others; now it merely means being able to compete at all in a business world that is more intense than ever before due to the enhanced capabilities of existing firms, as well as the emergence of new entrants from all over the globe.

Strategy has often been talked of as an either/or scenario, which may be described as an *outside-in* or *inside-out* approach. The outside-in approach is to see what changes are happening in the business world, including market requirements, and then to devise strategies around these. The inside-out approach is where firms – aware of terms like *core competencies* and *distinctive capabilities* – will then try to apply their particular abilities to market segments. Both approaches are fatally flawed. The outside-in approach means that the firm might well chase after markets in which it has no hope of being successful because it does not have operations capabilities; the competence approach can mean that the firm offers capabilities or competencies that nobody wants. That is not so say that this is what the original authors had in mind. Rather it has to do with the misunderstanding that firms have in trying to apply either approach to strategy.

There is a better approach, which combines both, simultaneously. I use the term *strategic resonance* to describe the process whereby a firm makes sure that resonance takes place in two ways:

- between strategic decisions and operations capabilities within the firm; and
- between the firm and its customers.

However, this process can be extremely difficult to do successfully because, as I mentioned earlier, those at the senior, strategic-decision-making levels of the firm are sometimes not fully aware of the potential strategic power – or severe weaknesses – within the firm's operations.

This book talks about enlightened and traditional plants. Enlightened plants are those that create and sustain strategic resonance and who outperform their traditional counterparts in all areas of operations. Traditional plants, by contrast, are those whose strategy processes are imbedded in the bygone age of mass production. As a consequence, these plants and firms fail to equip their operations with sufficient capabilities in order to compete against the best in the world and, just as important, to satisfy customer requirements. I have been in many traditional plants where, through a complete misunderstanding of lean and re-engineering initiatives, core areas of expertise have been wiped out. I have looked in the eyes of men and women who have been betrayed by senior managers who formerly sold ideas of total quality management (TQM), business process re-engineering (BPR), and Lean and Flexibility, to the workforce and then 'rewarded' their efforts with cynical downsizing. As a result, some of the traditional plants became anorexic rather than lean. These plants were unable to heal the damage inflicted on their workforce whose trust had been broken. Just as important was that the plants were then unable to compete.

In contrast, it has been a pleasure to see those plants that are enlightened. They are exciting, vibrant places to work in where operations are customer-focused. It is no coincidence that these plants are full of men and women who care passionately about what they do and who are rewarded – in a range of imaginative ways – for the quality of their performance.

Just a short while before this book went to print I gave a speech in front of a number of managers. I mentioned that one of the delights of being in an enlightened plant or firm was seeing how vibrant the place could be. I gave an example of how, in one of the reception areas of an enlightened plant, there were grown men and women playing basketball. I have visited many plants and seeing men and women having fun like this in the reception area is clearly a refreshing contrast to many other reception areas that are lifeless, unexciting places. However, the interesting point for me was that those who listened to the speech approached me afterwards and wanted to know answers to questions such as: 'How often should basketball be played – every day, once a week/month, etc.?' 'Who should play – should it be managers and workers, together?' 'Why basketball in particular – wouldn't another game be just as good?' Of course, these sort of questions miss the point. The basketball story was an anecdotal – but telling – account of how creative and different enlightened plants can be. It was curious to see how managers wanted to capture the 'magic' of such plants by writing a set of rules and procedures on how to recreate such fun and magic in their own workplace! But at least they wanted to become enlightened in their approaches to manufacturing – and that can only be a good thing.

This book is intended to be read by all levels of management in manufacturing firms, as well as by those intending to become managers in manufacturing. Manufacturing is no longer just about being lean or world-class, important as these are. It is about a radically different, strategically orientated approach to manufacturing. It is about becoming enlightened through creating and sustaining strategic resonance.

1

Strategy matters

Introduction

Strategy is vitally important; in this chapter, I will look at the reasons why it is important, and how strategy has changed over time. Many managers that I have spoken with, having previously been fed on a management diet of over-simplified, prescriptive recipes contained within many strategic models, have almost given up on strategy. You can certainly sympathize with those managers who have become indifferent to strategic models. Many of these models are static, some are irrelevant and others are, frankly, dangerous. Some strategy models come in what appear to be easy-to-use matrices consisting of four or more mutually exclusive boxes. This seems to appeal to managers and academics alike. These matrices may be of some use for teaching purposes, but the effective transfer from the classroom to the business world is suspect because the business world is a great deal more complex than some of these matrices suggest. We must not relegate strategy to a process of lining up the firm – either in its entirety or via its range of products – in a number of mutually exclusive boxes within a matrix. As you will see in this chapter, strategy is a much more dynamic process than that.

Some managers that I have interviewed have become stale and unenthusiastic about the potential worth and contribution of strategy. As a result, they seem incapable of crafting strategy that both aligns with, and makes best possible use of, existing and future capabilities of their operations. Strategy matters in spite of the fact that sometimes even well-intentioned strategies have failed to gain competitive advantage for the firm. The chief reason why these strategies fail is that they do not take on board the capabilities, or just as important, the non-capabilities, of the firm's operations. It is futile to have a strategy that cannot be achieved due to the incapability of operations within the firm or plant. Putting this more positively, the key to good strategy is that the strategy process will be fully aware of, and will make the best possible use of, capabilities and it will do so in order to satisfy customers.

This chapter asks the key question: 'What is strategy and does it matter?'[1] But the chapter warns against some of the popular approaches and argues for a radical departure from some of the previously perceived wisdom on 'how to do strategy'. Strategy matters in spite, or even because, of the continuing, massive amounts of uncertainty that many firms face in the majority of industries. Indeed, in such volatile environments strategy has become more important than ever before. Harvard's Hayes and Pisano were right when they stated:

> In today's turbulent competitive environment, a company more than ever needs a strategy that specifies the kind of competitive advantage that it is seeking in the marketplace and articulates how that advantage is to be achieved.[2]

Strategy matters because without it a firm does not have direction. Consequently, any successes that it may gain will be by fluke. For sure, there are success stories that appear to have been achieved by pure chance – or so the stories would have us believe. But get to the core of the success and you will nearly always find that a firm was poised and ready by its capabilities and then met a market opportunity. It was able to respond more quickly, or with better quality, or with a greater range of offerings than its competitors. All of these capabilities are what the firm does, and does via its company-wide operations.

Strategy has little to do with the degree of formality given to the strategic planning process. Nor is strategy dependent upon how well the mission of the strategy is articulated. Strategy includes understanding and securing the means by which the firm will satisfy customer requirements. The strategy formulation process can include inventing new markets; it will almost always mean rethinking the nature of the operations processes that the firm currently employs. This will sometimes mean radically rethinking operations processes in those firms that have not properly undertaken strategy planning for some time.

Getting rid of two myths of strategy

The top-down myth of strategy

It is clear that many practitioners, as well as trade and academic publications, treat corporate and business strategy as some sort of elitist activity, as if the CEO and very senior-level managers/vice presidents alone should determine it.[3] Take the personal computer (PC) industry as an example.

Throughout the 1990s, the business press continually reported on various changes of CEOs and made suggestions as to what each new CEO would need to do, almost single-handedly, to improve their respective firms. For example, in the early 1990s, there were vast numbers of articles on what Lou Gerstner would need to do once he became the new CEO at IBM in 1993. Similarly, the business press freely advised as to what various CEOs should do at Apple – the reality, though, was that both Splinder and Amelio were ousted from their posts after very short times. Steve Jobs later returned to take over the helm. Large amounts of press were dedicated to articles on CEO changes at both Hewlett-Packard and Compaq once Eckhard Pfeiffer and Lew Platt had left. Undoubtedly the role of the CEO is vital and crucial. But a CEO cannot articulate any sort of mission unless he or she has immense knowledge about, and a strategy for, the firm's operations. As you shall see, for some, strategic operations planning based on capabilities (or incapabilities) come as an after thought – a consideration to be put in place once the so-called business strategy has been devised. But this approach to strategy for a firm serious about competing in the new millennium is wrong, and it is old!

Strategy is seen by some as something that is devised at the highest levels of the firm – where, as you shall see in this chapter, in some firms there may not be any senior-level manufacturing, or operations management presence – and then simply 'passed down' through levels of hierarchy, with all the filters and blockages to accomplishing the strategy that this may bring. Pick up any textbook of strategy and the same old models seem to appear time after time. The model goes like this. Strategy starts at the top (the corporate level); it then passes down to business levels (where business strategy is devised), and then passes down again to functional levels, including operations. Some publications say that there should, ideally, be dialogue in the process – particularly where a resource-driven (not necessarily including operations capabilities, by the way) strategy is being pursued. However, in the main, the top-down model of strategy remains the dominant model – you will see it articulated especially when a new CEO is put in place. All eyes will be on how the person at the top of the hierarchy will create a strategy. But the model is fatally flawed because it:

- enforces the idea of different realms of strategy – each with its own agenda – within the three levels of the firm;
- assumes that corporate decisions will, somehow, line up with business and functional strategies to make some sort of perfect fit between them;
- assumes that corporate managers actually know something about operations capabilities and are able to leverage these capabilities as part of the strategic plan (as you'll see throughout this book, such an assumption is often totally without any foundation whatsoever);

- encourages a hierarchical, top-down approach where, as a result, there may be little or no ownership of the planning process and the subsequent strategic plan.

The net result to this is that *strategic dissonance* takes place. The dissonance will be there because corporate goals may be at odds with business strategies; these in turn may be completely at odds with operations capabilities. More importantly, these strategies will be at odds with market requirements. The problem is further compounded because of two factors concerned with the composition of senior level management within many firms:

- You will often search in vain for the vice president of operations or the vice president of manufacturing within large firms – though other functions will, typically, have senior level presence. This means that often there is no senior-level manufacturing/operations person in the firm whose presence might help to shape the strategic direction of the business.

- In any event, titles can be misleading. While researching this book, I spoke with two 'vice presidents of manufacturing', but the title was nonsense. They knew very little about manufacturing and, more alarmingly, they hardly ever left their corporate offices to actually see for themselves what manufacturing/operations capabilities there were within their plants. Instead, they were dependent on weekly and monthly reports that simply churned out numbers and provided reports that the VPs wanted to see.

So the problem with the top-down strategy process includes an over-dependence upon a small group at the very top of the firm; the lack of senior-level manufacturing/operations personnel whose presence might help shape the business strategy of the firm; and the fundamental lack of understanding of the strategic power, scope and contribution that operations capabilities can provide in the strategy process. Some firms have solved the problem by virtue of the fact that the firm's CEOs is also its chief operating officer (COO) as *Fortune* indicated:

> Note how many of today's best CEOs, the master executors, don't even have a COO: Craig Barrett of Intel . . . Michael Dell of Dell, Gerstner of IBM . . . Nasser of Ford . . . That's a multi-industry all-star team of CEOs who've put themselves squarely in charge of meeting their commitments and getting things done . . . The problem is that our age's fascination with strategy and vision feeds the mistaken belief that developing exactly the right strategy will enable a company to rocket past competitors. In reality that's less than half the battle.[4]

The real battle is in constantly ensuring that *strategic resonance* takes place between those decisions made at senior levels of the firm and the firm's capabilities, and between the firm's capabilities and customer requirements. Having *strategic operations* in place is the means by which strategy becomes operationalized and, to use *Fortune*'s phrase, 'getting things done'.

The second myth: strategy is either market- or resource-driven

In the past there was a tendency to see strategy in terms of an either/or scenario. The firm could either compete on its capabilities – a resource-based strategy[5] – or it could pursue a market-led strategy, in which case it would seek out and respond to market opportunities. However, this view is myopic and fatally flawed. World-class firms do not see strategy either as a market-driven or resource-based affair. World-class, enlightened firms are those that both seek new market opportunities and have in place capabilities that are poised to be used. Dell Computers is a perfect example. In his book, Michael Dell describes how he reacted to taunts from the revitalized Apple Computer Company:

> We reacted by continuing to do what we always have: focusing on the customer, not the competition.[6]

This is more than a bland dismissal of Apple by Dell. Dell knows that his strategy works because market opportunities are met by powerful, strategic, operations' capabilities:

> 'By spending time with your customer where they do business, you can learn more than by bringing them to where you do business,' he (Dell) writes. Visiting British Petroleum Co. in London, for example, Dell watched workers configure their machines with new software and networking capabilities – at considerable cost. BP asked Dell if he could do the work for them. The result was a new multi-million dollar business involving many such customers.[7]

Was this a market-led strategy or was it resource-based? The answer, of course, is that it is both, simultaneously. In other words, strategic resonance had occurred.

 ## Strategic resonance: the key to successful strategy

Enlightened firms equipped with enlightened plants are those that cause *strategic resonance* to occur. Strategic resonance is an ongoing, dynamic, strategic process whereby customer requirements and organizational capabilities are in harmony and resonate. Strategic resonance is more than *strategic fit*[8] – a term that has often been used (rightly in the past) to describe the 'fit' between the firm's capabilities and the market that it serves. Strategic fit may be likened to a jigsaw where all parts fit together. This is a useful view but it can have – and this was noted in interviews with key staff in this research – a very static feel to it. With strategic fit, it is as if once the 'bits' are in place, the strategic planning is done. By contrast, strategic resonance is a dynamic, organic process, which is about ensuring continuous linkages and harmonization between:

● the market and the firm's operations capabilities;

● the firm's strategy and its operations capabilities; and

● all functions and all levels within the firm.

Firms need to find and exploit their strategic resonance, between markets and the firm, within the firm itself, and between senior level strategists and plant-level, operations capabilities. Therein lies the problem – you will see in this book that often, those who are in a position to make strategic decisions may know little or nothing about the strategic opportunities and strategic power that lie within its operations' resources and capabilities. As a result, there is no strategic resonance between strategy and operations and consequently, senior-level strategists articulate a mission and a strategy that

Figure 1.1   Planning strategic resonance between market requirements and operations capabilities

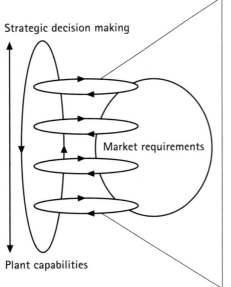

Strategic decision making

Market requirements

Plant capabilities

The essence of strategic resonance is that ongoing linkages are made between:

● strategic decisions and operations capabilities
● the firm's strategy and market requirements.

This ensures that there is no conflict between market-driven and resource-based strategies. Instead they operate simultaneously and resonate. This prevents the firm being excellent in the wrong things; it also prevents the firm chasing after business and markets in which it cannot hope to compete. The strategy process is ongoing and changing, adapting to ensure that customer requirements and organizational-wide capabilities continue to resonate.

Figure 1.2   Strategic imbalance and dissonance

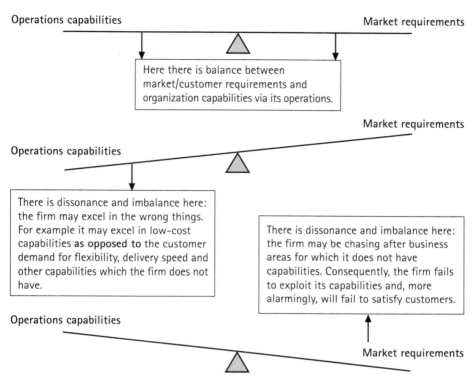

has no chance of being realized. It will not be realized because the firm does not know what the capabilities are in the first place, or does not possess the necessary operations know-how and capability, or seems incapable of seeking partnerships with other firms that do. Strategic resonance is illustrated in Figure 1.1.

A strategic resonance approach avoids strategic dissonance or imbalance, as shown in Figure 1.2.

 ## What strategy really is

Strategy is about three things. First, it is about satisfying and, where possible, delighting, customers. Second, it is about making the best use of resources, and to leverage these resources either alone or with partners. Third, it is about developing capabilities within operations which are superior to other competitors and which other competitors either cannot copy, or will find it extremely difficult, to copy. For example, Dell's 'secret' of the company's phenomenal success is not a secret at all, but no other competitor can quite emulate what Dell does via its operations capabilities. The same is true of Toyota. In an interview with a senior executive at Toyota, he stated bluntly: 'It's not that other auto firms won't copy the Toyota Production System, it's that they can't!'

There has been a vast array of publications discussing Toyota's capabilities but most of these fail to address the real reason for Toyota's success: its ability to create strategic resonance between customers and operations. It does this by having senior-level personnel who both protect and improve upon strategic capabilities.

The term 'strategy' as used in the 'corporate strategy' or 'business strategy' sense, clearly has strong associations with, and owes its origins to, military terminology. Strategy in the military includes devising plans in order to out-manoeuvre the opposition.[9] Some writers do not like the military analogy because, they argue, strategy is not about killing off other firms, particularly when there is strong industry growth.[10] This may be true on some occasions but we need to be realistic here. For example, in a fast-growing PC industry, it was IBM and not Wang who dominated PCs for long periods because the industry adopted the IBM and not the Wang standard; Wang was forced into Chapter 11. IBM won and Wang did not. Also, it was IBM who in turn, within a still vastly growing market, lost out to the likes of Compaq and Apple at the end of the 1980s and again to Hewlett-Packard and Dell at the end of the 1990s. Similarly, General Motors (GM) lost vast amounts of market share to both US and foreign competitors that attacked within an industry suffering from over-capacity in segments to which GM did not pay attention. These competitors created new niches as well as concentrating on existing, smaller segments such as turbos, four-wheel drive cars and mini-vans. Their gains were at the expense of GM's loss.

Undoubtedly, it makes sense to ensure that 'enemies' become friends or allies. By the beginning of the new millennium, there were numerous instances in the plethora of relationships and alliances which pervade many industries. But this only confirms the military analogy of strategy still further – one group clusters together against other, competing alliances or clusters, all of which are seeking to position themselves and gain some sort of defensive cover or competitive advantage.

We will see throughout the book that in order to be a contender as a player within these alliances, a would-be partner has to demonstrate some unique or outstanding operations capability that another partner does not have.[11] Clearly, world-class performance in operations has profound, strategic importance for firms in terms of alliances. Such alliances will be formed between world-class firms, who posses outstanding and complementary capabilities. But the ability to learn, adopt, and utilize world-class operations capabilities does not come about by chance. Instead it comes about by seeking out and accumulating capabilities. If a firm does not do this there will be a gap between strategic intent and strategic capability. It is this gap between intent and capability that remains a massive hurdle for firms. It has cost many CEOs their jobs. It was one of the key reasons for Compaq ousting Eckhard Pfeiffer at the end of the 1990s: it was one thing to assert back in 1994 that Compaq would 'build to customer order'; it was quite another thing for the firm to be able to do it. By 1996 only 5% of its PCs were built to order.[12] Moreover, Compaq had not improved dramatically on this by the end of the decade. Compaq had concentrated on low-cost production of PCs but the problem was that it was not doing what the market required. It excelled in the wrong things: strategic dissonance had occurred. Meanwhile Dell continued to thrive because it could build to order and could do so with great speed: market requirement and operations capability were in harmony and strategic resonance was in place at Dell.

Asserting the strategy

Sometimes the impetus for devising strategy comes from competitive threats. The reaction does not have to be stated in a wonderfully articulated manner but it needs to be focused and it needs to be supported by operations capabilities if it is to have any meaning. This was clearly the case at Honda:

> . . . when Honda was overtaken by Yamaha as Japan's number one motorbike manufacturer, the company responded by declaring 'Yamaha so tsubu su!' (We will crush, squash and slaughter Yamaha!). There followed a stream of no less than eighty-one new products in eighteen months. The massive effort nearly bankrupted the company, but in the end left Honda as top dog once more.[13]

Just for a moment, try to imagine the sort of elaborate and protracted strategic planning that would have taken place in many firms in the West faced with this threat from Yamaha. It is easy to imagine chief strategists undertaking all sorts of risk analysis with calculators in hand, with their strategies governed by accounting ratios such as net present values, internal rates of return and other ratios that can act as dangerous inhibitors to innovation. The key issue is that Honda had the capability to launch the range and volume of new products within such a short time. If it didn't, its assertion to overtake Yamaha would have been both arrogant and pointless.

In the PC industry, when Steve Jobs returned to Apple Computers, his message was clearly strategic and 'war-like':

> Mr Jobs, who returned after a long absence to take over the leadership of Apple . . . declared 'war' on Dell Computer, one of Apple's most successful competitors. 'We are

coming after you, buddy,' Mr Jobs declared as he displayed a huge image of Michael Dell, Dell founder and chief executive, with a target superimposed on his face. Mr Dell became the target of Apple's ire, Mr Jobs said, because he had refused to retract a statement that Apple should be dissolved. 'I'd shut it down and give the money back to the shareholders,' Mr Dell said . . . [14]

But Jobs' statement is more than mere words. For sure, his statement could be put down to a 'war of words' between firms but, as you will see in Chapter 2, both Dell and Apple had very clear, but different, strategies in order to enable the assertions to become realities. By 1999, Apple had supported its intention with vast improvements in its operations capabilities. However, by the end of the 1990s Dell had also put in place phenomenal operations capabilities which many envied but nobody, it seemed, could quite emulate (though a few have tried).

Likewise, Hewlett-Packard was not slow in announcing its strategic intentions:

Hewlett-Packard yesterday unveiled products and initiatives aimed at making it the world's leading business personal computer manufacturer . . . HP intended to vie for leadership in every key segment of the PC market over the next few years, Jacques Clay, vice-president, said. 'In 1994, before anyone knew HP was in the PC business, we set a goal to become one of the world's top five PC suppliers . . . By redoubling our focus on customer needs, we hope to reach our new goal . . . [15]

Whether or not Hewlett-Packard will actually achieve this depends entirely on its operations capabilities.

Becoming strategic, focused and holistic

As well as creating and sustaining strategic resonance, a firm has to ensure that it is strategic, focused and holistic in approach. Each of these three factors needs further explanation.

Strategic

First, strategy decisions really do need to be strategic. In the 1990s, many firms seemed to see cost-cutting and strategy as synonymous. Downsizing and cost-cutting may well be necessary, particularly where management ranks are bloated and where strategy implementation becomes painfully protracted and damaging for the firm and its customers. But cost-cutting by itself will not be a sustainable strategy and the full scope and possibilities of strategy must go beyond this. There are at least four characteristics that tend to distinguish *strategic* from *tactical* decisions.

Strategy must include, but not be limited to, senior-level management

Strategy formulation tends to be the prerogative of senior managers within the firm[16] and the final decisions regarding the direction of the firm will rest with these senior managers. However, other levels of the firm may be involved in the development of strategic plans and these other levels will certainly be involved in their implementation.[17] Thus the link with operations capabilities is both profound and of fundamental importance – it is not an afterthought once a strategy has been defined but is, instead, a necessary and central feature of strategic formulation.

Strategy should create competitive advantage

Strategic decisions are intended to create competitive advantage for the firm or, at the very least, to allow the firm to continue to compete in its chosen markets. A key means for doing so is via operations capabilities that both satisfy market needs and are superior to other competitors.

Strategic decisions can have profound consequences

A strategic decision can profoundly alter, and have major consequences for, the firm. Examples of such decisions might include massive financial investment, and radical reconfigurations of entire business structures. The strategy may include reshaping of the organization, in addition to outsourcing and insourcing operations, and configuring the entire supply network.

Strategy must have long-term horizons

Strategic decisions can have long-term implications for the firm and hence the factor of time is an important one for strategists.[18] It is important to note that strategic planning is not simply crystal-ball gazing into the far future; for strategy to be effective it also needs to have a sense of timing and urgency in its implementation.

Focused

Focus is essential when deciding which businesses and markets the firm wants to be in and then ensuring that strategic resonance occurs between this intention and plant capabilities. In a sense all firms have to focus to some degree because they do not have limitless resources and cannot therefore provide a limitless range or any volume of products or services in every market around the world. However, focus is much more specific than this and can have profound importance for the firm. In essence, focus is concerned with what the organization *will not do* as much as it is concerned with what it will do, and this intention can become part of its core mission. For example, in 1991 Hewlett-Packard intended to enter the PC market with great intensity and it has succeeded in doing so, reaching a position in the top four PC manufacturers in the US. Focus played a key part in Hewlett-Packard's phenomenal rise in the PC market. Hewlett-Packard decided that it would move away from being a manufacturer to being an assembler of products. This shift in focus places even greater emphasis on the need for excellent supplier relations throughout the supply chain, especially with those suppliers on whom Hewlett-Packard greatly depends.

The organization can focus in a number of ways including:

- Focusing on particular customer groups/market segments which it serves.
- Deliberately avoiding other market segments.
- Ensuring that strategic resonance occurs between customer requirements and plant capabilities and resources. Focusing the plant into a number of specified areas by customer, product, or process is important to ensure that strategic resonance takes place between customer requirement and plant capabilities.
- Divesting non-core areas of the business, which, in turn will impact on operations management. One of the easiest – and most dangerous – means of becoming unfocused is in acquiring other businesses. As you will see later in the chapter, this became part of Compaq's problems in the late 1990s.
- Concentrating on specific activities within the supply chain and forming strategic buyer–supplier relationships with other players in the supply network.

Focus also ties in with agility – by virtue of being freed up from areas in which it does not excel or have capability, the organization may concentrate on its core competencies and become agile by knitting these together with other operations required to satisfy simultaneous requirements of flexibility, delivery and cost. Very often, focus means concentrating on specific aspects of the supply chain to see where the organization really adds value and to subcontract whole areas in the supply process.

Holistic

The firm must become holistic in its vision and understanding of strategy. Holistic includes – but is not limited to – integration of functions within the firm. Undoubtedly the need to integrate various functions so that the firm moves in a unified fashion is vital if strategic plans are to be achieved. However, being holistic is wider than ensuring integration. Being holistic means that a firm is able to grasp the complete picture in its strategic vision. This includes understanding:

- The composition and changes within entire markets.
- Complete configurations of supply networks and how the firm will feature in the configuration.
- The fit that a particular alliance will have with the firm.
- The impact of growth or divestment, including downsizing of staff.

Being holistic in approach means that strategic resonance is more likely to be achieved simply because a firm will not make a decision in isolation which might cause strategic dissonance to occur but will, instead, go in a particular strategic direction only once it has undertaken an holistic audit of strategy.

Strategic, focused and holistic in practice

Being strategic, focused and holistic is a powerful approach. It enables the firm to position itself in a truly strategic position rather than embarking on a knee-jerk, cost-cutting frenzy. In addition, it will ensure that the firm will not suffer from internal myopia, by being pulled in different directions by the power of its internal functions. It will also prevent the firm from being pulled in different directions because it will be focused on businesses and markets instead of functions and marketing. Being strategic, focused and holistic in approach will enable the firm to understand the likely repercussion that a particular strategic plan will have on the firm's numerous stakeholders in the business. Although the three factors, strategic, focused and holistic, are separate to some degree, the extent to which a strategy will succeed depends on how these factors themselves resonate. Consequently the three entities should overlap to a large degree, as shown in Figure 1.3.

The problem for many firms is that strategic dissonance takes place between the firm and its customers. At the core of this is imbalance due to decisions being taken which are not strategic, or focused or holistic. Compaq's involvement in NT workstations, the high-powered computers, is a case in point. In 1998, Compaq's market share declined from 22% to 14%, and part of the problem was that the supposed benefit from the purchase of Digital simply did not materialize.

> Compaq thought Digital would help, but they found Digital didn't have a lot of expertise there, either. It used to, but lost it through years of downsizing.[19]

Figure 1.3   The strategic, focused and holistic approach

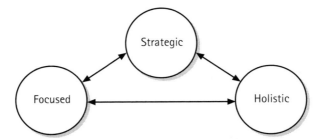

The strategy process now becomes a dynamic and interactive process.

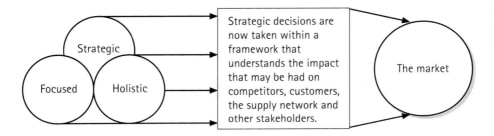

Compaq's acquisition of Digital caused it to become unfocused to some degree. Indeed, Compaq's overall acquisition strategy has caused a number of problems. The acquisitions are shown in Table 1.1.

In 1999, in an attempt to be more focused, Compaq replaced its matrix organization with a structure that aligns the company by various lines of businesses, each of which has profit-and-loss responsibilities. In other words, Compaq has become more focused. This was not always the case:

Table 1.1   Compaq's acquisitions 1995–99

Company	Product	Price	Date
Networth	network computing	$372m	November 1995
Microcom	remote access software	$280m	April 1997
Tandem	enterprise class servers	$3.6bn	June 1997
Digital	high-end computing	$9.6bn	January 1998
Shopping.Com	Internet shopping	$220m	January 1999

Source: Computer Weekly, April 22, 1999

We did not do a good job of telling our story. We had fragmented marketing messages. Compaq had stood for the world's most powerful personal computing brand. Then we added the very, very high-end Tandem side, and then we brought in Digital. The customer lost track of who we were.[20]

Strategic focus is exemplified at Hewlett-Packard. Its former CEO, Lew Platt, split HP into two: a $39.5 billion company selling computers, printers, software and services, led by Platt's successor as CEO, Fiorina, and a $7.6 billion unit in the business of medical products, and test and measurement devices. Fiorina's experience in managing strategic focus is an important feature:

'I have an ability to grow businesses,' she says, 'and the experience I had with the AT&T-Lucent split and what opportunities a split like that represents for both companies are very relevant for HP.'[21]

Fiorina's success will depend on her ability to leverage operations capabilities now that strategic focus is in place. Lew Platt stated the reasons for the HP split:

HP [is] not quite as focused as we should be ... More focused management time and energy, more focused messages, and greater visibility of the pieces will lead to a better outcome.[22]

In 1999, HP had around 124,000 employees, with a revenue of $47.1 billion comprising a range of products from high-end computers and competitively priced inkjet printers, to equipment for monitoring heart patients and analyzing chemical compounds. Focus was a strategic necessity and should allow Hewlett-Packard to become an even stronger player in computers.

Lack of focus has often been a problem for the large car firms. For example, Chrysler bought Gulfstream Aerospace and a small Texas defence contractor, both of which it eventually sold. General Motors acquired EDS and Hughes Aircraft. Both EDS and Hughes turned out to be valid investments, but not in the way that GM perceived it would, via proposed synergy outcomes. Instead, General Motors used the EDS stock to pay its unfunded pension liabilities, and the profits from the sale of Hughes' defence business to Raytheon were largely nullified by a $4 billion write-off which GM was forced to make.

In 1998, General Motors announced its most radical reorganization in the name of focus. But GM has struggled with reorganizations. The most catastrophic was the huge restructuring in 1984. As you will see in Chapter 4, this was the starting point for the $80 billion spending spree on technology, which provided little or no competitive advantage for GM. GM divided its American division into two groups – BOC (officially 'Buick–Oldsmobile–Cadillac'; unofficially tagged 'Big Overpriced Cars') and CPC ('Chevrolet–Pontiac–Canada', which again suffered from another tag,

'Cheap Plastic Cars'[23]). At the end of the 1990s, GM tried to become more focused by being far less integrated in the supply chain. One strategy was to sell Delphi, its components division. At the same time GM sought to centralize its vast sales, service and marketing system for the six main American car divisions that provide two-thirds of its sales volume. Such a strategy was aimed at saving around $300 million a year.[24] GM has tried to become more focused in its operations. For example, GM intended to build a network of new assembly plants, far smaller and better focused than before. These factories will rely on suppliers to pre-assemble 'modules', such as entire instrument panels. Thus the focus is on assembly rather than manufacture. In order to do this, GM will have to rely on strong and close relationships with suppliers, something which, as you will see in Chapter 6, it has failed to do in the past.

GM has tried to focus its innovation process too. In 1998, GM had 16 car platforms but aimed to have eight. As a point of comparison though, Volkswagen, Europe's largest car maker, planned to use just four platforms in its manufacturing.

Creating strategic resonance via strategic operations management

Ensuring that the firm is strategic, focused and holistic in approach is vital. However, to ensure that strategic resonance takes place between the firm's operations and customer requirements, a specific operations strategy has to be in place. Moreover, the operations strategy needs to be plant-specific. Again, if we take GM as an example, it is pointless having a strategy for its NUUMI plant (the GM/Toyota plant in Fremont, California) and assuming that this can be adopted in Detroit. Undoubtedly, lessons may be learned from another plant but the technology processes, human capabilities and often the nature of the supplier base will be peculiar to each plant. In order for this to be successful, the plant must have plant-specific operations strategies in place. This is where the role of senior-level manufacturing personnel can be vital – but this role is sometimes overlooked.

There's no doubt that production/operations managers have huge responsibilities. At the very least, they are responsible for utilizing something in the region of 80–85% of company assets, both fixed (plant) and current assets, especially materials. In addition, they have huge responsibilities, concerning managing costs: production/operations activity will account for 80% of company costs and inventory alone can account for over 60% of costs of sales in manufacturing. Also, if the plant is to perform well, technology and processes are not enough: production/operations managers are also responsible for gaining the best possible contribution from human resources. If that isn't enough responsibility, production/operations managers now have to deal with rapid ongoing changes and to respond to latest paradigms including lean production, mass customization and agile manufacturing. *The Economist* summarized the position very well:

> Manufacturing used to be pretty simple. The factory manager or the production director rarely had to think about suppliers or customers. All he did was to make sure that his machinery was producing widgets at the maximum hourly rate. Once he had worked out how to stick to that 'standard rate' of production, he could sit back and relax. Customer needs? Delivery times? Efficient purchasing? That was what the purchasing department and the sales department were there for. Piles of inventory lying around, both raw materials and finished goods? Not his problem. Now it is. The 1980s were the decade of lean production and right-first-time quality management. In the 1990s the game has grown even tougher. Customers are more and more demanding. They increasingly want the basic product to be enhanced by some individual variation, or some special service. Companies sweat to keep up with their demands, in terms both of the actual products and of the way they are delivered.[25]

In the future, the pressure put on production/operations managers will be greater than ever. An operations strategy must be in place to enable the firm to deal with such changes. But the problem for many firms is that they do not have manufacturing strategies. That is because in many firms manufacturing is seen as a function and is separate from the business and corporate strategy process, as mentioned earlier. You will search in vain for any real discussion on manufacturing strategy/operations strategy in the great majority of books on strategy. What you will see is a mindset that is anchored firmly in the hierarchical approaches to strategy of the past. This may well have been appropriate for mass production. It is entirely inappropriate for the current era. That is why firms will often fail when they attempt to become lean and agile and all of the other aspirations: they concentrate on operations characteristics such as quality, speed of delivery, space reduction and so on, but they do not have strategies in place to enable them to do so. Harvard's Whickham Skinner summarized the problem for many firms when he stated:

> Manufacturing is generally perceived in the wrong way at the top, managed in the wrong way at plant level, and taught in the wrong way in the business schools.[26]

To begin with, the very idea that operations should be seen as 'strategic' is still a problem for some firms whose overall strategy may be governed by a few people at the top of the hierarchy of the firm who might know very little about production and operations management. As a result of this, the rationale behind, and the measurement of the success of, business decisions may be driven almost entirely by short-term financial criteria and not operations capabilities. Over time, of course, operations capabilities will decline.

Coping with massive competition demands that strategies are in place because being prepared and poised to act rarely, if ever, comes about by accident. Strategies have to be in place to deal with key questions such as:

- What business is the firm really in?
- What does the firm do best?
- Should it outsource some of its activities, and if so why, to what degree, where and how?
- How can opportunities become quickly exploited, and how can the firm's capabilities help to ward off external threats from new and existing players?

Figure 1.4 The changing role of strategy in different manufacturing eras

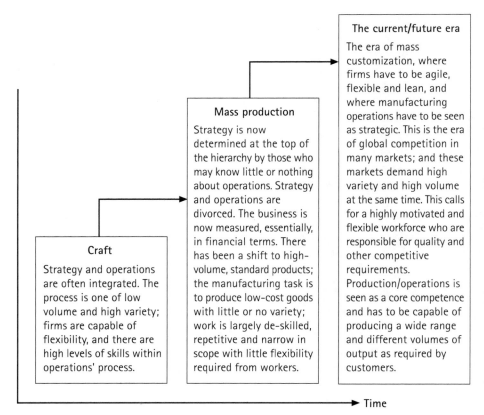

The degree to which these questions are answered successfully will depend upon:

- the strategy process itself;
- the content of the strategy; and
- the ability to operationalize the strategy.

We now need to see why strategy is important for operations managers and how this has changed over time because therein lies the major clues as to why strategy often fails within firms.

 ## The current and future era of operations management

The reason why strategy is so important is that the nature of most operations has undergone major changes over time, as shown in Figure 1.4. Often the differences between manufacturing eras are discussed in terms of changes in volume and variety from craft to mass production. But the nature of the transition is more profound than this and is concerned with strategy.

The first major era is now referred to as 'craft' manufacturing. Two factors are crucial here: first, many craft firms were owner-managed and so skilled operators were responsible for the business of the firm as well as the purely operations activities and capabilities. Second, there was integration between what the firms did, their highly skilled operations, and the strategic direction that the business would take.

The second major era is known as mass production, which developed in North America to accommodate three major goals of the US economy: the need to export, the need to provide employment for a massive, largely unskilled workforce, and the need to establish itself as a world player in industry.

The third era (which is the current and, for the foreseeable future at least, likely scenario) is more difficult to name and has been called various things. The terms used to describe the current era include:

- *Mass customization*[27] – reflecting the need for volume combined with recognition of customers' (or consumers') wishes.
- *Flexible specialization*[28] – related to the manufacturing strategy of firms (especially small firms) to focus on parts of the value-adding process and collaborate within networks to produce whole products.
- *Lean production*[29] – developed from the massively successful Toyota Production System, focusing on the removal of all forms of waste from a system.

- *Agile*[30] – emphasizing the need for an organization to be able to switch frequently from one market-driven objective to another.

- *Strategic manufacturing*[31] – in which the need for the operations to be framed in a strategy is brought to the fore.

Many publications dealing with the transition from craft to mass to the current era concentrate on how these changes of eras affected skill levels and the nature of the manufacturing process. This is an important clue to the nature of changes but an even more crucial and fundamental part of the puzzle is often missing. The biggest factor was how business strategy became divorced from the firm's operations. This then manifested itself in two different sets of criteria for 'success', which sometimes pulled the firm in different directions. The transition from craft, through mass production, to the current era, caused three major factors to emerge. First, we can say that operations personnel were often absent from the most senior levels of the firm as enterprises became larger and more functionally organized.[32] While there has been increasing importance placed on operations personnel in terms of their contribution to the firm's capabilities, this has not necessarily included involvement in terms of their seniority within the hierarchy of the firm, which is a telling indication of the operations management role in many Western plants.

Second, the role of operations managers often became that of a technical specialism rather than an involvement in the business of the firm. Often, manufacturing's contribution, in terms of its capability, is ignored until after strategic plans have been already formulated by an elite planning group whose understanding of the specifics of manufacturing or assembly may be very limited.[33]

Third, strategy formulation and planning became the prerogative of senior managers, and operations personnel were typically excluded from the process because of their position within the firm, so that operations strategies, where they did exist, were merely the means by which an already existing business strategy became translated into plant operations. This may have been appropriate for the mass production era but market requirements are now wholly different, as you will now see. This change demands that operations strategy is formulated and linked to the firm's business strategy.

The current era and its impact on the need for flexibility and agility

The need to move away from standard products in high volume and little variety, thus requiring some agility in operations, was first highlighted by Skinner:

On Monday, they want low cost. On Tuesday, they want high quality. On Wednesday, they want no backorders. On Thursday, they want low inventories. On Friday, they want maximum overhead absorption, so we have to work the weekend.[34]

As mentioned earlier, the current era in manufacturing demands that both high volume and high variety must be achieved simultaneously. In addition, the problem for the modern operations manager is that other requirements of cost, quality, speedy delivery with no backorders or queues, low inventories, and so on, are also all needed simultaneously. This is good for customers who may demand such requirements but it poses major potential headaches for operations managers who are charged with the responsibility of having to deliver all of these requirements simultaneously. This is a very different scenario from that of mass production. The initial reaction to this range of requirements was for production/operations managers to offer some sort of trade-off: for example, you could have low cost but not fast delivery as well, or vice versa. However, as Richard Schonberger stated in 1990 – by which time the current era of mass customization was in place – the trade-off solution was not a solution after all:

World class strategies require chucking the (trade-off) notion. The right strategy has no optimum, only continual improvement in all things.[35]

Operations strategy can be a driving force behind such continual improvements in all areas indicated by Schonberger, whereby the notion of trade-offs between various competitive requirements becomes redundant. Instead, accumulated operational capabilities, activated simultaneously, can equip and enable the firm to satisfy a wide variety of requirements. Companies have tried to do this in different ways. For example, in the mid-1990s, Hewlett-Packard's strategy for mass customization was to postpone the task of differentiating a product for a specific customer until the latest possible point in the supply network.[36] Hewlett-Packard then had to change this strategy. As you saw earlier, this was part of a massive company-wide change of strategy for Hewlett-Packard.

 ## The process of forming operations strategy

There is no single, prescriptive process plan in forming strategy. However, three factors are important:

- the process of forming strategy;
- the content of the strategy; and
- how the strategy becomes operationalized.

The process must be ongoing, dynamic and aiming always to ensure that strategic resonance takes place between the firm's overall strategy and the operations capabilities within its plant. For example, it is pointless for a firm to state that its strategy is to produce six million cars per year if there are no operations strategies in place concerned with factors such as capacity, location decisions, and manufacturing processes. The process should be strategic, focused and holistic as mentioned earlier. In real terms, this means that the process needs to be integrated across all functions and understood by all those involved in the strategic planning process. Often though, you will find that one functional group may have unequal power and will unduly influence the nature of the strategic decision. You will see this often when a CEO has come from a functional specialist area – such as finance or marketing – and then continues to see strategy through a particular functional lens. Unless this is redressed, strategic dissonance will undoubtedly occur instead of strategic resonance. The firm needs to be constantly fed with information on major trends – political, economic, social, technological and other major business forces. It needs to be constantly auditing changes in market requirements as well as competitive changes. Each change needs to be fed constantly into the strategic process. Although there may well be a specific strategic planning group – and this must include senior level operations presence – there may well be opportunities for *ad hoc* meetings, particularly where scenario planning may take place.

The quality of the strategic content is dependent upon how it creates resonance between all levels of the firm, and between the firm and its customer requirements. Thus the content of an operations strategy will include at least the following:

- Amounts of capacity required by the organization to achieve its aims.
- The range and locations of facilities.
- Technology investment to support process and product developments.
- The degree, extent and structure of strategic buyer–supplier relationships as part of the organization's 'extended enterprise' network.
- Organizational structure – to reflect what it 'does best', often entailing outsourcing of other activities.
- The extent and nature of alliances with other competitors.
- The rate of new product introduction.
- Ensuring that skill levels are in place to accommodate flexibility of volume, variety and other changes.

The means by which the strategy will become operationalized is where great management expertise is required among various functions but most notably in the firms' operations managers. The strategy needs to have a sense of urgency if it is to be operationalized and this means project managing specifics. This is a major task and many firms fail with it. For example, *Industry Week* summarized a report from its links with the American Production Inventory Control Society:

> The first and largest implication delivered by the IW Census is that there is a fundamental disagreement between the strategic level and execution of the business. This issue may have far-reaching effects for a company . . . Another large issue, that of management capability, also should be evaluated in the strategic-deployment process. Senior managers should be assessing whether plant managers have the ability to absorb the strategic direction of the business and turn the vision into operating reality . . . Manufacturing executives need to look at themselves in the deployment process as well. They must question whether their expectations have been communicated effectively to plant managers. Conversely, they also need to evaluate whether the degree of support they provide in terms of involvement could alter their perception of operational execution.[37]

Examples of how strategy becomes operationalized are shown in Figure 1.5.

However, in addition to ensuring that strategic resonance takes place between business and operations strategies within the firm, enlightened firms ensure that strategic resonance also occurs between operations capabilities and market requirements, as illustrated in Figure 1.6.

An important part of the process of ensuring strategic resonance between operations and market requirements is in ranking the importance of the market requirements. For example, if the chief market requirement is low cost and delivery reliability is assumed, then the operations capabilities must be focused on this bias. Terry Hill[38] speaks of order-qualifying and order-winning criteria. The former are those competitive factors that the firm must achieve to be considered at all in the market; without them the firm will lose orders. Order-winning criteria are those factors that will enable the firm to win in the market place. This is a powerful approach with one caveat, which you will see in Chapter 4 – it is not that easy to line up order-qualifying and order-winning criteria against the process technology that the firm has within its plants. However, this distinction between order-qualifying and order-winning criteria is one that firms should consider – undoubtedly it would help to focus their efforts.

Figure 1.5   Operationalizing the strategy

Overall strategic factors		Operation strategy
• Amounts of capacity required by the organization to achieve its aims.	◄──►	Ensuring that volume – through variety and variability of products – can be achieved. Capacity includes flexibility and range of volumes and not just output from a singe product. Measured in maximum outputs as well as various configurations of product mixes.
• The range and locations of facilities.	◄──►	Targeting strategic locations – close to the market; near to labour and other vital inputs to manufacturing. Measured in terms of how quickly a new plant can be manufacturing to world-class standards.
• Technology investment to support process and product developments.	◄──►	Understanding the required process choice, FMS and other advance manufacturing technologies to support the firm in the market. Avoiding technological myopia in the selection and acquisition of new technologies. Measured in terms of rapid changeovers, flexibility, quality and cost.
• The degree, extent and structure of strategic buyer–supplier relationships as part of the organization's 'extended enterprise' network.	◄──►	Understanding market requirements in terms of inventory and product delivery. Benchmarking, inventory carrying and inventory turns against competitors. Measured in terms of cycle times and hours of inventory.
• Organizational structure - to reflect what it 'does best', often entailing outsourcing of other activities.	◄──►	Re-engineering in the best sense, i.e. focus without necessarily firing staff will enable the operations to be more agile and to respond more rapidly and intelligently to market requirements. Measured in terms of sales per employee, speed of response to customer order and cost.
• The rate of new product introduction.	◄──►	Ensuring that operations are involved in new product development – in particular by close liaison with suppliers. Measured in terms of speed to market – and success – of new products.
• The extent and nature of alliances with other competitors.	◄──►	Finding other firms whose operations are complementary and add value to the firm's own capabilities. Ensuring that strategic resonance occurs between firms' operations. Measured in terms of enhanced quality, delivery and cost parameters.
• Ensuring that skill levels are in place to accommodate flexibility of volume, variety and other changes.	◄──►	Ongoing training and empowerment of staff to enable them to manage key areas of technology and quality. Measured in terms of suggestions per employee, percentage of personnel involved in CI groups and other parameters of quality and cost.

Figure 1.6   Creating strategic resonance between market requirements and operations capabilities

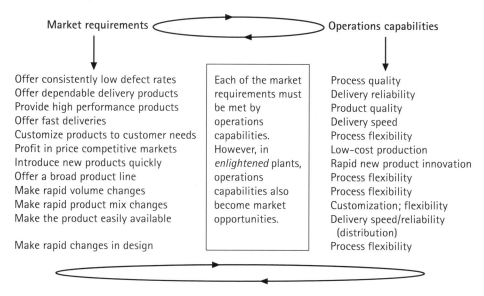

Offer consistently low defect rates — Process quality
Offer dependable delivery products — Delivery reliability
Provide high performance products — Product quality
Offer fast deliveries — Delivery speed
Customize products to customer needs — Process flexibility
Profit in price competitive markets — Low-cost production
Introduce new products quickly — Rapid new product innovation
Offer a broad product line — Process flexibility
Make rapid volume changes — Process flexibility
Make rapid product mix changes — Customization; flexibility
Make the product easily available — Delivery speed/reliability (distribution)

Make rapid changes in design — Process flexibility

Box in centre: Each of the market requirements must be met by operations capabilities. However, in *enlightened* plants, operations capabilities also become market opportunities.

Conclusions

There are a vast number of publications concerned with strategy. While many have been full of insight, many books and articles either ignore, or fail to understand, the strategic power and potential of operations. This has been redressed to some extent by a number of writers who have spoken of the need for manufacturing strategies.[39] However, the transfer from production/operations publications to mainstream strategy has not been completely successful and they are often seen as two different territories within strategy, which is fundamentally wrong.

Strategy is not an either/or scenario, between market-driven and resource-based approaches. Instead strategy is about creating and sustaining strategic resonance between the firm and its market requirements, and between senior-level strategy making processes and operations capabilities. One of the chief failures in many firms is that their strategy processes have not developed from the mass production era where, perhaps, the gap between senior-level strategy and operations was understandable. However, in a business world full of world-class players, the firm now has to move into more enlightened approaches and to be strategic, focused and holistic in its strategy planning and implementation.

NOTES AND REFERENCES

1. Whittington, R. (1993) *What is Strategy – and Does it Matter?* Routledge, London.
2. Hayes, R. and Pisano, G. (1994) 'Beyond World-Class: The New Manufacturing Strategy', *Harvard Business Review*, January–February: 77–86.
3. See, for example, *Fortune*, June 21, 1999, where the edition is dedicated to CEOs who have failed. *Fortune* provided a management failure grid against which various CEOs were scored. The grid included 'People problems, Decision gridlock, Bad Earnings news and Missing in Action'. They then listed eight attributes of the 'Superior CEO'.
4. *Fortune*, June 21, 1999.
5. The role of internal resource-based strategies was discussed by B. Wernerfelt (1984) in 'A Resource-Based View of the Firm', *Strategic Management Journal*, **5**(4): 171–180. This view has been developed further in a number of ways. See, for example: Hayes, R. and Pisano, G. (1994: see note 2 above); Prahalad, C. and Hamel, G. (1990) 'The Core Competence of the Corporation', *Harvard Business Review*, May–June: 79–91; Stalk, G. and Evans, P. (1992) 'Competing On Capabilities: The New Rules of Corporate Strategy', *Harvard Business Review*, **70**(2): 57–69; Collis, D.J. and Montgomery, C.A. (1995) 'Competing on resources: strategy in the 1990s', *Harvard Business Review*, **73**(4), July–August: 118–128.
6. Michael Dell with Catherine Fredman (1999) *Direct from Dell: Strategies that Revolutionized an Industry*. Harper Business, New York.
7. *Business Week*, March 8, 1999, p. 20.
8. A good discussion on strategic fit is provided in Johnson, G. and Scholes, K. (1999) *Exploring Corporate Strategy* 5th edn. Prentice Hall, Hemel Hempstead, UK.
9. See, for example, discussions on strategy in: Dodgson, M (ed.) (1989) *Technology Strategy and the Firm*. SPRU/Longman, London, UK; Gilbert, D., Hartman, E., Mauriel, E. and Freeman, E. (1988) *A Logic for Strategy*. Ballinger, Boston, USA.
10. See Kay, J. (1993) *Foundations of Corporate Success*. Oxford University Press, Oxford, as an example of an argument against the military analogy.
11. Excellent insight into the role of, and the risks contained within, strategic alliances is provided in: Das, T.K. and Teng, B. (1996) 'Risk types and inter-firm alliance structures', *Journal of Management Studies*, **33**: 827–843; Das, T.K. and Teng, B. (1997) 'Sustaining strategic alliances: Options and guidelines', *Journal of General Management*, **22**(4): 49–64; Das, T.K. and Teng, B. (1998) 'Resource and risk management in the strategic alliance making process', *Journal of Management*, 24: 21–42.
12. *Business Week*, May 3, 1999, 3627: 162(1).
13. Whittington, R. (1993) *What is Strategy – and Does it Matter?* Routledge, London.
14. *Financial Times* (1997) 'Companies and Finance: The Americas: Apple chief has Dell in his sights', November 12.
15. *Financial Times* (1997) 'Companies and Finance: The Americas: Hewlett-Packard aims to lead business PC market', September 10.
16. See the following for good insights into the role of senior managers in devising strategy: Chandler, A. (1962) *Strategy and Structure: Chapters in the History of the American Industrial Enterprise*. Irwin, USA; Evered, R. (1983) 'So What is Strategy?' *Long Range Planning*, **16**(3): 57–72; Mintzberg, H. (1994), *The Rise and Fall of Strategic Planning*. Prentice Hall, Hemel Hempstead, UK; Porter, M. (1985) *Competitive Advantage*. Free Press, New York; Porter, M. (1980) *Competitive Strategy*. Free Press, New York.
17. See the following for further insight into how strategy becomes operationalized: Hax, A. and Majluf, N. (1991) *The Strategy Concept & Process*. Prentice Hall, Englewood Cliffs, New Jersey, USA; Johnson, G. and Scholes, K. (1999) *Exploring Corporate Strategy* 5th edn.

Prentice Hall, Hemel Hempstead, UK; Bartlett, C.A. and Ghoshal, S. (1995) 'Changing the role of top management: beyond systems to people', *Harvard Business Review*, May–June, 132–142.

18. The factor of time in strategy decisions is discussed by Das, T.K. (1991) 'Time: The hidden dimension in strategic planning', *Long Range Planning*, **24**(3): 49–57; Itami, H. and Numagami, T. (1992) 'Dynamic Interaction Between Strategy and Technology', *Strategic Management Journal*, **13**: 119–135.

19. *Business Week*, May 3, 1999.

20. *Fortune*, August 16, 1999.

21. Ibid, p. 29.

23. *The Economist* (US), October 10, 1998, **348**(8089): 63(3).

24. Ibid.

25. *The Economist*, June 20, 1998, **347**(8073): 58(3).

26. Skinner, W. (1985) *Manufacturing, The Formidable Competitive Weapon*. John Wiley & Sons, New York.

27. Pine, B., Bart, V. and Boynton, A. (1993) 'Making Mass Customization Work', *Harvard Business Review*, September–October: 108–119.

28. Piore, M. and Sabel, C. (1984) *The Second Industrial Divide: Possibilities For Prosperity*. Basic Books, New York.

29. Womack, J., Jones, D. and Roos, D. (1990) *The Machine That Changed the World*. Rawson Associates, New York.

30. Kidd, P. (1994) *Agile Manufacturing – Forging New Frontiers*. Addison Wesley, Reading, USA.

31. Hill, T. (1995) *Manufacturing Strategy*. Macmillan, Basingstoke, UK; Brown, S. (1996) *Strategic Manufacturing for Competitive Advantage*. Prentice Hall, Hemel Hempstead, UK.

32. Lazonick, W. (1990) *Competitive Advantage on the Shop Floor*. Harvard University Press, Cambridge, USA.

33. Hayes, R. and Wheelwright, S. (1984) *Restoring Our Competitive Edge*. John Wiley & Sons, New York.

34. This quote from Skinner is reported in Wallace, T. (1981) *The Manufacturing Strategy Report* No. 4, June. T.F. Wallace Inc., Cincinnati, USA.

35. Schonberger, R. (1990) *Building a Chain of Customers*. Hutchinson Business Books, London.

36. Excellent insight into this is provided in: Feitzinger, E. and Lee, H.L. (1997) 'Mass customization at Hewlett-Packard: the power of postponement', *Harvard Business Review*, January–February, **75**(1): 116(6).

37. Details of this survey is provided in *Industry Week*, December 7, 1998, **35**(1).

38. Hill, T. (1995) *Manufacturing Strategy*, Macmillan, Basingstoke, UK.

39. The reader might find the following of interest; they have certainly made major contributions in the areas of manufacturing strategy: Anderson, J., Schroeder, R. and Cleveland, G. (1991) 'The Process of Manufacturing Strategy', *International Journal of Production and Operations Management*, **11**(3); Hayes, R. and Wheelwright, S. (1984) *Restoring Our Competitive Edge*. John Wiley & Sons, New York; Skinner, W. (1985) *Manufacturing, The Formidable Competitive Weapon*. John Wiley & Sons, New York; Skinner, W. (1969) 'Manufacturing – The Missing Link in Corporate Strategy', *Harvard Business Review*, May–June – this was a ground-breaking article on manufacturing strategy; Slack, N. (1991) *The Manufacturing Advantage*. Mercury, London.

Other articles which may be of interest include the following: Bates, K.A., Amundson, S.D., Schroeder, R.G. and Morris, W.T. (1995) 'The crucial interrelationship between manufacturing strategy and organizational culture', *Management Science*, **41**(10), October: 1565–1580; Corbett, C. and Van Wassenhove, L. (1994) 'Trade-offs? What trade-offs? Competence and competitiveness in manufacturing strategy', *California Management Review*, **35**(4): 107–120; Harrison, A. and Stovey, J. (1996) 'New wave manufacturing strategies: operational, organizational and human dimensions', *International Journal of Operations & Production Management*, **16**(2): 63–76; Hayes, R.H. and Pisano, G.P. (1994) 'Beyond world class: the new manufacturing strategy', *Harvard Business Review*, January–February: 77–86; Swink, M. and Way, M.H. (1995) 'Manufacturing strategy: propositions, current research, renewed directions', *International Journal of Operations & Production Management*, **15**(7): 4–26; Voss, C.A. (1995) 'Alternative paradigms for manufacturing strategy', *International Journal of Operations & Production Management*, **15**(4): 5–16; Ward, P.T., Bickford, D.J. and Leong, G.K. (1996), 'Configurations of manufacturing strategy, business strategy, environment, and structure', *Journal of Management*, **22**(4): 597–626.

2

The industries, the plants and the research

Introduction

This chapter is concerned with three things. First, I will provide a brief overview of the car and computing industries. This is because the plants operate within these industries and it is important, therefore, to gain insight into the industries. It is pointless homing in on the details of the plants without first understanding their business context. Second, I will develop some of the themes mentioned in Chapter 1, and discuss how they are relevant to these particular industries. Third, I will provide details about the plants themselves. In this section I will discuss how strategy is formed within their firms and describe the degree of strategic resonance that takes place between their business and manufacturing strategies within the plants. This section is pivotal for the book because I shall also discuss the nature of the strategy planning process within the plants themselves and how the plants became divided into the two profoundly different groups – enlightened and traditional. This will then set the background for the subsequent chapters in which I will discuss the operations capabilities of the plants.

Manufacturing matters

First, if anybody needs reminding of the critical importance of manufacturing we need only to look at the contribution of manufacturing to both the Fortune 500 (US firms) and the Fortune Global 500. It is important to bear in mind that it is not only those firms that we might think of automatically as manufacturing companies that count. The massive retail outlets are also very dependent upon manufactured goods – this may seem obvious but often people will classify retail as a service industry as if, somehow, it is an entity which is entirely independent of manufacturing. The fact is that retail is very dependent upon the manufacturing base. The 40 largest companies listed in the Fortune 500 and Global 500 in terms of revenues are shown in Table 2.1.

Table 2.1   The top 50 Fortune 500 and Global 500 companies, 1999

Fortune 500 Rank	Company	Revenues ($ millions)	Global 500 Rank	Company	Revenues ($ millions)
1	General Motors	161,315	1	General Motors	161,315
2	Ford Motor	144,416	2	DaimlerChrysler	154,615
3	Wal-Mart Stores	139,208	3	Ford Motor	144,416
4	Exxon	100,697	4	Wal-Mart Stores	139,208
5	General Electric	100,469	5	Mitsui	109,372
6	International Business Machines	81,667	6	Itochu	108,749
7	Citigroup	76,431	7	Mitsubishi	107,184
8	Philip Morris	57,813	8	Exxon	100,697
9	Boeing	56,154	9	General Electric	100,469
10	AT&T	53,588	10	Toyota Motor	99,740
11	Bank of America	50,777	11	Royal Dutch/Shell Group	93,692
12	Mobil	47,678	12	Marubeni	93,568
13	Hewlett-Packard	47,061	13	Sumitomo	89,020
14	State Farm Insurance Cos.	44,620	14	International Business Machines	81,667
15	Sears Roebuck	41,322	15	AXA	78,729
16	E.I. du Pont de Nemours	39,130	16	Citigroup	76,431
17	Procter & Gamble	37,154	17	Volkswagen	76,306
18	TIAA-CREF	35,889	18	Nippon Telegraph & Telephone	76,118
19	Merrill Lynch	35,853	19	BP Amoco	68,304
20	Prudential Insurance Company of America	34,427	20	Nissho Iwai	67,741
21	Kmart	33,674	21	Nippon Life Insurance	66,299
22	American International Group	33,296	22	Siemens	66,037
23	Chase Manhattan Corp.	32,379	23	Allianz	64,874
24	Texaco	31,707	24	Hitachi	62,409
25	Bell Atlantic	31,565	25	US Postal Service	60,072
26	Fannie Mae	31,498	26	Matsushita Electric Industrial	59,771
27	Enron	31,260	27	Philip Morris	57,813
28	Compaq Computer	31,169	28	Ing Group	56,468
29	Morgan Stanley Dean Witter	31,131	29	Boeing	56,154
30	Dayton Hudson	30,951	30	AT&T	53,588
31	J.C. Penney	30,678	31	Sony	53,156
32	Home Depot	30,219	32	Metro	52,126
33	Lucent Technologies	30,147	33	Nissan Motor	51,477
34	Motorola	29,398	34	Fiat	50,998
35	SBC Communications	28,777	35	Bank of America Corp.	50,777
36	Kroger	28,203	36	Nestlé	49,504
37	Merck	26,898	37	Credit Suisse	49,143
38	Chevron	26,801	38	Honda Motor	48,747
39	Metropolitan Life Insurance	26,735	39	Assicurazioni Generali	48,478
40	Intel	26,273	40	Mobil	47,678

Source: *Fortune*, August 2, 1999.

Undoubtedly, there are major service companies in both lists but the key issue is this: service exports have not managed to plug the gap between manufactured imports and exports in many countries, and this is especially evident in the USA. Although the USA managed to improve its manufacturing base dramatically during the 1990s, and now has many plants that can be termed world-class, the damage to the economy is ongoing because the USA still imports more manufactured products than it exports. The difference is not met by the export of services. This is shown in Table 2.2.

So we need to be clear that the idea that manufacturing can simply be replaced by service jobs without any harm coming to the economy is a myth. Fortunately for the USA, it has continued to be a power in two key industries: cars and computing. The vital importance, size and power of these industries are evident from the data shown in Tables 2.3 and 2.4.

As can be seen from Table 2.3, the major players in the computers and office equipment industry are from the USA and Japan. The car industry, by contrast, is much wider in the range of global players, as illustrated in Table 2.4.

Before looking at the plants themselves, we need to gain insight into the industries in which the firms operate. We will deal with each in turn, starting with the car industry.

Table 2.2   US international trade 1992–97

Year	Balance ($ millions)		
	Goods	Services	Total
1992	−96,106	56,899	−39,207
1993	−132,609	60,308	−72,301
1994	−166,192	61,776	−104,416
1995	−173,560	71,703	−101,857
1996	−191,170	80,130	−111,040
1997	−198,975	85,291	−113,684

Source: US Commerce Department.

The automobile industry

The auto industry has a total turnover of well over $1 trillion, and employs about 10 million people. Motor vehicle production at the beginning of the

Table 2.3   Major players in the computers and office equipment industry

Ranking	Company	Revenues (1998) ($ millions)	Profits (1998) ($ millions)
1	IBM	81,667	6,328
2	Hewlett-Packard	47,061	2,945
3	Fujitsu	41,018	(107)
4	Compaq	31,169	(2,743)
5	Canon	21,616	838
6	Xerox	20,019	395
7	Dell	18,243	1,460
8	Ricoh	11,156	240
9	Sun Microsystems	9,791	763
	Total	281,740	10,119

Source: Fortune, August 2, 1999.

new millennium was around 55 million units and these were manufactured in the areas shown in Figure 2.1.

The automobile industry is still the world's largest manufacturing business. But there are a number of major concerns for auto firms and there are vast differences between competitors in terms of their size, capabilities and financial performance. A small number have large cash reserves but the weaker members are saddled with huge amounts of debt, and in 1999–2000 only a quarter of the world's 40 car makers were profitable. Competition has become far more intense due to increased globalization efforts coupled with saturated capacity in several major geographic areas. Perhaps the key issue for the industry is over-capacity: in total, the car producers can produce 20 million more cars and trucks a year than it sells. Put bluntly, every car plant in North America could close, and the world would still have too many cars. A possible scenario is that by the year 2010, 40 car makers will have been reduced to a total of the Big Six:

. . . by 2010, the thinking goes, each major auto market will be left with two large, home-based companies – GM and Ford in the USA, DaimlerChrysler and Volkswagen in Europe, and Toyota and Honda in Japan. Players such as Nissan or Volvo may keep their brand names, but someone else will be running the show.[1]

The capacity problem is made even more acute because the Asia–Pacific region will add capacity to make an additional 6 million cars by 2005. Different firms will deal with the problem of over-capacity in various ways but an important development has been in the surge of mergers and acquisitions.

The merger and acquisition trend in the car industry

Mergers and acquisitions activity became an important feature of the car industry during the 1990s. Mergers and acquisitions are business strategies that may cause strategic dissonance to occur between business intent and manufacturing strategies. Particular manufacturing strategies may be serving and supporting the company. However, as you will see in the DaimlerChrysler example, the holistic approach may be ignored and the impact of such a merger – on suppliers in this case – may cause potential strategic weaknesses to emerge. Consolidation may well be a necessary feature of the automotive industry but the impact on infrastructure issues – especially with the supplier base – may be profoundly damaging and an holistic approach is vital if the merger is to be successful.

The merger between Daimler and Chrysler in 1999 created the world's fifth largest car company by volume with combined annual revenues of around $130 billion. The aim of the merger was to create strategic fit:

Chrysler makes moderately priced cars and light trucks; Daimler makes Mercedes luxury cars and heavy trucks. Chrysler is strong in North America and weak in Western Europe; Daimler, just the reverse. Chrysler is deft at design and product development; Daimler holds the upper hand in engineering and technology. This is a marriage of opportunity, not desperation.[2]

Figure 2.1   World motor vehicle production figures by country

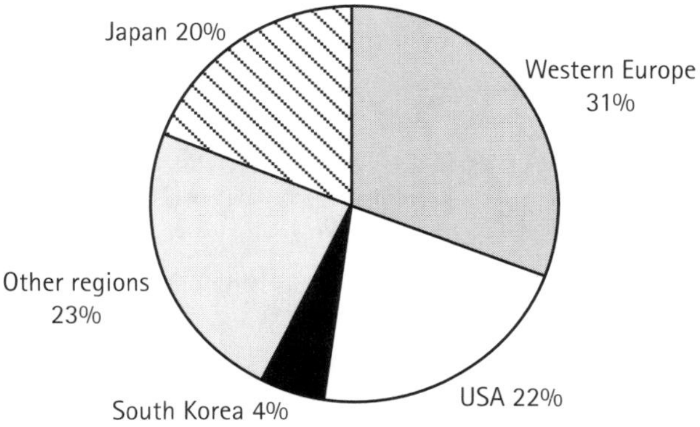

Japan 20%, Western Europe 31%, Other regions 23%, South Korea 4%, USA 22%

Source: Ward's Automotive Yearbook, 1999.

Table 2.4 Major players in the motor vehicles and parts industry

Ranking	Company	Revenues (1998) ($ millions)	Profits (1998) ($ millions)
1	General Motors	161,315	2,956
2	DaimlerChrysler	154,615	5,656
3	Ford	144,416	22,071
4	Toyota	99,740	2,787
5	Volkswagen	76,307	1,261
6	Nissan	51,478	(217)
7	Fiat	50,999	692
8	Honda	48,748	2,386
9	Renault	41,353	1,500
10	Peugeot	37,540	539
11	BMW	35,887	513
12	Robert Bosch	28,610	446
13	Mitsubishi	27,480	44
14	Volvo	26,773	1,086

Source: Fortune, August 2, 1999.

Chrysler had managed to position itself as a potential partner by its transition from a traditional to enlightened firm both in the way it formed strategy and how it subsequently performed in its operations capabilities. This is exemplified in its performance in costs – it drastically reduced costs while still managing to retain a strategic approach both within its plants and with its external partnerships, particularly suppliers. In 1998, Chrysler had profits of $1,468 for each sale compared with Ford's $1,000 and GM's $683. The link with Daimler was important for Chrysler because it needed to grow its business outside North America. But the strategic fit with Daimler will be a difficult one, as Maryann Keller, an American car analyst, observes:

> When it comes to the cultures of these two companies, how they think and act and what drives their decisions, they're oil and water.[3]

For example, Chrysler purchases 70% of its added value from mainly US suppliers and came closer than either GM or Ford to producing cars to

Toyota's lean standards. In contrast, Daimler is a fully integrated German producer of luxury cars. As a result of the merger, DaimlerChrysler set about reviewing the entire components supply chain in Europe and North America as a means to ensure strategic fit between the two companies. This very act may threaten one of the major foundations upon which Chrysler's success was built – its strategic relationships with suppliers.

Merger and acquisition activities directly impact strategic operations. For example, fewer car makers will result, in turn, in fewer (but more powerful) core components suppliers. Coupled with this development is the fact that, as you will see in Chapter 3, many car manufacturers are adopting new product 'platform' strategies – building a variety of vehicles from one basic set of designed components provided by suppliers. As large manufacturers do so, this will lead to fewer, but larger, contracts for those suppliers with the resources and global capacity to supply them. Contracts will not be awarded solely in terms of capacity and volume requirements. The nature of the buyer–supplier relationship will become more profoundly intertwined than ever before. For example, supplier involvement in ongoing develop- ments of new products will be an essential and central feature of the relationship. Mergers and acquisitions influence several key features of strategic operations including capacity, new product development and strategic relationships with suppliers in order to manage inventory.

If we take new product development as an example, it is clear that some mergers have resulted in the disbanding of former alliances involving joint designs. For example, the union of Renault and Nissan, by which Renault invested $5.4 billion for a 37% interest in Nissan, has impacted the minivan alliance between Ford and Nissan. Since 1992, Ford and Nissan have co-produced the Nissan Quest and the Mercury Villager. However, as a result of the link with Renault, Nissan then announced that it planned to end its relationship with Ford by 2004. Nissan intended, instead, to develop minivans with Renault, while Ford wants to engineer its own minivan for Mercury. Thus a business decision (a merger) has resulted in the demise of another strategic relationship which had been based on joint collaboration in design.

Ford has used mergers and acquisitions as a means to overtake GM as the largest car company. In January 1999, Ford bought the car division of Volvo for SKr50 billion ($6.45 billion). The purchase gave Ford the oppor- tunity to overtake GM as the largest player, the first time since the 1930s. Such an acquisition will place a great burden on other players to find strategic partners. These mergers will not be about simply seeking a match with another car firm's product portfolio. Instead, much will depend on the excellence of operations capabilities that each firm can offer to the part- nership. Indeed, such operations capabilities will need to be in place if a

Table 2.5   Possible merger strategies of major car firms

Company	1998 earnings ($ billions)	1998 revenues ($ billions)	Worldwide vehicle sales (millions)	Possible merger strategies
General Motors	2.8[a]	140	7.5	GM has a 49% stake in Japan's Isuzu and a 10% stake in Suzuki. Some speculate GM will rescue South Korea's Daewoo.
Ford Motor	6.7	118	6.8	Purchase Volvo.
DaimlerChrysler	6.47[b]	147.3	4	Daimler Benz and Chrysler have created a global powerhouse. But it needs a presence in Asia and is already talking to Nissan about a deal.
Volkswagen	1.3	75	4.58	VW has already acquired Rolls-Royce, Bugatti and Lamborghini. Hard-driving Piech is often rumoured to be eyeing BMW and Volvo, which itself is in talks with Fiat.
Toyota Motor	4	106	4.45	Toyota wants to strengthen its hold on Japanese auto maker Daihatsu Motor, truckmaker Hino Motors, and affiliated parts suppliers like Denso.
Honda Motor	2.4	54	2.34	Honda must grow bigger if it is to make it into the Big Six. Honda insists it wants to go it alone. But joining forces with luxury carmaker BMW could result in a dream team.

[a]Includes one-time charges for restructuring.
[b]Estimates of Daimler Benz and Chrysler combined results.
Sources: Merrill Lynch & Co.; Schroder & Co.; Salomon Smith Barney; J.P. Morgan; Wasserstein Perella; Company Reports; and *Business Week*, January 25, 1999, p. 16.

firm is to be even considered as a potential partner in an alliance or as a target for a merger.

The European car market saw mergers and acquisitions taking place. In 1998, Volkswagen made a number of purchases. It bought Rolls-Royce, after a protracted contest with BMW. Volkswagen also bought Automobili Lamborghini and Bugatti. Purchases also took place in Asia with Hyundai buying Kia. A list of possible mergers and acquisitions is shown in Table 2.5.

As well as mergers and acquisitions, various alliances took place that allowed major car firms to create a stronger presence than before in previously undeveloped territories. For example, Renault invested $350 million in OAO Avtoframos in Moscow by which 120,000 cars would be produced. Daewoo invested $1.3 billion in AvtoZAZ in the Ukraine. However, the success of these alliances and mergers is not dependent upon the size and subsequent volume that might be achieved. Instead, success will depend to a large extent on ensuring that strategic resonance takes place. This in turn demands that a range of strategic operations are put in place – this capability means that quality, rapid innovation, competitive costs, process technology, excellent inventory management and a trained and motivated work force are all poised and ready to be activated.

Strategic operations in transplants

Examples of strategic operations are clearly evident in the auto industry, particularly within transplant production in the USA. It is plain to see that Japanese and German firms have targeted strategic areas to set up production facilities within the USA and their emergence has been at the expense of US competitors. General Motors, Ford and Chrysler now produce fewer vehicles than they did in the 1980s, but the total number of cars produced in the USA has remained constant due to the emergence of Japanese and German plants. By the end of the 1990s, Toyota, Honda and Nissan assembled 2.3 million vehicles in North America. The former Big Three, GM, Ford and Chrysler (which is now the Big Two due to the Daimler–Chrysler merger), accounted for around 59% of passenger cars produced in the USA at the end of the 1990s. The other 41% came from foreign players in the USA. Toyota ensures that strategic resonance takes place between its business and operations strategies. Thus its aggressive growth strategy is underpinned by a clear vision regarding its strategic operations, including seeking out new production locations to satisfy capacity requirements. Toyota planned to increase production to around 6 million units by 2005. It therefore supported this vision with added potential capacity in new and existing plants. Toyota opened its first car plant in Brazil, while in Europe,

Toyota opened its second car assembly line in the UK, at a cost of £200 million and also built an assembly plant in Valenciennes in northern France. The UK is now merely a host country for foreign investment. However, the good news for the UK was that both Honda and Nissan announced expansion plans. But the strategic significance of this development for the UK is evident in the following:

> In the case of every plant, from General Motors' Astra-producing facility at Ellesmere Port, a few miles from Halewood on Merseyside, through Nissan's at Sunderland, Toyota's in Derbyshire, Honda's at Swindon, to the Rover and Land-Rover plants of the Midlands, ultimate decision-making lies not in the UK but in the boardrooms of Detroit, Munich and Tokyo. As global competition sharpens, whether these plants live, wither or die will depend almost entirely on performance.[4]

That is a telling, and rather damning, statement for the UK which, at one time, had an active, British-owned, car industry.

We saw earlier how General Motors had lost domestic market share. The company has responded to this loss by becoming more aggressive in new and developing markets. For example, during the 1990s GM made the largest foreign investment of all car firms in China. In 1997, a $1.6-billion, 50–50 joint venture was signed between GM and Shanghai Automotive Industry Corporation (SAIC), a state-owned firm. However, if this joint venture is to be successful then a range of strategic operations – and not just cheap labour costs – will be a key issue. China's main manufacturing advantage – cheap labour – is not the most important issue because labour accounts, typically, for around 10% of a car's cost. A range of strategic operations capabilities will need to be in place including strategic supplier relationships and world-class inventory management, quality, process technology and rapid introduction of new car designs. It will be many years before GM's local supply networks in China will match the quality and efficiency of those in Japan, South Korea or the USA. As we saw in Chapter 1, a feature of strategic decisions is that they can have both profound and long-term effects. It may well be, though, that this joint venture between GM and SAIC will test GM's patience to the full.

The personal computer industry

Enlightened manufacturing capabilities, which help to create strategic resonance between market demands and operations capabilities, are vital requirements within the PC industry. Although the industry saw remarkable price reductions during the 1990s, cost was not the only crucial strategic factor. Other strategic operations capabilities had to be in place including build-to-order configurations, expert inventory management, and managing relationships with other strategic partners. This calls for the very best man-agerial skills and, as you will see, some firms have struggled with having to deliver a range of customer requirements simultaneously. Another damning example of the demise of the UK's manufacturing base came in 1996 when ICL pulled out of the personal computer business. ICL placed its volume products operations under the control of Fujitsu, its Japanese parent. This meant that there were no British-owned firms in the PC industry. In 1990, another player, Apricot, sold off its manufacturing business to Mitsubishi, and a few years later its software and services operations were sold too. The service and software elements of the business did not compensate for the closure of its manufacturing activities. There is now no Apricot presence other than a mere badge put on to products made by Mitsubishi. Put bluntly – but accurately – Mitsubishi was able to do in its operations capa-bilities what Apricot itself could not do.

The PC industry has seen major developments in software and services in recent years but the hardware remains centrally important, particularly in the range of configurations that can be offered. The sheer size of the sales volume indicates how important manufacturing continues to be in the indus-try, as shown in Table 2.6.

Table 2.6   Worldwide computer hardware revenues, 1998 (based on factory shipments in billions of dollars)

Type of product	Revenues ($ billions)
PCs	170
Workstations	14.7
Entry-level servers	25
Mid-range servers	17.6
High-end servers	16.3
High-performance market	5.2

Source: International Data Corp.

Computer hardware has gone through a remarkable change, based on three interlinking attributes: smaller, faster and cheaper products. Computer power, which only a few years before would have taken up large amounts of space, is now available as a desktop unit. There have been a number of dramatic changes in the PC industry. IBM's PC, launched in 1981, although not the first PC, was an important breakthrough because it combined two important factors: microchips from Intel and software from Microsoft. This meant that from this point every PC producer would need to form strategic partnerships with these two firms. Intel and Microsoft continue to have a profound impact on the industry and they shape the step changes in technology to a large extent. It is not surprising then that in 1998, Intel and Microsoft's combined spending on research and development (R&D) amounted to $5.2 billion – about 12.7% of their combined sales. A PC manufacturer, in contrast, spends between 2% and 5% of sales on R&D. Intel's 386 chip, introduced in 1985, was important because for the first time, IBM-compatible PCs could use graphical user interface applications which formerly belonged solely to Apple units. With the launch of Windows in 1990, the industry became increasingly standardized. As a result, phenomenal growth took place and prices were greatly reduced. Growth in worldwide PC shipments averaged around 20% per annum between 1991 and 1995, and then declined slightly to 15% per annum for the rest of the decade; all signs are that this would continue into the next decade. However, increased shipments and increased sales in dollars are different entities. The worldwide PC market in 2000 consisted of three key units – servers, desktops and portables – as shown in Figure 2.2.

The volatility of the industry – and its dependence upon ongoing world-class operations capability – is evident in Apple. I shall discuss Apple in more depth later, but it is important to note here that in the early 1990s Apple seemed destined to be the largest player in worldwide shipments of PCs. However, it then slipped badly but then enjoyed a remarkable turnaround in its operations capabilities which, coupled with a plethora of new products – also aided by operations capabilities, helped to reverse the decline. Indications of changes of market share within the PC industry are shown in Table 2.7.

The number of worldwide shipments and revenues between 1983 and 1998 is shown in Table 2.8.

Figure 2.2   Server, desktop and portable units in the PC industry in 2000

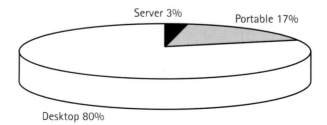

Source: Standard & Poor's Industry Survey, 1999.

Table 2.7   Top 10 marketers of PCs (worldwide shipments)

1992			1996			1997		
Rank	Vendor	Market share (%)	Rank	Vendor	Market share (%)	Rank	Vendor	Market share (%)
1	IBM	10.4	1	Compaq	10.4	1	Compaq	12.7
2	Apple	9.0	2	IBM	8.9	2	IBM	9.0
3	Compaq	5.1	3	Packard Bell NEC	6.1	3	Dell	5.9
4	NEC	4.5	4	Apple	5.4	4	Hewlett-Packard	5.6
5	Packard Bell	2.3	5	Dell	4.3	5	Packard Bell NEC	5.2
6	Dell	2.3	6	Hewlett-Packard	4.3	6	Toshiba	4.1
7	Toshiba	2.0	7	Acer	4.1	7	Fujitsu	3.7
8	AST	1.9	8	Toshiba	3.9	8	Acer	3.5
9	Olivetti	1.8	9	NEC Japan	3.8	9	Gateway 2000	3.4
10	Groupe Bull ZDS	1.6	10	Fujitsu	3.7	10	Apple	3.2
–	Others	59.0	–	Others	45.0	–	Others	43.6

Source: International Data Corp.

Strategic operations in personal computer manufacture and assembly

Manufacturing a PC demands that firms have to manage a range of strategic operations successfully. First, there is an extremely high volume of components. All of these components must meet quality requirements of customers who are now used to user-friendly and easily installable products. However, quality is not the only facet required in strategic operations within the PC industry. Careful production planning and strong strategic relationships with suppliers are vital ingredients. If these are not in place firms suffer. For example, in the period 1994–95 Compaq did not judge correctly how quickly customers would switch from 486 to Pentium units. As a result, Compaq had to drastically reduce prices for its 486 units because it had built up a large amount of unwanted inventories.

The need for agility and flexibility as core features within strategic operations is evident in the computer industry. We shall see how Hewlett-Packard (HP), IBM and Compaq dealt in different ways with the

Table 2.8   Growth in shipments and revenues in the PC industry 1983–98

Year	Shipments (thousands)	Revenues ($ millions)
1983	11,123	11,019
1984	15,044	18,496
1985	14,705	22,765
1986	15,064	22,968
1987	16,676	24,975
1988	18,061	33,367
1989	21,327	40,435
1990	23,738	46,000
1991	26,966	57,580
1992	32,411	64,095
1993	38,851	73,561
1994	47,894	94,457
1995	60,171	123,643
1996	71,065	150,414
1997	82,400	162,834
1998	97,321	181,544

shift to mass customization in their operations. Compaq, IBM and HP had to radically alter their respective manufacturing and distribution processes in order to help bring their PC pricing and delivery capabilities more in line with direct marketer Dell Computers. Compaq, IBM and HP had to change from a finished-goods inventory model to build-to-order and channel configuration processes, or varying combinations of both. Each was trying to emulate Dell's efficient inventory model by focusing on components rather than finished goods.

Let's now look at how a number of major players within the PC industry attempted to manage the huge competitive requirements placed on their plants.

Acer

Acer is an example where a range of strategic operations capabilities were put in place to ensure that strategic resonance took place between business strategies and plant capabilities. Acer America became profitable in 1994 and grew at an average of 70% between 1994 and 1999, and more than doubled its market share to around 4%, pushing it ahead of AST, NEC and Toshiba. At the core of Acer's development have been powerful strategic operations capabilities, particularly in inventory management. The Acer Group has 30 manufacturing sites worldwide, and has devised strategies to enable plants to assemble PCs to order. Acer devised manufacturing strategies centred on strategic locations to satisfy mass customization requirements, as their CEO stated:

> With 30 manufacturing sites around the world, we are in a much better position than anyone else for assemble to order.[5]

Acer chose not to outsource everything, preferring instead to make everything from memory chips (through a joint venture with Texas Instruments) to CD-ROM drives, monitors, keyboards, motherboards, video cards, scanners and printers. Acer manages inventory by having parts such as chassis and monitors delivered by ship to the USA every three weeks, while more time-sensitive components such as CPUs are purchased locally.[6] Assembly for the US market takes place in the USA. In 1998, its inventory cycle – the number of machines shipped in a year divided by the number on hand in current inventory – was 12 times per year, which was nearly double the turns of industry leader Compaq, although, as you will see, this figure was behind Dell and Apple.

Acer America understood the need to create strategic resonance: its 75,000 square foot plant has four assembly lines, which are then focused further into 16 different cells. This gives Acer the flexibility to produce numerous configurations, simultaneously. Capacity has been planned carefully. Acer America's assembly plants produce more than 50,000 PCs and servers a month, but there is capacity to increase to 150,000 systems. Acer clearly sees the vital importance of human resources to achieve world-class operations. Each employee associate assembles an entire PC, which gives employees a greater sense of pride in their work and ownership of the process. This in turn has impacted quality performance where defects found in final testing total less than 1%. Acer's phenomenal growth demonstrates the competitive capabilities that can come from powerful, strategic operations. Its growth strategy has been supported by a manufacturing strategy which includes strategic location decisions, build-to-order capabilities, focused manufacturing cells and expertise in inventory management. However, in spite of its remarkable growth Acer, like other major players, continues to lag behind Dell.

IBM

In 1998, IBM's PC group lost nearly $1 billion.[7] IBM's strategy includes engaging in a range of alliances to support its strategic operations efforts, especially in inventory management and new product development. For example, in 1999, IBM and Dell Computer announced a seven-year, $16-billion alliance that gave Dell access to a broad range of IBM hardware components; in return, IBM gained a new technology channel. The deal had direct impact on areas of strategic operations: Dell would purchase storage, microelectronics, networking and display systems from IBM and there would be broad patent cross-licensing and collaboration on development of new products between the companies.[8] As you will see in Chapter 3, although IBM has been prominent in developing patents it has often struggled with the speed of new product development and this alliance, therefore, could be an important enhancement in speed of innovation within its operations.

In another alliance, IBM and Acer agreed a far-reaching purchasing and technology-sharing alliance estimated to be worth $8 billion over seven years. The two companies agreed to collaborate on technology development and purchase components and PC peripherals from each other. Acer would do most of the buying including purchasing IBM hard drives for use in note-books, desktops and servers as well as some of IBM's eBusiness software for internal use. The companies also pledged to work together to develop system-on-a-chip technology, based on IBM's PowerPC chip and IBM agreed to purchase about $1 billion worth of the Acer's flat-panel displays.

These alliances were typical of several major computer and telecommunications agreements that IBM made. Another key part of the strategy has been in purchasing smaller companies. Between 1993 and 1999, IBM purchased 58 companies. However, as IBM's CEO, Lou Gerstner, stated:

The legacy of this management group will include the deals we didn't do.[9]

Undoubtedly, Apple Computer and Digital Equipment are two major firms who would be included in a list of firms not purchased by IBM. However, as can be seen from the alliances with Dell and Acer, IBM aimed to provide strength in key areas of strategic operations, particularly inventory management and new product developments.

Hewlett-Packard

We saw in Chapter 1 how Hewlett-Packard (HP) has seen the need for strategic focus by dividing itself into two separate business entities. HP has also seen the critical importance of having strategic operations in place. However, trying to change the actual nature and shape of its strategic operations – especially in its relationships with resellers – has been very difficult. In early 1994, HP conducted an analysis of its PC manufacturing and distribution strategies and found that the modular structure of the product and the production process would allow the company to post-pone all steps of the PC's final assembly. Integrating the PC board, processor, chassis, power supply, storage devices and software could be done by resellers. HP's distribution network could then build the product in locations close to customers and do so only in response to customer orders. In early 1995, HP abandoned its previous practice of stocking fin-ished goods or partially completed units, and implemented a build-to-order strategy within all of its distribution centres. Apparently, a Compaq executive stated in the trade press that HP was 'light-years ahead of the competition' in its ability to deliver products quickly and at a low cost.[10] As a result of its new strategy, HP did in fact deliver a highly cus-tomized product more quickly and cheaply than its competitors could. In 1997, the company announced plans to streamline its delivery channels further and intended to build all of its PCs on the basis of incoming orders rather than any forecast demand. About ten resellers were responsible for assembly, customization and delivery of products directly to customers. However, the problem for HP – along with Compaq, IBM and other PC makers who sell products through resellers – is that it faces a perfect dilemma concerning price and inventory factors. If all PC competitors could agree jointly to reduce inventories in the reseller channel down to similar levels, all of them would benefit. But the major players do not do so and, therefore, if one firm did take the initiative and reduced inven-tories to, for example, two weeks, that might merely provide opportunities for space for their competitors on their distributors' shelves. A major com-petitor would then reduce prices to gain market share, or to clear inventory, and HP would then have to follow suit.

In spite of being heralded as a model for mass customization through clever use of configurations via its resellers, HP finally decided in 1999 to embrace the direct-sales model used by Dell Computer. HP encouraged consumers to buy PCs direct from its website. This direct distribution strat-egy was for both consumer and corporate customer segments. Its rationale for the change was explained by one of its vice presidents:

We've been a product-centric company . . . Now we're going to be customer-centric.[11]

The intention may seem admirable but strategic dissonance has occurred and the strategy is potentially a dangerous one because it is at the expense of the resellers who stock HP's PCs. Something in the region of 80% of HP's PCs sales are dependent upon regional resellers for the installation and service of its products. The shift, therefore, from mass customization via its resellers, to direct sales not needing resellers will be a massive challenge for

HP. The only consolation is that it is a problem that all of the PC firms – other than Dell – must face. This fact alone means that a massive change in the industry – regarding strategic operations activities in inventory – is inevitable.

Compaq

As we saw in Chapter 1, Compaq has pursued an aggressive acquisition strategy including purchasing Tandem and Digital Computers. Undoubtedly, for some time Compaq's strategic operations capabilities allowed it to oust IBM in 1995 as the largest producer of PCs. Compaq created and, to an extent, *defined* strategic resonance within the PC industry by virtue of its massive price cuts throughout the 1990s. But over a period of time cost became less of a factor, and was replaced by customization requirements. In 1996, Compaq surpassed $20 billion in sales, nearly seven times its revenues in 1991, the year Eckhard Pfeiffer took over as CEO. Compaq sold a full line of machines, from low-margin, sub-$1,000 PCs to high-margin workstations and servers. Growth was the major business strategy and, as a result, Compaq could proudly state that in the mid-1990s, it had an astounding figure of $1 million sales per employee annually. However, inventory problems has remained a problem for Compaq. Its problems began in February 1994 when its former CEO, Pfeiffer, announced that Compaq would make all its PCs on a build-to-order basis by 1996; inventory problems have plagued Compaq since. At the time of the build-to-order statement from Pfeiffer, Compaq built less than 5% of its machines to order. In July 1997, Compaq announced a new business model that it promised would deliver the latest product innovation to customers at the highest quality and for a lower total cost of ownership. Known as Optimized Distribution Model (ODM), Compaq said it was designed to meet customer-specific orders while keeping down distribution costs. Unfortunately, it did not succeed in doing this.

The major problem with inventory in the PC industry is that the value of the components used to assemble a PC decrease by 1–2% a week. Consequently, a computer sitting in inventory for eight weeks commands a significantly lower price than one built with the newest components. Major cracks in Compaq's strategic operations abilities occurred in March 1998, when Compaq produced and distributed far too many PCs for its resellers, resulting in excess inventory levels.

In November 1998, Compaq faced a similar problem to Hewlett-Packard when it announced that customers could buy direct from Compaq, thus upsetting resellers. Compaq stated that its ProSignia desktop PCs would be sold only over the company's website. However, by March 1999, as a result of poor sales, Compaq reversed the decision.

Compaq's inventory management has been a major and constant problem. Its annual rate of inventory turns – the number of machines shipped in a year divided by the number on hand in current inventory – at around seven turns in the late 1990s, was way behind other players. In the period 1998–99, Compaq's inventory on occasions backed up to an estimated eight to ten weeks' worth resulting in an inability to launch new products until its distributors sold existing models. By the end of the 1990s, Compaq attempted to overhaul its distribution system, trying to cut the amount of PC inventory held by its wholesalers and resellers to two or three weeks. Unfortunately, Compaq's operations incapabilities became increasingly visible.

By the beginning of the new millennium, Compaq was way behind Dell in build-to-order capabilities and Dell had surpassed Compaq in desktop PC sales to US businesses for the first time. The Optimized Distribution Model struggled with no significant reductions in distribution and manufacturing costs or increases in PC revenues. Compaq has frequently been caught with outdated computers on retailers' shelves, forcing it to slash prices to move the inventory. A telling quote comes from one of Compaq's vice presidents:

A computer is like fruit or fish . . . You have to sell it before you smell it.[12]

The replacement CEO for Pfeiffer at Compaq was Capellas, whose background is in information technology (IT), supply chain management and manufacturing. He stated:

Strategy is about solving business problems . . . I've been in IT for many years, [so] I'm confident that I can do that.[13]

The major requirement for Compaq is to restore strategic resonance between its operations capabilities and market requirements. At the beginning of the new millennium, Compaq had strategic operations that excelled in the wrong things – low-cost production. What Compaq needed to do was to put in place capabilities of customization without pressuring costs. At the same time, it needed to increase direct sales without causing major problems for reseller in the process. Not surprisingly the task facing Compaq was similar to other layers and Compaq's size alone would not help. Excellence in its strategic operations capability, through a strategic, focused, holistic approach, would be the key challenge for Compaq.

Dell

Dell's remarkable strategic operations capabilities have practically reinvented the PC industry. Dell is more focused than any rival on speedily manufacturing and delivering inexpensive, top-quality PCs. An example of Dell's remarkable operations capabilities was at the end of 1997 when Dell shipped 2,000 PCs and 4,000 servers loaded with proprietary and multimedia software to 2,000 Wal-Mart stores in six weeks – just in time for the Christmas season.[14] Dell turns its inventory around 50 times in a year, in contrast to other companies who boast of stock turns of 6–10 times a year. In addition, Dell does not compete purely on price because Dell serves mainly corporate technology buyers, who are less sensitive to price and more concerned with performance. This accounts for why Dell's average sales price is $500 more than Compaq's. Clearly, Dell does not suffer any conflict between market demands and operations capabilities and, indeed, Dell measures success not only in financial terms but also in strategic operations performance:

> He now wants to measure parts inventory in hours instead of days. Seven days doesn't sound like much inventory, but 168 hours does . . . In a business where inventory depreciates by 1% per week, inventory is risk. A few years ago no one in this business realized what an incredible opportunity managing inventory was.[15]

Dell's clear understanding of the importance of focus in ensuring strategic operations are in place is evident in the following:

> 'We have put a big X through traditional manufacturing,' says Dell. 'We focus on how fast we can deliver product, and we have designed manufacturing to be a continuous flow with customer-specific aspects such as loading proprietary customer software built into the process.'[16]

Likewise, the holistic approach was evident when Dell stated:

> 'Both suppliers and customers must be treated as partners and collaborators, jointly looking for ways to improve efficiency across the entire spectrum of the value chain, not just in their respective businesses,' insists Dell. 'You have to approach the relationship with both the customer and supplier from the standpoint of what is the most efficient way to accomplish things rather than the old traditional view of 'if we don't control things, it won't work'.[17]

This is further endorsed in an interview in the *Harvard Business Review*, when Dell mentioned how:

> The supplier effectively becomes our partner. They assign their engineers to our design team, and we start to treat them as if they were part of the company. For example, when we launch a new product, their engineers are stationed right in our plants. If a customer calls in with a problem, we'll stop shipping product while they fix design flaws in real time.[18]

In the same interview, the combined strategic, focused, and holistic approach is exemplified in Dell's approach to managing inventory:

> Inventory velocity is one of a handful of key performance measures we watch very closely. It focuses us on working with our suppliers to keep reducing inventory and

increasing speed. With a supplier like Sony, which makes very good, reliable monitors, we figure there's no need for us to have any inventory at all. We are confident in putting the Dell name on them, and they work fine. We don't even take these monitors out of the box to test them because we've gotten them to under 1,000 defects per million. So what's the point in having a monitor put on a truck to Austin, Texas, and then taken off the truck and sent on a little tour around the warehouse, only to be put back on another truck? That's just a big waste of time and money, unless we get our jollies from touching monitors, which we don't. And because we build to our customers' order, typically, with just five or six days of lead time, suppliers don't have to worry about sell-through. We only maintain a few days – in some cases a few hours – of raw materials on hand. We communicate inventory levels and replenishment needs regularly – with some vendors, hourly.[19]

You have to admire not only the dramatic growth that Dell has enjoyed but also the remarkable way in which market requirements are woven into the core of operations capabilities so that strategic resonance takes place. Market requirements and operations capabilities result in supreme strategic resonance, better than any other company in the PC industry. However, as you will now see, Apple has surprisingly re-emerged as a contender to challenge Dell.

Apple

You saw in Table 2.7 how Apple had slipped from second to tenth position in worldwide shipments between 1992 and 1997. One of its core problems was poor strategic operations, particularly in inventory, which it has now improved to a great degree:

Apple's problem was a supply-chain management problem. As a result, the company either missed potential sales because it couldn't fulfil demand or piled up huge excess inventory that later had to be written off at a crippling cost. For years the company struggled with the twin demons of insufficient supply and excess inventory.[20]

Indeed most of Apple's huge financial losses can be attributed to poor inventory management:

The company lost $1 billion in 1997 mainly as a result of asset problems, such as being too long on inventory . . . We had five weeks of inventory in the plants, and we were turning inventory 10 times a year.[21]

This figure was consistent with other players – except Dell, of course. One of Apple's vice presidents claimed that by the end of 1999 Apple had surpassed Dell:

We've gone from 10 turns to 180 turns . . . That's a direct metric of your supply chain. We've now gone past Dell. In a year or two, I'd prefer to be able to talk inventories in terms of hours, not days . . . And we're not letting up . . . I consider any internal inventory to be a defect . . . Now, instead of building hundreds of thousands of computers in advance to meet a sales forecast, Apple projects sales each week and adjusts production schedules daily. 'We plan weekly and execute daily,' says Cook. 'I'm relentless on that.'

The dramatic improvement in Apple's inventory management is shown in Table 2.9.

Table 2.9 Apple's inventory management 1996–98

Year	Inventory value ($ millions)	Days of supply
1996	662	33
1997	437	31
1998	78	6

Inventory was the key issue for Apple, but another issue was innovation, which Apple has also managed to radically improve. In 1999 alone, Apple managed to enhance the already phenomenally successful iMac with three new models: iMac, iMac DV and iMac DV Special Edition. The operating system was upgraded to Mac OS 9 and the iBook – a notebook computer with easy Internet access – was also successful. The PowerBook G3 provided desktop performance in a notebook computer.

If Apple does ever manage to surpass Dell it will be through the dramatic improvement in its operations capabilities. In short it will need to create even stronger strategic resonance between its operations capabilities – which it has clearly improved upon since the mid-1990s – and customer requirements.

 ## From industries to individual plants

Thus far we have looked at the industries and commented on how particular firms have attempted to create strategic resonance between themselves and their customers. As you will have seen, much of this depends on strategic operations capabilities. But there is a key issue: these abilities do not come about by mere chance. Instead, they have to be put in place and this comes about by seeing the range of activities within operations as strategic. However, as we saw in Chapter 1, there is often a gap between those who make strategic decisions and those who manage operations capabilities. It is as if an assumption is made that strategic operations capabilities will somehow naturally follow on from a particular strategic decision. Of course this simply will not happen. A major reason for going to the plants, then, was to see how they ensure that strategic operations are put in place. We have seen that the computer and automobile industries are very powerful, dynamic and exciting, noted for continuous change and innovation. But there were other reasons for choosing them. First, they have formed a major part my consulting activities in the past. Second, they are both high volume producers. As a result, both industries tend to share the same, core manufacturing processes – based largely around line processes, with flexible manufacturing, group technology and other hybrid systems in place. Third, the industries tend to be at the forefront of developments in manufacturing technologies and practices. These practices include total quality management (TQM), just-in-time, MRP, and other developments, which are more or less established in the industries and are seen as quite common. This contrasts with other industries where such developments have not been so readily adopted. We now need to look at the plants.

The plants

How the information was gained will be of interest to the reader. There were 24 plants involved – 16 from the car industry and eight from the PC industry. The car plants consisted of nine plants in the USA and seven in the UK. There were six Japanese transplants within the 16 car plants, three from the UK and three from the USA. The essence of this book was to ask a number of questions, and to seek answers concerning strategy and plant performance. This was done in three stages: Stage 1 looked at how plants devised strategies; Stage 2 looked at how plants performed in a range of operations capabilities; and Stage 3 examined if there were links between how firms – and their plants – formed strategy and subsequent performance in the range of operations capabilities.

The key questions in Stage 1 included:

- How do firms develop strategy – in particular how do firms link with their plants in forming strategy?

- Who is involved in the strategy process? The fact that strategy is formed by 'top management', as we saw in Chapter 1, says very little about who is actually involved in the process.

- Are senior-level manufacturing personnel involved in the strategy process? If so, does their role really include involvement in business decisions, or does the role centre on 'technical' or 'production' decisions?

- Where does manufacturing strategy line up in the overall strategy process? In particular, how does manufacturing strategy link to business strategy?

In essence, the aim of Stage 1 was to establish:

● The level of seniority, and role of manufacturing personnel within the plant;
● The existence and scope of a manufacturing strategy within the plant;
● The extent of common links between business and manufacturing strategies.

In order to assess the common links a massive search was undertaken among over 300 books and journals devoted to business strategy to establish major business areas. Eight core business areas emerged. These were:

● The nature of the supply chain – including the degree of vertical integration and buyer–supplier relations for the plant.
● Fundamental process decisions: the degree of manufacture, as opposed to assembly, within the plant (including make/buy decisions).
● Adding to, or reducing, plant capacity within the *existing* plants. This included decisions on downsizing, or adding to, the number of manufacturing personnel.
● New facilities/location decisions – including how these new plants would complement existing manufacturing capabilities.
● The degree of, and rationale behind, investment in new process technology for plants.
● Levels of productions of *existing* products and models of the firm's product portfolio.
● New product development in existing markets.
● Entering totally new product markets both by repositioning existing products or by developing new products.

But commonalties between manufacturing and business strategy was only one part of the puzzle. It was also important to find answers to the following:

● Time horizons for the business strategy.
● Time horizons for the manufacturing strategy.
● How often business plans and manufacturing strategies were reviewed – both measured in months.

The emergence of two very distinct groups: traditional and enlightened

As part of Stage 1 of the analysis on profiling, two very distinct groups emerged. These groups had to be termed in such a way as to do justice to the distinction between them. One of the problems in writing about differences in groups is particular terminology used to tag them and the rationale behind the terms 'traditional' and 'enlightened' developed over the three stages. The term 'traditional' was used because these plants are consistent with previous research on 'typical' Western plants which we saw in Chapter 1, namely:

- the relegation of manufacturing to a functional, reactive role, rather than involvement in business planning; and

- the inability, partly as a result of the former point, to develop manufacturing strategies which support the overall business of the firm.

Another term had to be chosen in stark contrast to traditional. The term, 'non-traditional' does not do justice to the difference between the groups and the 'enlightened' approach is indeed just that – a massive contrast to the traditional approach to manufacturing which has been, typically, short-term, reactive and tactical in approach. Without trying to pre-empt what is to follow in subsequent chapters, using the term 'enlightened' was fully justified once the second stage of our findings – performance measurements – was in place. However, let's be fully clear that the use of the terms at Stage 1, merely denoted differences in approaches to formulating strategy and had no bearing on links to plant performance. Utmost care was taken to ensure that no bias or contamination of data took place in the second stage of the research – the performance measurements.

Stage 1: Identifying traditional and enlightened plants

Of the 24 plants, 13 may be labelled 'enlightened', and all of the Japanese transplants, of which there were six in this research, are included in the enlightened group. These plants are enlightened because of five, combined factors:

- They have manufacturing personnel in place at senior management/director level.

- These senior manufacturing personnel are actively involved in the business strategy planning process and are not employed purely as technical specialists.

- They have explicit, plant-specific, manufacturing strategies.

- These manufacturing strategies feed into, and form part of, the business strategy – they are linked completely with the eight business areas mentioned earlier.
- There is cohesion in timing between manufacturing and business strategies.

By contrast, 11 plants are traditional because they fail in various degrees to match the five-fold criteria of the enlightened plants. For example:

- Eight plants had no senior-level manufacturing presence within the plant.
- Three plants did have senior-level manufacturing staff but the role of these managers did not include involvement in developing business strategies.
- Seven of the 11 plants had no manufacturing strategy at all.
- Of the four that did have what they called 'manufacturing strategies', these 'strategies', when examined, were essentially reactive plans on a purely operational level, rather than of any real strategic intent or content.

An important point to make here is that enlightened and Japanese are not one and the same thing. Enlightened included non-Japanese plants. Two points need further explanation: the level of seniority and role of manufacturing personnel; and the contribution of manufacturing strategy.

The seniority and role of manufacturing personnel within the plants

Trying to establish links between senior-level manufacturing staff and business strategy is a difficult and demanding task for two reasons:

- From the plant view, there is very little consistency in the role of manufacturing managers. Some managers within plants have constant links with either the parent company or corporate offices and are in continuous dialogue and involved in business decisions, while others clearly are not.
- From a corporate or business level, away from the plant (which is how many firms are organized in their hierarchy) the title of the senior-level manufacturing manager provides little in the way of clues to the role that a person may have. For example, I found instances of vice presidents of manufacturing who seemed to spend little or no time in plants and consequently any links between business strategy and would-be manufacturing strategy were very thin.

However, in spite of these difficulties, distinctions between traditional and enlightened plants became very clear. Although all of the enlightened plants had senior manufacturing personnel in place, it must be noted that six of the traditional plants also had senior manufacturing personnel. In some plants that were part of a multi-plant group under the direction of the parent company, the most senior position might be that of manager rather than director. Nonetheless, manufacturing personnel were positioned at senior levels within some of the traditional plants. We may conclude that having senior manufacturing personnel may be necessary, but is not sufficient, to distinguish enlightened from traditional plants. The level of seniority does not by itself explain the differences of the role and contribution that manufacturing personnel might have within a plant. However, the role and scope of responsibility that manufacturing managers have in translating planned strategic aims into operational capabilities does distinguish enlightened from traditional plants. In short, senior manufacturing personnel within the traditional plants saw their role as technical specialists. Enlightened manufacturing managers/directors, by contrast, saw their role as much more than mere technical support, and were involved in, and central to, wider business issues of the plant.

Another key issue is that it was possible to have two plants – one enlightened, the other traditional – within the same company. In one, the role of the senior manufacturing manager would be limited to that of a technical specialist; in the other, much more contact and dialogue took place between the senior manufacturing manager and the parent company on a range of wider business issues relating to the plant.

The role of manufacturing strategy within the plant

The role and importance of the manufacturing strategy was, perhaps, the most important issue in distinguishing enlightened from traditional plants. In enlightened plants, manufacturing strategy helped to translate the business strategy of the plant into a range of plant-specific action plans. Essentially, manufacturing strategy in enlightened plants would be the important bridge that linked together business strategy and operational capabilities. In the enlightened plants, manufacturing strategy was clearly linked to the business plan, coherent with the business plan in time, and included business areas such as the extent of vertical integration, sourcing and developing supplier relationships, new product development, and involvement in selecting partners in alliances. In the traditional plants, manufacturing strategy either did not exist at all or, if it did, was essentially technical in nature.

From Stage 1 onwards

Thus far I have divided the 24 plants into two groups – one enlightened group, consisting of 13 plants, including six Japanese transplants. The other, traditional group consisted of 11 plants. But this only provided clues about how strategy is developed. The question needs to be *so what difference does this make?* The answer to this follows in the next chapters, where the operations capabilities are examined and measured. Chapter 3 examines innovation within the plants; Chapter 4 is concerned with how plants manage process technology; Chapter 5 looks at quality performance within the plants; Chapter 6 examines inventory and strategic partnerships; and Chapter 7 looks at the contribution of human resource management to strategic operations capabilities. Each chapter will provide background material for each operations area and then I shall look at how enlightened and traditional plants performed in each area. You will see that I have not named the firms or given clues about the plants' locations, other than by country, when it comes to the operations capabilities. This is for two reasons:

- I agreed this with the plants and it is important to honour that agreement, especially, as you will see, in the case of the traditional plants.

- The point of this book is to describe how a firm can transform from being traditional to enlightened. It is not the intention to describe how your firm can transform itself into a Dell or Toyota, because this simply will not be achieved.

NOTES AND REFERENCES

1. *Business Week*, January 25, 1999.
2. *Fortune*, June 8, 1998, **137**(11): 138.
3. *Financial Times*, March 1, 1999.
4. Standard & Poor's Industry Survey, June 3, 1999.
5. *Financial Times*, October 1, 1997.
6. *PC Week*, June 3, 1996, **13**(22).
7. This figure is given in *InternetWeek*, March 8, 1999, though the figure is higher than my estimates.
8. This was taken from a quote from Lou Gerstner in *Business Week*, June 14, 1999.
9. A good description of the extent of the alliance is given in *PC Week*, June 14, 1999, **16**(24): 7.
10. Feitzinger, E. and Hau, L. Lee (1997) 'Mass customization at Hewlett-Packard: the power of postponement', *Harvard Business Review*, January–February, **75**(1): 116(6).
11. *Forbes*, June 14, 1999.
12. This is a quote from Compaq's senior vice president, Edward Straw, in *Fortune,* August 16, 1999.
13. *PC Week*, July 26, 1999, **16**(30): 1.
14. *Industry Week*, November 16, 1998: 57.

15. *Fortune*, May 11, 1998, **137**(9): 59.

16. *Industry Week*, November 16, 1998: 57(1).

17. Ibid.

18. Magretta, J. (1998) 'The power of virtual integration: an interview with Dell Computer's Michael Dell', *Harvard Business Review*, March–April, **76**(2).

19. Ibid.

20. *Industry Week*, March 15, 1999, **248**(6): 34.

21. Ibid.

3

Innovation

 ## Introduction

Innovation is of fundamental importance for firms. This chapter looks at the uncertainty concerning innovation, and some of the things that can be done to manage it, and answers a number of questions, including:

- How is manufacturing's role and involvement in new product development perceived within the various plants?
- What are the methods used by the plants to enhance the speed and success of new product introduction?
- How did the plants view failure of innovation – as a waste of resources, or as a learning experience, or as something other than these two possibilities?
- Do enlightened plants perform better than traditional plants in terms of both the speed and amount of innovation within measurable timeframes?

In his book, *The Foundations of Corporate Success*,[1] John Kay states that innovation is one of the major factors needed to achieve competitive success. Tom Peters[2] put it more succinctly when he stated: 'Get innovative or get dead.' Both are right – without ongoing commitment to innovation in all of its forms, a firm will collapse. It has become increasingly important in the last 50 years. More innovations have taken place since the Second World War than in the combined total of innovations before then. Such an assertion is alarming but true, and with the combination of increasing technological and globalization issues, there are no signs that the rate and speed of innovation will decline. Just the opposite, in fact. For example, the consulting firm Deloitte and Touche reported in *Industry Week*,[3] in their survey of global manufacturing executives, that product innovation was seen as the major driver for growth and customer retention. The ability to innovate is certainly one of the major challenges facing managers and the inability to do so has major repercussions for firms. Since 1985, over 50% of firms that were then listed in the *Fortune* 500 have disappeared. Were they all poorly managed? No: the main issue was that the majority of them were unable to innovate either at the speed, or at the rate, of the success of their often new competitive rivals. Does this mean that the firms that disappeared were stupid? Again, no: what it does mean is that innovation of all kinds – and new product development in particular – is a messy, uncertain business as Keith Pavitt summarizes:

> It is not clear before the event who is in the innovation race, where the starting and finishing lines are, and what the race is about.[4]

In Kay's book, he states how EMI, the electronics manufacturer, declined in televisions, computers and radiology scanner technology. This was in spite of the fact that:

> EMI was one of the most effectively innovative companies there has ever been. It was a pioneer in television, a leader in computers, its music business was at the centre of a revolution in popular culture, and its scanner technology transformed radiology. Today only its music business survives.[5]

The major reason here was the inability to translate innovation of ideas and one-off designs into a sustainable advantage through its manufacturing and marketing capabilities. The inability to translate one-off designs into volume manufacture is a major issue. It accounts for so many failures of attempted new product developments. Yet this inability is still not dealt with sufficiently and it is not given the attention it deserves. As you'll see later, this ability is at the very core of enlightened plants' innovation successes.

The rate of new entrants has shaken many markets and resulted in new rules being written on how to compete. As consumers we take this for granted. Gary Hamel,[6] from the London Business School, reports how:

> As an individual consumer, you may well take a flight on Virgin, buy a computer from Dell, and buy insurance through Direct Line. There are dozens of things you buy today from vendors that didn't even exist a decade ago. Never has the world been a better place for industry revolutionaries; and never has it been a more dangerous place for complacent incumbents.

He rightly goes on to say that speed is a critical issue:

> Indeed, the dividing line between success and failure is today measured in months, not decades. What evidence supports these bold assertions? The telephone took almost 40 years to reach 10 million customers in the US (and that industry still seems to move at

a glacial pace). Yet the Web browser reached 10 million customers in 18 months. Sun Microsystems Java software platform was populated on 100 million computers in only 13 months.

This rate of change is scary stuff for many firms. Basically, a firm is damned if it doesn't innovate and almost sure to be damned if it tries and fails. Even if it does succeed in translating designs into volume production – and that's a big if – there is no assurance until after the product is launched that customers will actually want the product. Innovation is one of many areas where traditional management wisdom – of feeding in numbers, and crunching them through various ratios, in order to come up with a magic formula – cannot hope to provide solutions. Innovation, in its broadest sense, is neither just product nor process development but is, instead, simultaneous improvements in both. These improvements happen as a result of the firm being poised and able to innovate. It demands that firms organize, reorganize and, if necessary, entirely reconfigure and reinvent themselves in order for innovation to occur. The firm must allow the creative abilities of all its resources to be translated into end products for customers.

Innovation is essentially justified by faith, and its success or failure is known only after the event. Industry is littered with failures and the reasons for some of these failures, in retrospect, seem obvious. Take the British 'car' known as the Sinclair C5, a much mocked target of abuse, which I will refer to again later in the chapter. Nobody knew what the C5 was: it certainly was not a car as we know it, but it was supposed to be a friendly-looking vehicle, with a small box-like design, powered by an engine the size of a sewing machine. It failed for many good reasons, including, most fundamentally, the lack of market research. But what if it had succeeded? We would then be singing the praises of Sir Clive Sinclair as a man of vision who brushed market research aside in order to spot a much-needed gap in the market – which is exactly what major innovating firms do who are involved in pushing their technology to customers. But the Sinclair C5 failed and the rest is history.

We are, of course, all wise after the event and no more so than in innovation. Some academics, blessed with perfect 20/20 hindsight vision, will run case after case in business schools of both success and failures in innovation as though the derived lessons can then be packaged together and transplanted to other situations. But very often they cannot, and therein lies a major factor of innovation – it is a firm-specific process[7] in terms of the initial scope, vision and ultimately the actual achievement of an innovation. There are lessons that can be learned – and learning is important, but this often comes more from what not to do in order to avoid failure, rather than a prescriptive list of ingredients that will guarantee success.

Innovation should be an organizational-wide activity. It should also involve other key players – customers, suppliers, various types of strategic alliances, and so on. Innovation is not the prerogative of one department or special-ist group, either in terms of the initial generation of ideas or of the management of the process through to successful (or otherwise) product launch. However, in spite of all that has been written about the need to integrate teams into multi-functional innovative groups, problems remain when it comes to organizing and managing such teams. Again, this was a clear feature of enlightened plants – they were able to manage multi-func-tional team efforts and to unite these groups into innovative units. As you will see, one key area was in the involvement of manufacturing personnel from the early stages of development, an element missing from traditional plants.

Are patents enough?

Patents can provide important indications of breakthroughs in firm-specific – or joint venture – developments. The problem is that there is often a gap between the initial breakthrough resulting in a patent and launching a product, which might utilize the patent, for customers. Undoubtedly a firm may wish not to develop a patent to final product, preferring instead to license its patent to others who do. But often there is no choice. The option is not really an option at all because the firm simply does not have the abil-ity to translate ideas into volume products – as you just saw with the EMI example. However, one of the key reasons behind Japan's phenomenal success in innovation was in the ability to utilize patents within a plethora of new product designs. In spite of being able to 'invent' patents, Britain has often failed to utilize this capability to successfully launch new products. One of the reasons is that its manufacturing base eroded dramatically between the 1950s and 1990s. Indications of patents for various countries are shown in Table 3.1.

The problem of transfer from initial patent to final product has plagued many firms. For example, although IBM was second in the number of patents that it launched in the period 1969–97 (*see* Table 3.2), it still strug-gled with converting these patents into end products in the computing industry. As a result, it was behind Apple with the PC by four years; it was behind Digital with the mini-computer by 11 years; and it lagged behind Toshiba with the PC laptop by five yeas, and behind Sun Microsystems with RISC workstations by three years.

Table 3.1   Countries receiving most patents for inventions 1963–97

Country	Number of patents	Country	Number of patents
Japan	359,496	Switzerland	40,756
Germany	202,663	Italy	29,357
UK	90,975	Sweden	25,660
France	77,904	Netherlands	24,215
Canada	47,671	Taiwan	13,186

Source: US Patent and Trademark Office.

Table 3.2   Corporations receiving most patents for inventions 1969–97

Company	Number of patents
G.E.	24,440
IBM	20,926
Hitachi	16,951
Canon	15,061
Toshiba	14,511
AT&T	14,409
Eastman Kodak	13,916

Source: US Patent and Trademark Office.

The strategic importance of innovation

Innovation is a major strategic issue for firms. Innovation will determine whether a firm can grow in, or will have to exit from, a particular market sector. You saw in Chapter 2 how Chrysler merged with Daimler, but how Chrysler's own improvements in the innovation process resulted in a remarkable turnaround. In 1991, Chrysler was nearly bankrupt; at that time, Chrysler would take about five years to launch new products. The turn-around since then owes a great deal to new models such as the Chrysler Concorde, the Eagle Vision and the Dodge Intrepid, as well as the success of existing, but modified, designs of minivans and Jeeps. The first break-through was with the Viper, which was created in three years. But this speed of innovation was improved further with Chrysler's Neon, which took 30 months to introduce. Such dramatic improvements in innovation demonstrated the intense learning that Chrysler had undertaken concerning Japanese approaches. This learning enabled both the Chrysler Cirrus and Dodge Stratus models to come to market less than three years after the project had won formal approval within the company. Their development costs of $900 million were less than one-sixth of that for Ford's competitive car, the Mondeo. As a result of these models, by 1995 Chrysler had 14.8% of the North American car market, its best rating for 23 years. In addition, in the mid- to late 1990s, Chrysler had the highest margins per vehicle and the best-performing stock of any American carmaker. Chrysler was also seen as the most innovative of the Big Three car makers in the USA.

The strategic importance of innovation is evident at Ford. Although the Ford Taurus had been the biggest selling car in the USA between 1992 and 1996, Ford had to then radically change its approach, as former CEO Alex Trotman stated:

> The economies of scale that come from purchasing materials from a simplified buying list, the single manufacturing system, the benefits of using best practice worldwide, all those things hold true . . . [but] what is a big issue is the number of platforms you have, how many drivelines, and how many people you have designing those products.[8]

Ford has attempted to deal with increasing pressures of globalization by introducing 'world cars'. World cars are designed around a single (or very small number of) platform and the car will then be sold to multiple areas of the world. At the time of writing, Ford's attempts with world cars have not been great successes. In the early 1980s, the Ford Escort had two platforms, one in the USA and one in Europe, but they did not share enough common components and Ford lost money on the Escort. The more recent world car development – the Mondeo/Contour/Mystique model – also lost money, even though there were 70% common components. The idea behind the development of a world car is to share best practice among various divisions and plants that make the car as well as trying to gain some scale economies. This sounds straightforward enough but as Standard & Poor's Industry Survey rightly stated:

> . . . while the rationale for building a world car is straightforward, the ability to do so successfully is not. For example, local tastes, infrastructure, government regulations, and other factors may make it difficult for a manufacturer to keep variations to a minimum.[9]

There is another factor: as we saw in Chapter 2, it is possible to have a firm with two plants – one enlightened and one traditional. There are no guarantees that 'best practice' will be transferred from one to the other.

Attacking markets

Chrysler's example shows how fundamental innovation can be to the firm's entire business fortune. Sometimes a firm equates innovation with being first to market and there are some good reasons for being first:

- The firm's image can be enhanced within the industry.
- The firm might be able to charge premium prices (if the market is willing).
- If other firms cannot copy the innovation, the innovating firm can enjoy sustained profitability, which can then be used for yet further research and development and product innovation.
- Patents can be used as a barrier to entry. For example, Polaroid successfully kept out Kodak from the instant-photography market. In 1991, Kodak had to pay $925 million to Polaroid for patent infringements.

But there are dangers with wanting to be first and it is a perfectly good and valid strategic move to want to be second. Again, the key to this is manufacturing capability – an innovating firm may well have the design expertise but lack the other vital ingredients and assets[10] to sustain the initial innovation – in other words, manufacturing capability with all of its requirements.

A firm can gain advantage by targeting products in focused market segments in the following ways:

- Going geographically where existing competitors have little or no presence.
- Attacking segments where marketing efforts are weak or neglected.
- Attacking by offering perceived added quality features.
- Attacking where there is little brand loyalty.
- Attacking where there are gaps in the product line.

The failure to pay attention to particular segments can be a big problem. For example, *The European* mentioned how:

> GM have badly misread the changing car market in Europe, where traditional Opel and Vauxhall customers are moving either upmarket to VW or downmarket towards the new breed of ultra-compact cars. GM is singularly weak in both of these vehicle classes . . . its most deadly rival of all, Ford, was busy reinventing itself. [CEO] Trotman . . . has given his European subsidiaries freedom to launch a bold new range of design-led cars – the Ka, Puma and Cougar – which have transformed the company's fortunes in Europe.[11]

So GM faces a major challenge in terms of launching products in certain parts of Europe in which it has either become lethargic or has chosen to avoid. We should be careful, though, not to charge only Western car manufacturers with such neglect. Japanese auto firms also became less than spectacular in innovation in the early 1990s. Honda in particular struggled, but its turnaround has, like Chrysler, been dependent upon major strides in innovation. *Fortune* reported how:

> Honda, the fairy-tale come-from-nowhere auto success of the Eighties, suddenly started falling apart in the early Nineties when the Japanese economy sank back to reality. Business dried up . . . The sport-utility boom? Honda missed it — completely. The company lost its famous sense of Japanese tastes. Honda's car sales fell in 1993 and again in 1994. Yet now, just two years later, Honda is zooming ahead of competitors to enjoy the greatest success of its 48-year history [CEO] Kawamoto says that before the bubble burst, 'Honda was in tune with the times. Everything it did was a roaring success. Then the environment changed, and we had to change the organization.'[12]

Note that Honda's success was not just about a particular product development but organizational-wide change and redevelopment. Honda's success was due to the ability to change the organization itself. Such change has brought benefits in terms of resources and speed:

> Honda builds its RVs cheaply from existing Civic and Accord platforms and parts . . . And Honda gets them to market so quickly — in as little as 18 months from design studio to the start of production . . .[13]

While Honda has improved it still has some way to go (as does the rest of the auto industry) before it can hope to emulate the sort of successes found at Toyota. In 1997 *Fortune* stated how:

> Like everything else at Toyota, product development is changing too . . . Two years ago Toyota reorganized its engineers into three groups — front-wheel-drive cars, rear-wheel-drive cars, and trucks . . . In the past two years it has introduced 18 new or redesigned models, including the new Corolla, which is made in different versions for Japan, Europe, and the US. Several Japanese models, like the Picnic and the Corolla Spacio, went into production as little as 14 1/2 months after their designs were approved – probably an industry record. Toyota also caught the auto world napping by announcing a breakthrough in engine design. The 120-horsepower engine in the 1998 Corolla uses 25% fewer parts than its predecessor, making it 10% lighter, 10% more fuel-efficient, and significantly cheaper.[14]

Such innovation is scary for other auto manufacturers. Like the Honda example before, innovation at Toyota comes about as a result of organizational-wide redesign rather than concentrating on particular product development. Innovation is evident not only in the surge of new end products – 18 in two years – but in the redesign of engines and parts that go into cars. Thus a whole range of innovations has taken place simultaneously. This is difficult for firms who think that somehow a new product will, by itself, cause innovation, and that a radical cultural change will take place around a particular product development. It won't. Rather, the organizational factors, including an innovation culture, supported by remuneration and reward for ideas, have to be in place.

The need for rapid and ongoing innovation – and the intense learning that can accompany this – sometimes comes through crisis. Take Kodak's response to Fuji, for example. In 1987, Fuji launched the QuickSnap 35-mm single-use camera in the USA. At this time Kodak simply did not have a comparable product in a market that was destined to grow dramatically for the next eight years (from 3 million in 1988 to 43 million in 1994). By the time Kodak did introduce its first model almost a year later, Fuji had already developed a second model, the QuickSnap Flash. For some time, Kodak was way behind Fuji, but by 1994 Kodak had won market share back from Fuji and had captured more than 70% of the US market.[15]

The success of Kodak's response resulted in part from its strategy of developing many distinctively different models from a common, base platform. Between April 1989 and July 1990, Kodak redesigned its base model and introduced three additional models, so that all four had common components and production processes. As a result of this, Kodak was able to develop its products faster and more cheaply. More to the point, it allowed Kodak to have twice as many products as Fuji. As you will see, this technique was one used by enlightened plants.

The strategic importance of innovation at national level

Innovation is not just of strategic importance to a particular firm. In the long term it is of strategic importance for whole countries. I mentioned earlier how Britain had lost out with the example of EMI's scanner, an invention then developed to final product in the USA. Penicillin, discovered by Alexander Fleming, was developed and exploited in the USA, and even the video recorder, one of the great examples of Japanese development, was invented in Britain and also developed in the USA. The strategic importance of loss by the originating company to the development by another competitor is shown in the Table 3.3.

America's Ampex, which pioneered video technology in 1956, is a case full of insight. Ampex charged about $50,000 for its early models and sold very few. It made little effort to cut costs and expand its market. By contrast, Japan's Sony, JVC and Matsushita saw the potential for mass-market sales, via their manufacturing capability, and set out to make a video

Table 3.3   Examples of innovators and followers

Product	Inventor	Developer
Transistor radio	Regency	Sony
VCR	Ampex	Sony, Victor
TV	RCA	Matsushita
Rotary engine	Vanchel	Mazda
CD	Philips	Sony

recorder that would cost $500. The goal took them 20 years to achieve. Ampex, the actual innovator, was content to have pioneered the technology, in the belief that its breakthrough was enough to bring market leadership. But it wasn't. Ampex did not have the ability to manufacture the designed product in any volume. The USA's loss was Japan's gain. The USA and UK are both littered with such stories. In the UK, John Bessant described how:

> Whereas in 1900 Britain made 60% of the world's shipping, she now accounts for less than 3%. In 1948 the UK was the largest steel producer, yet she now only just manages tenth place . . . over 50% of cars and 98% of motorcycles are imported.[16]

By the 1990s, the USA was $5 trillion in debt. A major part of this was due to the decline in manufacturing as described by Harvard's Wickham Skinner:

> By the late 1970s it was clear that the United States had lost its century-old dominance in manufacturing in dozens of industries. Our competitive edge was destroyed by lower costs, better quality, and product and process technologies of global competitors. Imports were surging into the country from Japan, Korea, Singapore, Taiwan, and many countries of Western Europe.[17]

The warning was loud and clear:

> Unless the United States gets its manufacturing operations back in shape – and fast – it could lose any hope of maintaining the foundation on which tomorrow's prosperity rests.[18]

Fortunately, as it enters the new millennium the USA seems to have heeded the warning, and parts of its manufacturing capabilities – including rapid and successful innovation – have undergone necessary change to compete against the world's best. The success stories included the enlightened plants.

Successes and failures in innovation

There are many reasons why new product innovations fail. These include the sheer cost of the project, the difficulty in managing the process, and lack of rewards – especially when a 'me-too' imitator comes in and steals the idea, developing it via its superior manufacturing capabilities. The dangers facing innovation include:

- There is no real market for the product.
- A need exists but the product does not match the need.
- The product is capable of meeting the market requirements, but the perception is not clear to the market and is therefore replaced by a better marketing effort from a competitor.

Not surprisingly, there have been lists provided of great success stories and their reasons for success. We saw in Chapter 2 how the manufacturing base has declined in Britain. But for some time there were success stories involving British designs in the automobile industry. For example, *The Independent*[19] provided lists of successes and failures. The successes were as follows.

- **The Mini** (1959) Its small dimensions, front-wheel drive and transverse engine started a trend which every small car now follows. But typical of British economic ineptitude, its maker lost money on every one it sold.
- **Jaguar E-type** (1961) One of the most beautiful, best-value, fastest and most desirable cars ever. Perfectly in tune with the Sixties, a decade it represents as surely as the Beatles.
- **Austin Seven** (1922) Cheap, simple, reliable; a car which helped to motorize Britain. It also helped to get BMW and Nissan into the car making business through overseas assembly deals.
- **Range Rover** (1970) Handsome and extraordinarily competent (considering its bulk), the Range Rover sired the upmarket 4×4; a type of car still booming in markets as diverse as the US, Britain and Australia. It also proved perpetually superior to a host of imitators.
- **Rolls-Royce Silver Ghost** (1907) The first (and probably only) time that Rolls-Royce built 'the best car in the world'.
- **Vauxhall 20hp** (1908) The first quality 'affordable car'. Allowed the middle classes to enjoy the sort of mechanical refinement then only available to the rich. In those days, Vauxhall was a British company. It is now owned by General Motors, and all Vauxhalls are engineered in Germany.

▶

- **Austin/ Morris 1100** (1962) Tough, mechanically advanced, roomy for its size, this car should have been the saviour of BMC. Instead, the strife-torn factories destroyed any chance of it enjoying the international success it deserved.
- **Jaguar XJ6** (1968) In various iterations, this car lasted until the early Nineties. It brought new levels of refinement to the class, but was repeatedly dogged by poor build quality. If Mercedes had built it, rather than a strike-ravaged, politically sensitive Coventry car maker, it would have been easily the best luxury car in the world.
- **Lanchester** (1900) Although the first Lanchesters were tested from 1895, production cars weren't sold until 1900. It was incredibly advanced, especially in that it was designed as a car from the ground up (where previous cars were often based on horse carriages, and used engines designed for stationary work) and in its use of counter-rotating shafts to dampen engine vibration.
- **Jaguar XJR** (1994) The best car currently made in Britain, if one of the most expensive (£47,000). Cosseting, comfortable, gorgeous and fast; proof that great British car firms (or at least some of them) can prosper under foreign ownership.

Note that the Mini was seen as successful in spite of losing money. It was a success for customers and it was a success for British Leyland in terms of design, if not in financial terms. In that sense, a narrow view of success would judge the Mini as a failure. The failures are listed below.

- **Morris Ital** (1982) BL's nadir. Hopelessly outdated engineering (based on the 1950s Morris Minor) mated with amazing marketing ineptitude. The Morris Marina, its closely related predecessor, was bought mainly for nationalistic reasons. So the gurus at BL gave its replacement an Italian sounding name. Brilliant.
- **Austin Allegro** (1973) Its nickname was 'all aggro'. It had a rectangular steering wheel, and it was more aerodynamic when going backwards than forwards. Enough said.
- **Austin Ambassador** (1982) Last and worst of the imaginative 'Landcrab' cars, that began with the fine-but-ugly Austin 1800. Ancient mechanicals, chronic unreliability and plug-ugly looks all spelt inevitable showroom failure.
- **Rolls-Royce Camargue** (1975) Looking a bit like a cousin of Lady Penelope's six-wheeled pink Rolls-Royce, the Camargue was top Italian stylist Pininfarina's only job for Rolls. Clearly, they must have drafted in the B-team for this one while the top guys were getting on with their Ferraris. It was a big ugly lump of a coupe that few people outside America bought.

- **Nissan Bluebird** (1985) First of the Tyneside-built Nissans, the Bluebird was B-grade Japanese technology mated to typically nondescript Japanese styling. It was miles behind the Sierras and Cavaliers of its day, but at least was well-made. Now a favourite of mini-cabbers.
- **Reliant Robin** (1974) Proof that four wheels are better than three.
- **Jaguar E-type 2+2 Series 3 V12** (1970) The gorgeous E-type was past its best when the Jaguar guys made it longer, heavier, soggier and fitted a massive fuel-thirsty V12. It ruined a great car.
- **Ford Cortina Mk3** (1970) Cheapskate engineering was the hallmark of British Fords in the 1960s and 1970s – even if the cars were reliable. But the Mk3 was a new Scrooge-like landmark in Ford's determination to give its customers as little technology as possible. Build quality, too, from Ford's strike-ravaged Dagenham factory was dismal.
- **Toyota Carina E** (1994) The dullest car made in Britain today, and a source of enormous relief for all those European makers who were petrified when Japan's most successful car maker set up shop in Derby, UK. They're not so worried now.
- **Sinclair C5** (1985) Sir Clive thought that the future of motoring was a single-seater with no protection (for weather or accidents) made out of glass-fibre and powered by a washing-machine engine. He was wrong.

The criteria for failure includes the style of the design and not just the basic quality (i.e. fitness for purpose) of the car. So the Ambassador is dismissed as 'ugly', the Rolls-Royce as a 'big ugly lump', and the C5 is dismissed out of hand. So-called product disasters are popular material for the business press. *Fortune*, in its article *The ghastliest product launches*, reported on these, including Gerber's attempt to move away from baby food:

> They probably wish they could forget the experiment, but they once tried to market a line of meals for adults. Unfortunately, if predictably, it flopped . . . Similarly, when Miller Brewing tried to cash in on the clear-products fad with Miller Clear Beer – it just turned out, again unsurprisingly, that beer drinkers didn't want a colorless beer. And as for Nestea's launch of a yellowish carbonated beverage called Tea Whiz – well, you can see the problem.[20]

Forbes[21] too, in its article *Famous flops*, described early computer products, the Osborne and Kaypro:

> Osborne 1 and Kaypro II – homely and huge by today's standards, the Osborne 1 and the Kaypro II were among the first portable computers. The pioneering Osborne was a market hit when it was introduced in 1981. At $1,795, it cost 40% to 60% less than other computers (say, from Zenith or Radio Shack), and it had disk drives. But an absurdly small 2.6-by-3.6-inch screen limited users to just 24 lines of text. The Kaypro,

on the scene a year later, weighed in at 25 pounds (having your own Sherpa was useful). Its keyboard was integrated into the lid. Both looked like military hardware or boxed sewing machines. But they had defined a need, and sold like crazy. Osborne shipped more than 11,000 machines in the first eight months; revenues skyrocketed to $100 million-plus by July 1982.

What, then, was the problem?

Ultimately, neither newcomer had the stamina to go the distance. They didn't keep up with the more sophisticated technology that soon came to market. Apple, for example, introduced the Mac in 1984, and its grace and ease of use made trailblazing models like these instantly obsolete.

But *Forbes* have only told some of the story because the failure with Osborne computers had as much to do with its manufacturing incapability as its purely technical shortcomings. For example, there was a great deal of inventory in stock of the Osborne I. However, the founder, Adam Osborne, announced that there would be a launch of the new product, Osborne II, in late 1982. The market responded by cancelling orders of Osborne I, and consequently its inventory level remained very high. So, outdated inventory – a key manufacturing concern if ever there was one – was a huge problem. Scheduling was another problem brought about by the late development of Osborne II. The combination of the slow sales of Osborne I, together with the late introduction of Osborne II, caused severe cash flow problems, and, in spite of the previous technological advances, Osborne filed for Chapter 11 in September 1983. The story of the failure of the Osborne computers is typically couched in terms of a 'marketing failure', but get behind the data and it becomes clear that manufacturing incapability was the core of the problem.

Similar manufacturing problems occurred at IBM with the PC Junior in 1984. In order to ensure adequate inventory to meet demand during introduction, IBM stockpiled IBM PC Juniors prior to the introduction date. However, due to technical problems and the limited number of software applications, sales of IBM PC Junior failed to reach expectations. Like the Osborne Computer example, IBM's inventory level remained high despite price cuts, and the IBM PC Junior died in 1985. Again, it's interesting that the myth surrounding this failure is told in terms of poor marketing. This *was* part of the problem, but the real core of the failure was in the lack of cohesion and co-ordination with manufacturing. As a result IBM's costs were huge both in terms of the failure of the product launch itself as well as the attendant stockpiling. Close cohesion between various functional areas, including manufacturing, was, as we have seen in other chapters, one of the central approaches of enlightened plants. This was clearly evident in all aspects of the development process of innovation. As a result, there was not one case of a disaster in terms of stockpiling, poor scheduling or other calamities within the enlightened plants. The reasons behind such capabilities are discussed later, but one of the issues was in attitudes toward perceived failures in innovation.

Are failures really failures in innovation?

I have noted problems of innovations, but sometimes problems can be opportunities for learning. By certain sets of criteria, both Hewlett-Packard (HP) and Apple had disasters with their early computer products. For example, the HP 3000 flopped when it was first introduced in 1972, and HP withdrew it from the market. By spring 1973, total development costs had reached $20 million. In October 1973, HP re-released the HP 3000, this time to much acclaim. The HP 3000 continues to survive, and there is an installed base of between 65,000 and 70,000. Similarly, Apple Computer's Lisa was launched and withdrawn in just one year. The 1983 computer was overpriced at $10,000. This was because it took a reported $20 million and 200 man-years to develop. After selling just 6,000 units in its first year (the Apple II would sell up to 30,000 per month), Lisa was abandoned in 1985. But before dismissing Apple's Lisa as a failure, it's important to note that it was the first commercially produced computer to use a graphical user interface. It also had pull-down menus and a mouse. Apple introduced the first Macintosh with the same features as Lisa. This time the computer was successful, the main issue being the price (around $2,500).

However, the success of the Mac following on from the 'failure' of the Lisa was in direct contrast to what happened with Xerox. In the late 1970s, Xerox's Palo Alto Research Centre developed a computer that included a mouse, laser printer, and a graphical user interface, and packaged them into the Alto. This qualified as the first true, but never commercially manufactured, personal computer. Again, the inability to transfer from one-off design to volume manufacture was the major problem.

Some companies would have seen success purely in terms of particular product launches and would have written off the experience as a failure. In the examples of Hewlett-Packard and Apple, the companies were willing to learn from mistakes and to then develop ideas into yet new products.

The problem with prescriptions for innovations

I mentioned earlier that innovation is a firm-specific affair and that it can be very difficult to transfer one set of achievements to another firm. That does not mean that firms cannot learn from each other. In fact, learning is crucial to innovation. But there are difficulties with the actual nature of what might be learned. The business press is fond of providing prescriptions for success and the difficulty in doing so is shown in the headlines from two journals that contradict each other. Imagine being a CEO faced with these two prescriptions: *Industry Week*[22] prescribed its formula with the headline 'Listen, then design (listening to customer needs before designing products)'. In this article, *Industry Week* provided success stories of firms who had deliberately paid great attention to customer requirements before launching products.

In direct contrast, *Fortune* announced that, in order to be successful, a firm should 'Ignore your customer' and began with the assertion that:

> A growing number of companies and consultants now believe that it's time to start ignoring the customer. That's the only way, these experts argue, to create the kind of breakthrough products and services that can catapult you far ahead of the competition.[23]

All well and good, but you can guarantee that those firms who pursue such strategies will then become the focus of future business press headlines and academic case studies. The subject for the class? To study how those firms, who ignored their customers, then failed.

Even when there are success stories, it's very hard to determine just why they were successful, let alone how this could be transferred to other firms. For example, the Post-it success at 3M is legendary. The case is described by Charlan Nemeth in the *California Management Review*:

> One of 3M's classic stories is the development of Post-it notes – which, in fact, was aided by a failure. The glue eventually used for Post-it notes was a failed attempt by Spencer Silver to develop a super strong glue. Art Fry, singing in his church choir, had trouble marking his hymnal with pieces of paper; they would slip out. Then came the idea: 'What I need is a bookmark with Spence's adhesive along the edge'. And thus Post-it notes were conceived. It should also be mentioned that marketing was initially skeptical, but the case was made when they found that the notes were already being used extensively among 3M's internal staff.[24]

So what can be learned from this? That success always comes from failure? That innovation is dependant upon going to church or that some other form of divine guidance is a necessary ingredient? That initial marketing scepticism is crucial? That internal customers should be the 'test market' for all new products before they are launched to a wider target customer group? Yes, the questions border on the sarcastic, but the point is that although you gain a certain warmth from success stories, the transfer of learning from these cases is almost impossible to achieve.

The culture of innovation

Firms who are innovative will boast of their achievements and these will be picked up in the media. For example, in 1996 3M introduced 500 new products – an accomplishment that made the business press headlines at the time. But innovation is not about headlines. It's about organizational capabilities. Although CEOs will sometimes state the obvious, they also can reveal something about a particular firm's culture. For example, *Forbes* quotes Johnson & Johnson's CEO, Ralph Larsen, as saying: 'New products are our lifeblood.' Clearly that statement is true for all firms, but the difference is that at Johnson & Johnson the assertion seems to go beyond mere rhetoric. The evidence is compelling:

> New products, defined as those introduced within the past five years here and abroad, account for 36% of the company's sales today. The ratio is up from 26% in 1988 . . . Over the past five years J&J's earnings have compounded at 17%; its return on equity has averaged 32% – over double the medical supplies industry average and several points ahead of such great companies as Procter & Gamble (19.5%) and Kimberly-Clark (20.6%).[25]

This is useful because comparisons are made with competitors in the same industry and Johnson & Johnson's record is impressive. However, the pharmaceuticals industry shows how uncertain innovation can be. It also shows that there is little correlation between the amount spent on research and development and subsequent successes, as a survey undertaken by *Fortune* showed:

> A Fortune analysis of 143 companies, comparing R&D expenditures as a percent of sales and rank on this year's innovation list, reveals that there is very little correlation between R&D spending and standing on the list. For some, the relation between R&D dollars and perceived innovation is downright perverse. Pharmacia Upjohn spends over 18% of revenues on research, more than almost any major company in any industry. But the pharmaceuticals company ranks 339th in innovation this year.[26]

The pharmaceuticals industry, like the computers and automobile industries, demonstrates that the rationale for investment cannot be justified by management calculations but by a commitment to innovation that goes beyond managerial logic.

But innovation – and new products in particular – can sometimes be the first casualty of a firm's bottom-line mentality. For example, in 1996 Apple Computer announced that it would halve the number of models it offered as part of a restructuring programme aimed at returning to profitability. By contrast, at the same time Compaq Computer aimed to launch a number of models in portable personal computers (PCs), particularly with the introduction of a broad new range of laptop PCs. Such innovation came from necessity. Compaq had led the market for portable PCs in the 1980s, but had then lost its market leadership to Toshiba and other manufacturers. So Compaq's re-entry demonstrated organizational ability to intensify new product launches. Market re-entry was also evident at IBM. IBM announced its re-entry to the market for low-end computer printers, five years after it had withdrawn from the business by selling off its printer division. In IBM's case, its capabilities were in place only as a result of the painful reorganization that it had to go through in the early 1990s. This change, like Kodak's response to Fuji, was brought about by intense competition. Such intense competition demanded change of the entire organization at IBM and not just one function. In fact, this reorganization took place twice in a four-year period and involved two CEOs – John Akers and Lou Gerstner.

Helping to manage the process – specific techniques

Although specific transfer of learning from one case to another is difficult, there are some things that can, and must, be done to help the innovation process. These were the sort of approaches adopted by the enlightened plants.

To begin with there are certain techniques that can be employed. These include quality function deployment (QFD), robust design (Taguchi methods), failure–mode–effect analysis (FMEA) and much better use of computer-aided design/computer-aided manufacturing (CAD/CAM) than has often been the case. At Black & Decker in Maryland, FMEA is now 'a requirement in all new designs and processes'.[27] The FMEA method is linked to quality. FMEA is a 'right-the-first-time' methodology that anticipates and prevents failures by designing them out of products and processes. Linked to this is a design process that embraces manufacture from the very beginning of the process rather than as a reactive, after-thought once the product has already been designed. So FMEA links to modular design and design for assembly (DFA). This has strategic importance because it will reduce parts, assembly costs, including labour, as well as improving quality.

CAD has profoundly affected the design process and can have strategic consequences because it influences areas such as flexibility, the speed of new product development and cost, all of which in turn are competitive, and are, therefore, strategic factors. In particular major benefits of CAD include:

- *Product quality:* CAD allows designers to develop alternatives and to be aware of possible problems at early stages of design. It therefore links with robust design (Taguchi methods), and FMEA.

- *Shorter design time:* this clearly influences both cost and actual development times to market where speed is critical.

- *Manufacturing cost reductions:* design changes are facilitated easily, and methods such as group technology enable families of components for manufacture to be combined. Standard or commonly used parts can be called up and transferred to a new design.

Ford has used CAD to great effect. Years ago it used to make a clay model for all new products. This would take 12 weeks and 12 people. Now, however, an idea can be transformed into a fully automated video within three weeks by using CAD.

Sometimes firms will embrace several of these approaches. For example, in the early 1990s Eastman Kodak re-engineered its process based on best practices, including robust design and QFD. QFD, a Japanese concept applied widely at Toyota, is important because it brings customer requirements directly to manufacturing by a series of what/how matrices developed by a multifunctional team.

There are other specific things that can be done. For example, the following methods can help to speed up the innovation process and make it more effective:[28]

- Overlapping development phases – instead of the sequential process that has caused many Western companies to be late to market, it is clear that some of the developments can be made concurrently. Not all phases are linear, and some phases are not dependent on what has preceded. Concurrent development therefore compresses the real-time development making it quicker.

- Fewer development phases can be implemented – this is made possible through computer-aided design/computer-aided engineering (CAD/CAE) which allows parts and sub-assemblies to have been 'tested' without prototyping.

- Incremental development, along the lines of kaizen, sees progress evolving from a core product. Constant small developments, particularly in cross-functional teams, result in large developments over a period of time.

- Better use of prototyping – not just as a one-off unit – will show how easy or otherwise the product will be to manufacture. The 'normal' approach to prototyping is to use one unit only as a means of 'debugging' and then to go from this to volume manufacture. Small batches will allow problems of producing to be highlighted which is important when manufacturing in large volumes.

Specific indicators of design efficiency include:[29]

- Minimizing the number of parts used (thus avoiding over-design).
- Percentage of standard parts should be large.
- Using existing manufacturing resources.
- Reducing the cost of the first production run will indicate whether the design is realistic.
- Monitoring the first six-month costs of design changes.
- The total product cost will show targeted cost and reveal over-design factors.

The human factor in innovation

More important than the actual techniques and processes themselves described above, is the fact that they encourage team work from multifunction areas in new product development. This factor is an important one in innovation. In new product development the process has changed over years from that depicted in Figure 3.1 to that in Figure 3.2.

Figure 3.1   The sequential (traditional) approach to new launches

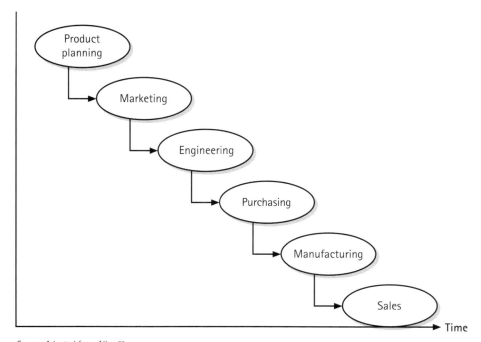

Source: Adapted from Allen.[30]

Figure 3.2   Enlightened approches to innovation

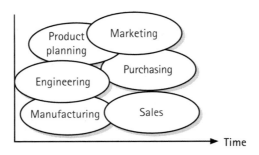

This is not just a case of getting people from different functions in the same room. If this approach is to be successful, sometimes a complete organization-wide change has to take place. For example, in 1991 Ford created the Design Institute and gave it a charter 'to change the fundamental way of doing our design, development, and manufacturing'. Similarly, Renault's reorganization of its development process was a fundamental change to its past approach. Renault's Technocentre was designed to house 7,500 engineers, designers and supplier staff and to bring together the group's entire car development staff, formerly split between numerous Parisian locations. Renault's intention was to reduce costs by FFr1 billion a year on its R&D budget. It also sought to reduce product development times to a target of 24 months.

Another example comes from Daimler where, prior to the link with Chrysler, Daimler's design centre aimed to house personnel previously split between 18 sites. The rationale behind this development was given by Helmut Petri, the group's head of passenger car development:

> We will become much faster in processes – although speed for itself was not our first aim . . . Product development has already got 30 per cent faster, but we see scope to do more.[31]

There is no single, fixed way to manage cross-functional teams. Some firms successfully innovate using cross-functional teams to focus on a particular product development. This was central to the success of the Ford Taurus. Other firms will use cross-functional teams and not limit them to a particular product but will have a more fluid, *ad hoc* arrangement. This approach works well at Toyota as we saw earlier. Toyota's approach is explained here:

> Cross-functional teams . . . work well within individual projects, but the temporary, personal nature of these teams makes it hard for them to transmit information to teams on other projects. Toyota, by contrast, seems to go to the opposite organizational extreme . . . Toyota has added a number of twists to ensure that each project has the

flexibility it needs and still benefits from what other projects have learned. The result is a deftly managed process that rivals the company's famous production system, lean manufacturing, in effectiveness.[32]

The cultural issue

Reorganization is vital but it is not sufficient. An innovation culture has to be in place, supported by financial incentives for creative ideas. Major innovating firms have cultures that encourage ideas for innovation. For example, 3M's culture regarding innovation is:

1. Set goals for innovation.
2. Commit to research and development.
3. Inspire intrapreneurship.
4. Facilitate, don't obstruct.
5. Focus on the customer.
6. Tolerate failure.

Other firms do not have cultures that encourage innovation. Harvard's Rosbeth Kanter sarcastically provides a list of cultural ingredients guaranteed *not* to bring innovation:[33]

1. Be suspicious of any new idea from below. After all, top management thinks of all the good ideas.
2. Make people go through several organizational levels before getting your approval.
3. Give criticism at every opportunity.
4. Keep people in the dark about what's going on in the firm.
5. Manage tightly; control everything to the nth degree.
6. Have the attitude that you (top management) already know everything there is to know.

Highly innovative firms support a positive culture with 'pay for ideas'; again, 3M shows the way. 3M has a '15% rule', which allows research and development (R&D) employees to spend 15% of their time on their own ideas. This was explained by a director of R&D at 3M:

The 15% rule is something that gives permission, but it is not something you push or monitor . . . You want people to be free to pursue their own ideas, but you believe that if it is too structured, too formal, or too exposed, you will lose the innovative entrepreneurial activity.[34]

This gives employees freedom to innovate and 'lets loose' ideas within the organization. Other firms' have also benefited from encouraging innovation at all levels. Texas Instrument's IDEA scheme contributed an estimated $500 million in profits and cost savings over a 23-year period from a total investment of about $20 million. Where there are rigid hierarchies in place, or where the culture is like that described by Rosbeth Kanter earlier, innovation, if it takes place at all, will be a slow, laborious sequence of events. It was an approach which, for years, was exemplified at IBM and was the cause behind the massive reorganization that it had to go through:

> But it's hard at IBM to do anything that hasn't been done before. New things tend to get shot down, or at least debated to death as IBM's marketing forces and related product groups raise objections . . . Anyone at IBM wanting to do something with any kind of speed finds himself using old ideas.[35]

Manufacturing involvement in innovation

As we saw in Chapter 1, manufacturing's role has often been relegated to that of a technical/functional specialist within firms. This is evident in many firms' approach to new product development where the main responsibility for manufacturing is to 'go away and make the product' in volumes demanded by marketing, to a design created by design specialists. We have now seen that cross-functional teams are important; manufacturing's involvement in these teams is vital. At some stage, manufacturing must be involved in the process simply because they have to actually make the product. It will be manufacturing personnel who need to ensure that capability is there to produce the range, volume and mix of new and existing products. But the crucial question is, *at what stage should manufacturing be involved in the development process?* The evidence from the enlightened plants will show that it makes good sense to involve manufacturing personnel from early, conceptual stages. Clearly, one of the important roles for manufacturing is in liaising with suppliers and, where such links are in place, with joint ventures and alliances with other firms in product development.

Techniques such as design for manufacture and modular assembly have become increasingly important and demonstrate manufacturing's pivotal role. These methods demand close relationships with suppliers to ensure that modules and sub-assemblies are delivered to the quality and quantities needed.

Companies of all sizes are developing strategic partnerships because of the uncertainties of innovation. For example, AT&T needed the assistance of Japan's Marubeni Trading Company to bring in the expertise of Matsushita

Figure 3.3   The marketing/manufacturing interface in new product development

Marketing's role	Stages of development	Manufacturing's role
Market assessment Volume requirements	Initial screening	Ensuring that capacity, process technology and skills are poised and costs can be met
Developing marketing strategy and product concept	Initial design	Integrated design – with other functions and with supplier involvement
Refining market strategy in terms of buyers, pricing and promotion decisions	Development	Design development; prototype testing; enhanced CAD usage
Executing marketing strategy	Product launch	Full-scale production capability; continuing product and process improvements

Electric to develop the Safari notebook; MCI Communications uses up to 100 partners to bid on contracts with large customers; and IBM, Apple Computer and Motorola formed alliances for developing new computer microprocessors. So what were once simply competitors are now co-innovators.

Manufacturing's role in helping to ensure the strategic fit between firms linked in an alliance is significant. Their role in linking with suppliers and alliances is vital in new product development. Furthermore, the internal links between manufacturing and other functions within the firm is crucially important, as shown in Figure 3.3.

Contrasting enlightened and traditional plants in innovation

A number of important issues emerged in interviews within the plants. The dramatic changes in many markets put ever greater emphasis upon the ability of operations to respond to volume, variety and flexibility requirements of the markets in which products are being manufactured. For the enlightened plants, this was seen as an opportunity; for the traditional plants, it was a threat brought about by the realization that their technology was not able to satisfy these needs. The shift in manufacturing – from mass production to the current era – that I outlined in Chapter 1 has direct relevance for the process of product innovation within the plants. In the current era of manufacturing, products have to be innovated more rapidly than before, with increased quality requirements – in addition to low cost – and all of these requirements have to be done simultaneously. This presents massive challenges for organizations.

The role of manufacturing personnel in new product development was an important indication of differences between traditional and enlightened plants. Enlightened plants involve manufacturing in all stages from early concept onward; traditional plants do not. (There were varying degrees of involvement from manufacturing according to particular plants.) Insight into the success of innovations within the plants was gained by asking questions about percentage of turnover from current and future products. I asked two questions concerning five-year spans:

1. What percentage of your current turnover comes from products launched in the last five years?
2. In five years' time, what percentage of turnover will come from products not yet launched?

There was no real difference between traditional and enlightened plants at this point. However, I then asked two further questions and focused these into a two-year timeframe:

1. What percentage of your current turnover comes from products launched in the last two years?
2. In two years' time, what percentage of turnover will come from products not yet launched?

It then became clear that there were major differences between traditional and enlightened plants when data concerning products that had actually been launched in a two-year period came to light. This shed light on another key factor, namely the differences in terms of the *speed* of innovation between traditional and enlightened plants. While it would be too cynical to dismiss any possibility that the traditional plants would achieve their future targets, if data from the past two years provide clues to the future, then their plans are, to say the least, optimistic. Dramatic improvements will need to take place within the traditional plants if future targets are to be met.

The speed of new product development within enlightened plants exceeds that of the traditional plants; this is true of both industries. However, it is important to see the differences between traditional and enlightened plants within the industry-specific settings, because speed of innovation is faster within the computer industry than it is within the automobile industry. These differences are illustrated in Figures 3.4 and 3.5.

Figure 3.4 Contrasting enlightened and traditional plants in innovation within the automobile industry

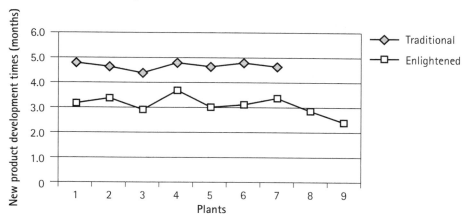

Figure 3.5 Contrasting enlightened and traditional plants in innovation within the computer industry

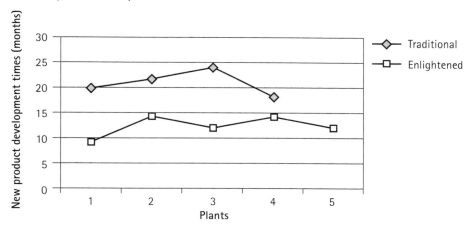

Further findings within the plants

In addition to the actual data, further insight came from the following:

Manufacturing's involvement in the development process

By virtue of the role that manufacturing played in the enlightened plants – that of involvement in the whole business and not merely technical areas – production/operation's early input into innovation of new products (together with modifications to existing products) was seen as central and vital. Approaches such as design for manufacturing and modular assembly were common and viewed as a means to satisfying market requirements. A Japanese transplant manager, whose plant belonged to the enlightened group remarked:

> We are eliminating component variations that do not add value for our customers. Our aim is to reduce variety of parts by 30% for each new model . . . one of the models we have launched did just that . . . 30% less parts variations than its predecessor.

Reducing the numbers of components used in a product was a feature of enlightened plants with manufacturing input being an important factor. One transplant production manager explained:

> We can make as wide variety as any on earth but customers don't actually require this variety so we have used fewer types of parts in our new models than we did before.

Another added:

> We used to have 20 different types of signal switches which was way over the top . . . we now have 7 and they use the same components in them. Our customers are still happy.

This consolidation also extended to the finished product variation:

> One of our cars had over 90 variations in one way or another . . . less than half of these accounted for over 95% of sales of that model. The other 40-odd accounted for less than 5% of sales . . . that's not good for us and, more to the point it's not what customers require.

However, it should be pointed out here that this does not mean a return to the good old days of mass production – even if this transplant reduced to 40 variations, this is still way beyond the 'have any colour of car provided it is black' mentality of Henry Ford's mass production system. In addition, such variations still exceed the capability of all of the traditional plants, some of whom could achieve very limited ranges of models in comparison to their enlightened counterparts.

We can contrast the differences between enlightened and traditional regarding linkages between manufacturing and marketing personnel. One of the enlightened plant's marketing managers commented:

> We always involve Manufacturing in the early stages rather than in just testing and assembly . . .

Another enlightened plant's marketing director stated:

> When manufacturing contributes to the process what is actually produced is more likely to be what customers want. We ensure that manufacturing get direct feedback from customers . . .

The same plant's senior manufacturing manager added:

> The other functions know what manufacturing can and can't do. This plant won't make promises to our customers that we can't deliver . . . our involvement from the start develops real commitment from us throughout the process.

The contrast between these quotes and what follows from the traditional group was striking. One of the traditional marketing managers stated bluntly:

> Manufacturing people know nothing about marketing and so they don't know what's out there and what needs to be developed.

Another added:

> Developing a new product is frustrating work as it is. If you get [manufacturing] involved it just won't happen – we'd be clashing all day instead of getting the thing up and running.

In language that endorsed how easily caught up manufacturing personnel can be with technicalities, one marketing manager stated:

> In the early stages of a project, manufacturing get too caught up in technical details and ask questions about how it will be made . . . they hold up progress . . . they have nothing to bring, really.

It became clear that when manufacturing personnel were seen in a purely 'technical' sense, problems occurred. When manufacturing personnel were viewed in a wider, 'business' sense, speed of innovations was enhanced.

The role of manufacturing strategies

In addition to the role of personnel, another important feature was that of manufacturing strategy within the enlightened plants. In each case, manufacturing strategy included new product development as part of its scope and contribution. Process technology was also important in terms of managing the commitment to existing products as well as facilitating the introduction of new products. Early involvement from manufacturing in product development was not merely assumed but was also encouraged on a division-wide basis from other functions in enlightened plants.

The recognition that constant innovation was a requirement was explicit and seen as a challenge. By contrast, in the traditional plants, the role of manufacturing was one of reacting to new designs devised, essentially, by design specialists; manufacturing's task was to satisfy subsequent volume requirements as determined by marketing. In these plants, there was conflict between departments, which did not add any value and which often reduced the speed of the innovation process. I can add that in the enlightened plants, manufacturing's early involvement also helped to satisfy the 'good criteria' cited earlier: parts were minimized, standardization across products was encouraged, and the static, function-to-function approach was replaced by simultaneous developments across functions, with manufacturing being seen as a key player in the development process.

The role of alliances

Another distinguishing factor was in the role of alliances with other firms. For the enlightened plants, alliances were a key means of organizational learning which would result in, but not be limited to, new products. For the traditional plants, alliances – where they existed – were much more product-specific and task-oriented in nature. The underlying theme here was that alliances could be abandoned once a particular project had been completed and that no further benefit could be derived from learning. It cannot be emphasised enough how important the role of alliances will be in developing new products in high-tech industries, as well as the automobile industry.

The involvement of manufacturing personnel in alliances

In the enlightened plants, senior manufacturing personnel were central in helping to decide who would be appropriate technological partners. This often meant close liaison with corporate headquarters before such links could be made. This link was missing in some of the traditional plants.

Attitudes towards failure

For the enlightened plants, learning from failure was integral. While neither traditional nor enlightened plants were very forthcoming in terms of the amounts of new product failures, the difference between the groups was one of attitude to failure. Fear dominated traditional plants and in two different plants personnel had been fired through 'failure' of new product innovation. The enlightened plants, by contrast saw failure of particular products both as inevitable and as something from which lessons could be learned. However, enlightened plants had more success both in terms of speed and volume of innovations than the traditional plants.

Conclusions

The 'strategic, focused, holistic' model developed in Chapter 1 was clearly evident in the approaches of enlightened plants to innovation, as shown in Figure 3.6.

Figure 3.6   The enlightened approach to innovation

Strategic innovation entails viewing innovation as an ongoing competitive factor. Innovation is not limited to new products only but will include processes, know-how, learning and experience. Senior personnel need to ensure that an innovation culture is in place. Furthermore, senior managers need to be constantly searching for new opportunities in terms of products, markets, and strategic partners as part of the ongoing commitment to innovation.

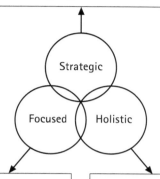

Focused innovation means focusing on particular market segments and concentrating on either pushing new ideas - 'technology push' - or by responding to market-pull requirements via cross-functional teams. The intense efforts do not need to be limited to one product.

Holistic innovation means thinking laterally for new market opportunities. It also involves integration of all departments within the firm as well as long-term relationships with suppliers and other alliances in order to develop processes and products.

We have seen that enlightened plants performed better than their traditional counterparts. While this chapter does not pretend to provide an instant panacea or checklist for successful innovation, it is clear that the enlightened approach is a minimum requirement to compete in markets full of chaos, turbulence and rapid new product requirements. For the enlightened plants, innovation is a strategic factor that includes cross-functional senior management involvement. The process is fluid and not sequential – functions combine simultaneously in the process. An important feature is learning, which is an ongoing part of the development process. Alliances can play a key role in process-learning as well as enhancing the development of particular products.

Enlightened Western plants seem capable of matching the speed of innovation of their Japanese rivals; traditional Western plants do not. Central to this development is the positioning of senior manufacturing personnel involved in the process of new product development, together with manufacturing strategies that include new product development as part of their content, the aim of which is to support the plant in the market. Again, it must be noted that these two factors are often missing or, at best, are only implicit in the literature on product development. These two areas are critical to both product and process technology. We will see in subsequent chapters that the business role of senior manufacturing personnel, together with explicit manufacturing strategies, are also central to other manufacturing areas.

NOTES AND REFERENCES

1. Kay, J. (1993) *Foundations of Corporate Success*. Oxford University Press, Oxford.
2. Peters, T. (1991, 1992) 'Get innovative or get dead' (parts 1 & 2), *Engineering Management Review*, **19**(4): 4–11 and **19**(5): 7–14.
3. *Industry Week*, July 6, 1998.
4. Pavitt, K. (1990) 'What We Know About the Strategic Management of Technology', *California Management Review*, Spring: 17–26.
5. Kay, J. (1993) *Foundations of Corporate Success*. Oxford University Press, Oxford.
6. Hamel, G. (1998) 'The challenge today: changing the rules of the game', *Business Strategy Review*, **9**(2): 19–27.
7. Pavitt, K. (1990) 'What We Know About the Strategic Management of Technology', *California Management Review*, Spring: 17–26.
8. *Ward's Automotive Yearbook*, 1998. Ward's Communications, Southfield, MI.
9. Standard & Poor's Industry Survey, June 1999.
10. Teece, D. (1986) 'Profiting from Technological Innovation: Implications for Integration, Collaboration, Licensing and Public Policy', *Research Policy*, **15**(2): 24.
11. 'The wheels come off GM in Europe', *The European*, February 2, 1998, p. 20.
12. *Fortune* (1996) **134**(5): 92.
13. Ibid.
14. *Fortune* (1997) **136**(11): 100.
15. Robertson, D. and Ulrich, K. (1998) 'Planning for product platforms', *Sloan Management Review*, **39**(4): 19.
16. Bessant, J. (1991) *Managing Advanced Manufacturing Technology*. Blackwell, Oxford.
17. Skinner, W. (1985) *Manufacturing, The Formidable Competitive Weapon*. John Wiley & Sons, New York.
18. Evans, J., Anderson, D., Sweeney, D., and Williams, T. (1990) *Applied Production and Operations Management*. West Publishing, St. Paul, MN.
19. *The Independent* (1996), 'Motoring: The ten best and ten worst cars of the century', January 20.
20. *Fortune*, March 16, 1998.
21. *Forbes*, June 2, 1997.
22. *Industry Week*, February 17, 1997.
23. *Fortune* (1995) **131**(8): 121.
24. Nemeth, C.J. (1997) 'Managing innovation: when less is more', *California Management Review*, **40**(1).
25. *Forbes* (1996) **157**(4): 56.
26. *Fortune*, March 3, 1997.
27. *Industry Week* (1996) **245**(21): 34.
28. Brown, S. (1996) *Strategic Manufacturing for Competitive Advantage*. Prentice Hall, Hemel Hempstead, UK.

29. Schonberger, R. (1986) *World Class Manufacturing*. Free Press, New York.

30. Allen, D. (1993) *Developing Successful New Products*. Pitman, London.

31. *Financial Times* (1998) 'Survey: Autotomobile', December 3.

32. Sobek, D.K. II, Liker, J.K., Ward, A.C. (1998) 'Another look at how Toyota integrates product development', *Harvard Business Review*, July–August, **76**.

33. Brown, S. (1996) *Strategic Manufacturing for Competitive Advantage*. Prentice Hall, Hemel Hempstead, UK.

34. *Industry Week* (1998) **247**(4): 47.

35. Carroll, P. (1993) *Big Blues: The Unmaking of IBM*. Crown, New York.

4

Managing the manufacturing process

Introduction

This chapter is about managing operations processes – in particular, the transformation process, or process choice as it is often called. In the previous chapter, we saw how difficult the task of innovating new products can be. But innovation is not just about launching new products: it also includes acquiring and managing new process technology. Process and product technology are often equal partners in innovation. Process technology must be in place to support new product innovations, and without this capability new product developments will fail. New technology will also have important influence on the wider issue of the firm's overall capacity. For example, at the end of the 1990s, Toyota made around 4 million vehicles a year in its home base, and a further 1.2 million outside of Japan, the main centre of which was the USA. Its five-year plan taking it into the new millennium included projected production of 6 million cars a year – with all the growth taking place outside of Japan. Toyota either owns or has investments in three factories in Europe, six in the USA, three in Latin America, and 14 around Asia and Australasia. Outside North America and Europe, these operations focus on assembly of imported 'car kits'. Part of Toyota's strategic plan included new plants in Australia and Turkey, and expansion in Taiwan and Thailand. In spite of over-capacity within the industry, other major car firms announced huge investments. The 'Big Three' in the USA invested heavily in technology in their plants.[1] General Motors (GM) spent $9.3 billion in both 1998 and 1999. GM's average expenditure on automation in the early 1990s had been $5.4 billion per annum. Ford typically spends $8 billion per annum. Chrysler's investment of $4 billion in 1998 and 1999 tended to be smaller and incremental in comparison to the more dramatic investments of Ford and GM. Chrysler committed $1.2 billion to build a new Jeep in Toledo, Ohio, in addition to $300 million to add 60,000 square feet to its existing 1.1 million square feet axle plant in Detroit. All of this aspiration to greater levels of capacity demands massive, ongoing investment in new process technology to support the volume of production. But investment in technology *per se* is not enough. As Toyota and other world-class manufacturers have shown, an important part of the innovation process is in ensuring that there is sufficient human know-how and learning in place to accompany and complement the investment in new process technology. It was this ability to match process investment with human skills into an integrated framework that enabled two of Ford's plants to be ranked in The Economist Intelligence Unit's top ten plants worldwide in 1997. The Taurus plant in Atlanta and the Sable plant in Chicago were the only two US plants on the list.

Capacity should not be seen just in terms of volume but also in the variety of products that the firm can provide. The capability to produce a variety of products is an important link to the overall output of the firm.

As we saw in Chapter 1, there have been three major eras in manufacturing, namely craft, mass production and the current era. This current era has been called a number of things, including flexible specialization,[2] mass customization[3] and agile manufacturing,[4] all of which have been linked to lean production, although they are not the same. Flexible specialization, mass customization and agile manufacturing attempt to describe the simultaneous requirements of volume and variety that have posed a major challenge to manufacturing firms who must satisfy these customer requirements. There are, of course, added customer requirements such as fast and assured delivery, and low cost. However, the key point to bear in mind – and one which some firms continue to struggle with – is that with the current turbulence in markets it is inappropriate to use methods and processes adopted under mass production. This is particularly noticeable in the use of technology in the transformation process – or process choice, as it is sometimes called. Market requirements now demand manufacturing capability in terms of flexibility, and this flexibility comes from an array of possibilities under the heading of 'flexible' manufacturing which is discussed in this chapter.

The key questions that I explore in this chapter are:

- Are process technology and investment viewed differently between enlightened and traditional plants and, if so, how?

- How do the two groups use technology to cope with the chaos and turbulence of markets?

- How does process technology help to support the competitive position of the plants?

● How are major technological areas, such as flexible manufacturing systems, used by the plants?

As you will see, what emerges is that although investment in process technology is a common characteristic for both traditional and enlightened plants, the motives, scope and expectations of this investment differ greatly between the two groups.

Figure 4.1   Gaining strategic resonance from plant processes

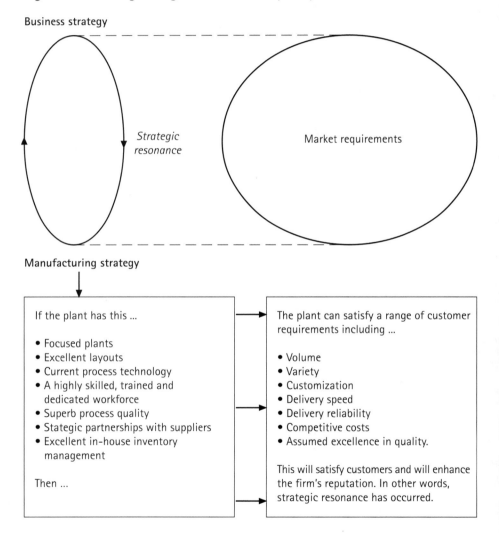

Managing technology is a difficult task because technology is, among other things, uncertain, dynamic, and must integrate with other areas such as human skills and capabilities. It is not suggested that enlightened plants will always get it right with technology. However, what we will see is that there is far greater cohesion in attempting to use technology as a means to gaining competitive advantage within the enlightened plants than in traditional plants. Enlightened plants use process technology to ensure strategic resonance takes place between plant technology and market requirements. It is axiomatic that it is pointless having technology that can ensure unit cost reductions but not delivery speed, when what is required by the market is delivery speed. Traditional plants tend to view technology as almost an end in itself, often championed by technical specialists, without realizing the need for a more integrated and holistic approach.

Process choice – the means by which technology transforms inputs into products within the plant – is a major strategic decision. This is because no amount of reactive, tactical measures can hope to compensate for inappropriate investment in 'wrong' processes which do not match the market requirements in which the firm/plant is competing. Decisions have to be based on current and future market demands and must not be swayed by technical or engineering indulgence by a particular group within the firm. As we will see, this can be the case, and was a feature, of traditional plants.

The essence of investment in technology is to help to create and sustain strategic resonance, as illustrated in Figure 4.1.

The financial consideration

Put simply, there is no choice between whether to invest in technology or not. The only choice – if a firm is to remain in business – is in the type and extent of process technological investment. But two equally dangerous steps can be taken when it comes to investment in process technology. The first is to not invest; the second is to 'throw money' at technology in the hope that, somehow, this will ensure success. If a firm does not invest, the reality of course is that it is then incapable of competing against other competitors over time. Lack of investment is one of the easiest financial traps to fall into. The plant's capabilities will decline and the fact is that other competitors will invest and will, therefore, be in a better position to meet a range of customer requirements. For a while the plant will muddle along and, more alarmingly, its return on assets – one of the most dangerous of all accounting ratios if used myopically – will appear to be financially strong. It is difficult to justify investment: typically, large sums can be invested and there is often a considerable gap between the time of investment and the benefits that might be attained. Various attempts have been made to justify accounting criteria including the payback period, break-even analysis and net present value. The problem with these accounting measures is that there is often a static and fixed feel to them. For example, payback criteria ignore any return that might be forthcoming beyond the payback period. Net present value (NPV) assumes that factors such as market share, price, labour costs and the company's competitive position in the market will remain constant over time. However, the fact is that all of these factors will change and, more importantly, will degenerate if the company retains out-dated production methods which will not allow it to compete in key competitive factors such as cost, delivery speed and reliability, and new product innovation.

Sometimes, the justification for investing is that subsequently there will be a reduction in the workforce. But justification for investment has to go beyond replacing labour costs to the idea of competitive advantage in other areas such as product quality, and delivery speed and reliability. Direct labour costs account for only a small percentage of total manufacturing costs – typically no more than 10% in high-volume manufacturing. Besides, human capability is often a very necessary complementary asset to the technological hardware.

Ultimately, the greatest cost is not investing. But the puzzle of how much to invest in technology is made more difficult because in many Western manufacturing firms, there is no senior-level technological/manufacturing presence involved in business strategy decisions and whose input might help in guiding the extent and appropriateness of technological investment decisions. The consequence of this is that sometimes there have been massive amounts of investments in technology that have gained no benefit for the firm. Part of this has to deal with senior management's ignorance of the role and contribution of manufacturing strategy. As I have noted throughout this book, manufacturing strategy is a major feature of enlightened plants. But the failure of senior management to understand the role of manufacturing strategy is common and is described by Harvard's Hayes and Wheelwright:

> The greater the variety of manufacturing strategies, the less likely it is that senior-level managers will develop a detailed understanding of manufacturing's potential contribution. This is due both to the fact that there are not enough common threads for them to exploit from their position and because they are unlikely to be familiar with all the technologies involved.[5]

This is only part of the puzzle and does not fully explain the failure of technology. As we saw in Chapter 2, several of the traditional plants *did* have senior manufacturing presence. But these plants still failed to successfully implement new process technology which would bring any competitive advantage. As we will see, the major factor was concerned with the rationale behind, and the expectations of, investment in technology.

So the key issue is that the actual sums invested in technology and process choice can be substantial, and purchasing fixed assets for manufacturing can have huge financial implications for the firm. However, the alternative problem is that in many firms there is a lack of investment and plants are consequently incapable of competing.

Substantial investment in process technology does not, in itself, guarantee competitiveness. For example GM's most automated plant in Hamtramck, Michigan, was known for having lower productivity and poorer quality performance than GM's labour-intensive plant at Fremont, California – the NUMMI project. Marianne Keller provides insight into the inappropriate investment at General Motors:

> While Smith provided the money for automation and supported it completely, he clearly didn't understand it . . . With its 260 gleaming new robots for welding, assembling, and painting cars; its fifty automated guided vehicles to deliver parts to the assembly line; and a complement of cameras and computers to monitor, inspect, and control the process, the plant put stars in Smith's eyes. He believed it held the promise of a new era of efficiency and quality and would eventually become a model for all assembly plants. What it became was a nightmare of inefficiency, producing poor-quality vehicles despite the heroic efforts of workers to correct mistakes before they were shipped to dealers.[6]

Fortune noted how:

> Infatuated with technology and given a nearly bottomless account, Smith spent the company dry and got almost nothing to show for it.[7]

GM spent $80 billion throughout the 1980s on automation. Did such investment bring enormous benefits to the company? Hardly, not if market share is any measurement to go by. In 1979, GM had a domestic market share of around 61%; by the end of the 1990s it was around 32% in a market where overall capacity had not increased. What had happened was that other rivals – particularly the Japanese – invested in the right technology for the right reasons. One of the reasons behind GM's investment disaster was that the decision to invest included wanting to radically reduce the workforce. It did just that – from 876,000 in 1986 to around 750,000 in 1992.[8] But GM's problem during this period was the lack of importance given to process technology as a complementary feature to skills and inventiveness of humans, rather than a wholesale replacement for them. This is directly relevant because the use of technology to complement rather than wholly replace labour was a feature of the enlightened plants, whereas in the traditional plants technology was viewed with great suspicion by manufacturing personnel who saw investment as a threat to their jobs. Clearly, the benefits of appropriate automation are widespread and not just in labour costs savings and, in fact, there does not have to be reduction in the workforce merely because of technology investment.

Technology *can* replace humans and this has always been a concern, ever since the early nineteenth century when the Luddites destroyed the looms and jennies that threatened their livelihood. Computers have always been seen as a threat. For example, in the late 1940s, Norbert Weiner, a pioneer of computing, forecast that this new technology would destroy enough jobs to make the depression of the 1930s appear tame by comparison. But as *The Economist* stated:

> Are such fears justified? In one way, yes. Millions of jobs have indeed been destroyed by technology. A decade ago, the words you are now reading would have reached you from two sets of hands: those of a journalist and those of a typesetter. Thanks to computers, the typesetter no longer has a job . . . Although the typesetter no longer has that job, he may well have a different one. John Kennedy put it well in the 1960s: 'If men have the talent to invent new machines that put men out of work, they have the talent to put those men back to work.' That is as true now as it was then, and earlier.[9]

Investment in technology can provide benefits for the firm and its workforce. The firm can gain from consistent process quality, and faster change-overs which will then result in greater flexibility. There are a number of benefits to workers in that robots can free-up humans from tiresome and repetitive, monotonous tasks in order for them to be involved in creative activities. That was certainly the case for the enlightened plants who used technology to free-up humans from mundane tasks, allowing them to be involved in far greater creative roles. With specific regard to manufacturing technology, *The Economist* manufacturing technology survey noted rightly that:

> . . . robots have not displaced men and women . . . despite the fact that their advent gave rise to yet another wave of speculation about the workerless factory. They have a role in manufacturing and have been used well in Japan . . . The Japanese have understood that, if work is designed properly for robots, they will do it well – but they are not able to replace people at jobs that have evolved to need a human's innate ability to fit the world and ideas and intentions to that of deeds and objects.[10]

It is clear, then, that the justification for technological investment must go beyond cost reductions that might be gained by reducing the numbers in the workforce. Instead, it must follow on from an awareness of, and the ongoing desire to satisfy, market requirements.

The impact of markets on process choice

Investment decisions are critical and must be made with the aim of equipping the firm or plant to be more competitive in the market. We know for sure that wrong investment decisions in automation will result in wasted funds – often many millions of dollars. Furthermore, wrong decisions regarding the plant's processes will cripple the company's capability to satisfy customer demands in particular markets. Process choice and technology are vital because key competitive factors for customers including cost, and delivery speed and flexibility, can be enhanced by appropriate technology. If appropriate investment in technology and the choice of process is made this will become a central part of the firm's competitive weaponry. Consequently, investment in technologies such as computer-integrated manufacture (CIM) and advanced manufacturing technology (AMT) is of strategic importance because it provides competitive options for the firm:

> In most cases, AMT investments are irreversible because they are highly specialized, durable, and dependent on the firm's specific operating routines, information flows and knowledge surrounding both product design and process technology. However, the strategic options allowed by AMT help the firm recoup its investment . . . The fragmentation of markets, the development of new market segments or niches, as well as faster design . . . all contribute to the need for strategic flexibility. Thus, flexible manufacturing technologies provide a strategic real option . . . in which high levels of economies of scope and a 'design for response' capability position the firm to enter a broader range of different markets at its own discretion.[11]

For example, Motorola's original AMT investments in the flexible manufacture of components for cellular telephones were applied successfully to other electronic component applications. This is typical of the sort of strategic opportunities that technology investment can present to the firm. As a result, AMT investments can enable the firm to provide a range of products or components based on group technology or shared design characteristics. This in turn provides strategic options based on economies of scope, rather than economies of scale.

We know there have been three eras of manufacturing: craft, mass and the current era. All three have direct relevance to the nature of the transformation process and process choice. In essence, process choice will provide major clues about how the firm competes and what it can – and cannot – do. The five types of process choice are: project, job, batch, line and continuous process. The basic distinction between these is shown in Figure 4.2. (For a more in-depth discussion on process choice and its link to types of layout, *see* Brown[12] and Hill.[13])

Figure 4.2   The key distinction of volume and variety outputs from process choice

Increase in volume – typically competing on cost via scale economies

| Project | Job | Batch | Line | Continuous process |

Increase in variety – typically competing on capabilities of scope

So the choice of the transformation process choice actually dictates, to a large extent, what the company 'sells' in terms of its capabilities, and how the company can then compete. Although there may be more than one process type being used within the same company, there will often be a dominant core process that is best suited to support the company in the market. This link between process choice and corporate and marketing strategies is shown in Figure 4.3.

Figure 4.3   The link between process choice and marketing strategy

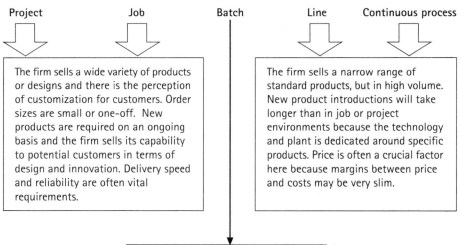

| Project | Job | Batch | Line | Continuous process |

The firm sells a wide variety of products or designs and there is the perception of customization for customers. Order sizes are small or one-off. New products are required on an ongoing basis and the firm sells its capability to potential customers in terms of design and innovation. Delivery speed and reliability are often vital requirements.

The firm sells a narrow range of standard products, but in high volume. New product introductions will take longer than in job or project environments because the technology and plant is dedicated around specific products. Price is often a crucial factor here because margins between price and costs may be very slim.

Batch can be difficult because of its 'middle' ground and is managed initially by mapping products according to their job (low-volume) or line (high-volume) characteristics. The plant is then further focused into production cells. Recent step changes to deal with this include FMS and other forms of advanced manufacturing technology (AMT).

Figure 4.4   The manufacturing eras and their impact on process choice

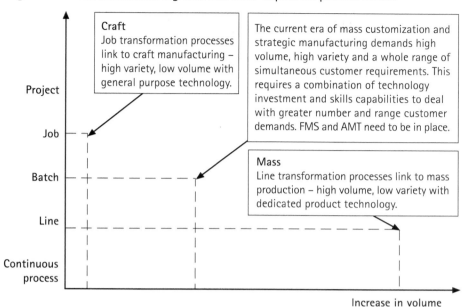

We can take this one stage further by mapping the previous and current eras of manufacturing on to types of process choice as shown in Figure 4.4.

So the traditional line process, which mass-produced one product in high volume (the 'you can have any colour of car provided it's black' mentality) clearly fails to meet the requirement of variety. This then changes the requirements needed from manufacturing, as summarized in Table 4.1.

Table 4.1   The changing task of manufacturing management

Period	Production range	Production task	Volume level	Finished product made
1950–1970s (line processes)	Narrow	Achieve supposed economies of scale by large production runs of limited range	Very high	To stock (just in case)
1980s+ (hybrid systems – FMS)	Wide	Meet specific customer needs, including cost, delivery, range and flexibility	As required – volume and variety	For customer requirements only (just in time)

The move towards flexible manufacturing was one of the major competitive advantages of Japanese car manufacturing for some time, and has now appeared in the best of Western manufacturing. Segments of the car industry are frequently fragmenting due to the manufacturing ability of firms to provide a wide variety of models. So whereas at one time GM could have produced 1 million of one model, by the 1990s it was rare to exceed 250,000 of a particular model. In consequence, if processes are structured around old fashioned ideas of vast economies of scale based on narrowly defined line processes, this has to change to more customer-driven processes, including FMT. We should not be overly critical of past approaches around line processes. It's just that they no longer serve the current market requirements. Line processes (mass production) was entirely appropriate for past market requirements. As *Industry Week*[14] rightly points out:

> In the early days of the automotive industry, Henry Ford reportedly was able to produce a Model T Ford in less than 56 hours – from the conversion of iron ore into steel and through final assembly operations.

But things have changed dramatically since then:

> But when a manufacturing organization bases its competitive strategy on offering customers greater product variety, that elevates the level of product and process complexity considerably . . . Supporting an endless flow of new products can trigger a chain of effects inside the organization that can burden it to the breaking point.

However, a word of caution is relevant here: as we saw in the previous chapter there has been a slight reduction in the amount of variation of products offered by manufacturing plants. This reduction of variation became common even in the very best of manufacturing plants – and was certainly evident in the enlightened plants. *Forbes* reported how IBM had reduced the component range of its products:

> . . . to paraphrase Ford, you can have any CD-ROM drive you want as long as it's black. IBM has reduced the number of motherboards in its PCs from 15 to 8, and the number of hard drives from 52 to 12. That still gives the customer a lot of choice, but not an infinite amount. Already, IBM is seeing results. During the past year finished-goods inventory has dropped 65%, and inventory turns have doubled. Turnaround from order to delivery has shrunk 40% in the past year.[15]

This does not mean that there is a return to mass manufacturing. Instead of mass production through narrow dedicated lines, modifications around the 'middle' area – associated with batch – are the solution where flexible manufacturing systems (FMS) and group technology are employed. However, both FMS and group technology are different approaches, or 'step changes', and they are not just a modification of 'traditional' batch manufacture. They are, instead, radical solutions where both variety and volume may be achieved. This radical solution demands equally radical differences in how the workforce is employed in the process – training, empowerment and responsibility are all required.

The mass production system has had to change to suit a volatile, ever-changing environment with new competitors coming in from all over the globe. Mass production's process 'strategy' emphasized efficiency in production; world-class strategic manufacturing firms, on the other hand, emphasize the need to provide product quality, speed, differentiation and any other offering perceived to be important by their customers.

Flexible manufacturing and its impact on competitive strategy

Flexible manufacturing is based essentially around high-volume batch processes. Standard FMS includes the following:

- A number of workstations, such as computer numerically controlled (CNC) machines that perform a wide range of operations.

- A transport system that will move material from one machine to another, and loading and unloading stations where completed or partially completed components will be housed and worked upon.

- A comprehensive computer control system that will co-ordinate all the activities.

But the advantages that FMS can provide go beyond the mere hardware, important as this is. The real advantage comes with the plant-specific know-how and enhanced skills that accompany FMS. Moreover, investment in FMS and other advanced manufacturing technologies provides strategic scope for the firm:

> Flexible manufacturers are in a rather interesting position in the marketplace. When non-flexible manufacturing firms are asked, 'What business are you in?' they list the products they produce. When flexible manufacturers are asked the same question, they respond, 'Whatever business you want us to be in!' In a rapidly changing marketplace, the ability to almost instantly change what the firm can offer its customers can be a formidable competitive weapon.[16]

This is true to some extent but we must be careful here. A firm cannot really state that it is any business that any customer wants. Sure, Toyota and other world-class manufacturers can build thousands of variations around a single base model, but a customer could not say to Toyota: 'If you're so flexible, build me a computer or an aircraft,' because the technology remains focused on car production and nothing else. So the term 'flexible' has to be seen within product-specific boundaries.

What FMS allows the firm to do is to compete on economies of scope rather than economies of scale. Because technologies are more flexible, allowing numerous product variations to be made, the overall volume achieved can be almost as efficient as manufacturing large volumes of standardized products. This means that the basis of competition moves from a strategy of low-priced, commodity products to an emphasis on low-cost special options and customized products. This profoundly changes the rules of the game. Michael Porter's book, *Competitive Strategy*,[17] stated rightly for its time – in 1980 – that firms were faced with two options of either low cost or differentiation in order to be profitable. This reflected industrial economic theory of the time but the reality is that now firms have to compete on both fronts, among a range of other customer requirements. Due to the nature of competition, what were once differentiated features able to provide sustained competitive advantage (for some time at least) now become an even playing field in many markets. This is because technology is often easy to copy. The computer industry is a perfect example. For years, Apple was able to charge premium prices for its differentiated products. But once others emulated the technology, price became critical and the basic software available now is not only vastly superior to before but is common to all PCs. So neither low cost nor differentiation are sufficient by themselves. Instead, a range of new competitive requirements including speed, flexibility and customization, have emerged as the key competitive drivers. This flexibility has become a central capability of world-class manufacturers. For example, in September 1995, when the 1996 Honda Civic was launched in Ohio, the assembly line was geared essentially to 1995 Civics. However, every twenty-second car was a 1996 model inserted in a production line allowing it to achieve remarkably fast changeovers:

> These changeovers on the fly are what make first-rate manufacturing firms continue to claim bragging rights to high-quality, low-cost new product launches. In the case of the 1996 Civic changeover, that meant not just maintaining quality, but going from 1.5 millimetre to 1 millimetre tolerance, and it cost Honda 30% less to launch the 1996 Civic than it did for the 1992 model change. Some companies still use the old method of plant or line shutdown to change over a model or product, but those days are ending.[18]

Honda's flexibility extends beyond technology alone into what has been termed 'Honda's flexifactory', which is based on three major factors:

- flexible machinery.
- flexible people, often rotating jobs on a two-hourly basis, with a willingness to be retrained; and
- flexible organization from the vehicle assembler to the parts suppliers.

Flexibility has spilled over to customer response times. In the past, in addition to the old 'any colour provided it's black' mentality from manufacturers, there was also the mentality of 'you'll have the product when we're ready'. This has had to change because if one firm does not respond quickly, another one will. Computer integrated manufacture (CIM) is an all-embracing term that includes electronic data interchange and other information technology tools, including intranet, which has resulted in greater speed of customer response. *Fortune*[19] describes how Ford has made great use of intranet:

> Ford Motor's intranet is an example of a bigtime manufacturer getting the technology right. The intranet connects about 120,000 of Ford's computers around the world to Web sites containing proprietary company information such as market research, rankings of suppliers' parts and analyses of competitors' components. The network has enabled Ford to bring new models into full production in 24 months compared with 36 months before. The intranet is expected to save the company billions of dollars during the next few years. Ford plans to use its intranet to move closer to manufacturing on demand, a process that involves coordination of delivery and assembly of thousands of components. The company plans to manufacture most of its vehicles on a demand basis by 1999, requiring linking of its 15,000 dealers around the world via its intranet.

Fortune also mentioned how Ford has had to speed up its customer response and provide greater choice for customers simultaneously:

> . . . this is all part of a sweeping manufacturing reengineering process that Ford has undergone in the past couple of years. The results are clear: in 1996 . . . it took more than 50 days to get the Mustang of your choice delivered from the plant to the dealer; today you'll get that Mustang in 15 days. Ford's goal is to manufacture the majority of its vehicles on a demand basis by the end of 1999, with delivery in less than two weeks after the order. This would save billions of dollars in current inventory and fixed costs.

The actual arrangement of production cells provides insight into how manufacturing becomes flexible. Flexible manufacturing systems are typically arranged in small, U-shaped cells. The reason for this shape include reduction of space, increased teamwork and better communication and motivation brought about by seeing a completed product in the cell.

Workers are divided into teams and a single cell can manufacture, inspect and package finished products or components. Every cell is responsible for the quality of its products and each worker will normally be able to perform a range of tasks. Again, process choice is the key insight to cell arrangements: in line processes, introducing variety or changing the product meant stopping the entire assembly line. Such breakdowns and shortages are very costly overheads for mass-producers, intent on low-cost production. To compensate for this, they have to carry large stocks of parts and spares, just in case. I will discuss the critical importance of 'just-in-time' – which is linked to cell manufacturing – in Chapter 6, but it can be mentioned here that stocks of partly finished products also tend to be high under traditional line processes. Components that have undergone part of the production process often sit idle, waiting for the next stage. This is a major source of waste. Large amounts of inventories, some sitting in large warehouses, are a feature of mass production. By contrast, flexible manufacturing, via U-shaped cells, and low inventory levels go hand-in-hand.

The Economist mentions how Harley-Davidson benefited from cellular production:

> . . . before Harley-Davidson introduced cells at its engine-and-gearbox plant, components were machined and stored repeatedly by the firm's 900–strong workforce. The parts meandered along the assembly line, often corroding while they sat idle. A cylinder-head took a week to make. Now, manufactured by a two-man cell, the process takes less than three hours. That means that the firm no longer has to carry big stocks so as to be ready if demand suddenly jumps . . . the floor space occupied by the factory has fallen by a third. It now turns over its stock 40 times a year, compared with just 4.5 times in 1981.[20]

Other equally impressive benefits were found: Compaq replaced three of its 16 Houston assembly lines with 21 cells; productivity rose by 20–25%. The cost of converting to cells was paid back in six months. Similar productivity increases were noted at Lexmark, the manufacturer of computer printers – it converted 80% of its 2,700-employee factory in Lexington, Kentucky, to cells and productivity soared by 25%.

But changes like these are driven by demands of competition and customer requirements. Harley-Davidson and Compaq didn't change for change sake. Harley was being attacked by aggressive, world-class manufacturers, and Compaq is in an industry that increasingly demands razor-thin margins but where customization is also required. Other examples are shown below:[21]

- **Motorola** – Motorola's Bandit Plant in Florida formed a cross-functional 24-member group nicknamed 'Team Bandit' to establish a world-class CIM operation within 18 months. The result was a high-volume CIM operation that produces radio pagers in lot sizes as small as one. A group of 27 programmable robots handles all of the production process including parts inspection, soldering, assembly and inspection. Despite the customized nature of the product, manufacturing cycle time has been cut from several days to about two and a half hours. Entering a rush order can activate the first robot in as little as 17 minutes. Quality has improved dramatically. A defect problem is found in 20 minutes compared with several days using conventional process.

- **Allen Bradley** – In 1983, Allen Bradley, a subsidiary of Rockwell International Corporation, formed a CIM task force to manufacture motor contactors conforming to world standard. Today, the facility is capable of producing over 600 units per hour in any of more than 1,000 variations in lot sizes of one with zero defects and zero direct labour. Allen Bradley's CIM showcase uses stockless production, advanced machine diagnostics and next-day shipping. As a stockless production operation, the facility minimizes material handling and warehousing needs. Once an order is placed, the CIM facility automatically manufactures, tests, packages and ships the product within 24 hours. Building on the success of the CIM contactor facility, Allen Bradley's new automated printed circuit board centre is another company showcase. Milwaukee's newest 'plant within a plant' has reduced production introduction time from two to three years to as little as five months. Circuit board throughput has been reduced to one day resulting in greater customer responsiveness. Inventory turnover has been increased from 2–4% per year to more than 12% per year contributing to just-in-time (JIT) production and lower inventory costs.

All of these benefits come from manufacturing capability. This includes the ability to gel technology hardware with human capability into a potent set of competencies which give the firm strategic options and power. It is strange, then, that in many firms the scope, capability and impact of such potential are ignored or glossed over by senior managers who either do not understand or are not interested in the technological abilities for the firm. Some firms are not so ignorant. Lew Platt, former CEO of Hewlett-Packard (HP), termed manufacturing and distribution the 'core competences' of his company.[22] It is not surprising that there are many success stories demonstrating HP's manufacturing capability. For example, HP was able to beat its Japanese rival NEC by being first to market with a line of inkjet colour printers. HP's units forced NEC to withdraw its own printers. NEC's products were deemed as uncompetitive just four months after they had belatedly entered the market.

Similar strategic manufacturing responses came from Caterpillar. Their competitor, Komatsu, talks of 'surrounding and killing the Cat' as part of its strategic intent, but this has not been quite the formality that many may have assumed from such a declaration by a Japanese manufacturer. A $1.8 billion overhaul of its factories has enabled Caterpillar to regain pre-eminence in earthmoving machines. By 1995, Caterpillar was in third position, after Boeing and Intel, among the top 50 US industrial exporters, in percentage of sales derived from abroad. Caterpillar makes two-thirds of its products in the USA, but nearly half its $12 billion taken in sales in the mid-1990s came from abroad. More significantly, Caterpillar managed to capture a larger market share in Japan than its Japanese archrival, Komatsu, had in the USA. The benefit that Caterpillar gained derived from its willingness to radically reconfigure its approaches to manufacturing. Undoubtedly, this was driven by competition in the first place but the turnaround in manufacturing capability prevented Caterpillar from being yet another casualty of Japanese assaults on Western markets.

Process technology and organizational learning

The importance of organizational learning in the firm's technological accumulation is critical. The acquisition of technology will not, by itself, bring benefits to the firm. Rather, the successful application of the technology is brought about by know-how and experience that will provide advantage for the firm.[23]

Learning is not just firm-specific – more precisely, it is plant-specific. Learning gained in one particular plant is not guaranteed to be transferred to another plant within the same company. For example, there is no evidence to suggest that the success of the GM/Toyota plant (NUMMI) in California has been transferred to all other GM plants – or indeed to any of GM's plants. The fact that the means by which plants learn to utilize process technology is a plant-specific affair is evident: in an interesting case of contrast within the same company, one traditional plant clearly saw automation as a stand-alone cure-all package, able to solve all manufacturing problems, where returns would be immediate. The other plant (within the same company) saw that there would be a required learning process – which would include possible failure and mistakes – and that this learning process was central to the plant's development and advancement. The contrast between these two plants goes against any notion that learning and subsequent transfer of know-how is somehow automatic and to be assumed simply because they belong to the same firm.

However, manufacturing plants can become a valuable learning laboratory. This is described as a place where there is:

> . . . problem-solving, internal knowledge, innovation and experimentation, and external information . . . A learning laboratory is an organization dedicated to knowledge creation, collection and control.[24]

The problem is that firms do not take time to learn. Industry is littered with examples of firms that spent sufficient sums but failed to take the time to learn from successes and failures in using technology. As a result, the investment became a financial millstone. For others, such investment created leverage, brought about by advanced technology allied to enhanced skills, know-how and learning.

Data from the plants

In the light of all the discussion on appropriate investment and use of technology, I wanted to see how plants sought to utilize technology. While I asked for details about the numbers of robotics, machine tools and other technology, the essential point was to discover the rationale behind investment in the plants. This is because this sets the whole tone for the manufacturing plant. The question of justification for the investment in technology provided more insight than other questions such as 'What percentage of operations are automated?' or 'What is the average age of equipment?'. These sorts of questions have been probed and published by others.[25] But the concern with that approach is that it may be argued, or at least inferred, that the more recent the age, the better the plant. Clearly this is not justifiable because, as I noted earlier, many GM plants, were 'young plants' due to the huge investment that took place in the 1980s, yet these plants performed poorly in relation to other plants with older equipment. The same criticism may be made in trying to determine the percentage of operations that are automated within a plant – a higher percentage may be viewed as good or better than other plants. However, as we saw earlier – again with GM plants – other, less automated plants sometimes performed better than their highly automated plants. I aimed to get behind the numbers and to explore the rationale for investment in automation.

Findings within the plants

Plants were invited to rank the rationale behind their investment in technology within the plant. The list included low unit cost, process quality, delivery speed, delivery reliability, flexibility and variety, and potential for customization. In essence, the rationale behind all of the traditional plants' investment was to reduce costs. This is in spite of all the volatility in markets discussed earlier in the chapter. For the enlightened plants, unit cost reduction was ranked last – other factors such as enhancing process quality, flexibility, delivery speed and delivery reliability were seen as priority factors in investing and all of these scored ahead of cost reduction considerations. A number of additional factors emerged and the differences in attitudes between traditional and enlightened plants were radical and dramatic, rather than a slight variation of opinion.

Linking process technology and human resources

How technology would gel (or not) with human resource capability, and how it would satisfy wider, business requirements, was an important issue. Basically, enlightened plants used technology to support the business – investment was not made as a calculated means to downsize the workforce. The traditional plants talked in terms of low cost and one traditional plant boasted how automation had enabled the plant to downsize by 20%. This downsizing had been the major justification for investment – was not a real aspiration to greater flexibility or other market needs. The ability to redress and reset the balance between technological investment (once it had been made) and human resources was, by itself, a distinctive feature between the groups. In short, enlightened plants were willing to redress this balance. As one enlightened plant manufacturing director stated:

> We used to be guilty of technical indulgence and I was as guilty as anyone . . . we were fascinated by what could be possible and we just got carried away with it all. We put the brake on that, though, and now we start from what the customer wants rather than how clever our technology might be.

One of the enlightened Japanese transplants admitted that they, too, had been caught up in the early stages of their pursuit of technology investment:

> We got carried away with it . . . we automated some work that could have been done more economically manually, but we've now got the balance right.

In fact, these sentiments were echoed within the technical documents of another enlightened transplant when alluding to a particular process:

> The work is simple and takes an employee only a matter of seconds to perform. It's less impressive to watch than the fully automated feeders in some of our plants . . . but it makes sense to do it like this.

The technophilia problem

There was a technophilia problem[26] – the love of technology for its own sake – with traditional plants. One of the 'guilty' traditional plants had a strong-minded manufacturing person who viewed technology as an end in itself. Moreover, this technical knowledge and supposed expertise were used by him to blind others with science in management meetings. In the interviews with other managers, it was clear that such an approach was neither appreciated nor welcomed by his management colleagues. Moreover, decisions on technology then became a contest between managers, some of whom were suspicious of possible potential benefits and who were far from clear what value such investment might provide. A telling statement came from one of the traditional plants:

> We've spent all this money and the plant is great from our engineers' point of view but I'm not sure if we all understand it . . . I certainly don't so I'm not sure how the whole company will benefit.

However, by contrast, an enlightened transplant explained:

> We'd rather not be at the leading edge of technological innovation – it's unproven, much of it . . . apart from robots for our tyres, body and welding applications few of our operations are fully automated.

The pace and frequency of investment

The pace and frequency of investment was a telling distinction between enlightened and traditional plants. While there was no great distinction between enlightened and traditional plants in terms of amounts spent, what did become clear was that traditional plants tended to spend large amounts sporadically. Several of the traditional plants boasted that large amounts had been spent but on closer inspection it emerged that this investment had been made at specific, irregular times. In the enlightened plants, investment tended to be more incremental but steady and regular. Investment in the enlightened plants was an ongoing but smaller incremental approach in contrast to some of the sporadic but dramatic investments that had been made by traditional plants.

The role of learning

Learning was an important issue. In enlightened plants, learning went hand-in-hand with investment, and technology was not used as an attempt to mask current performance. It was instead employed to enhance manufacturing performance across a number of competitive variables chosen by the plant. The enlightened approach came from managerial ability to integrate a number of skills. Such an approach is discussed by Prahalad and Hamel who, when talking of technology, suggest that:

> The real sources of advantage are to be found in management's ability to consolidate corporate wide technologies and production skills into competencies that empower individual businesses to adapt quickly to changing opportunities.[27]

This is true, but the caveat with this statement is that the technological advantage can be at plant level, rather than corporate-wide. In other words, the ability to manage technology is not just firm-specific. Instead, this capability must be focused further into divisional/plant-specific ability, brought about by learning.

The role of senior manufacturing personnel and manufacturing strategies

The nature of the involvement from senior manufacturing personnel – coupled with the role of manufacturing strategies – were key factors in determining differences between enlightened and traditional plants. The view of the enlightened plants was that technology was central to meeting business requirements. The difference is that whereas the traditional plants used technology essentially as a means to cut costs, technology took on a far broader perspective within the enlightened plants. Financial criteria were used but finance was seen as part of a wider justification process. Passion and commitment to compete and win in markets were not constrained by mere accounting numbers.

This link between market needs and technological capability was an explicit feature of the enlightened plants. Flexibility within the plant was the central issue, not the meticulous precision of a particular robot. The role of manufacturing strategy was critical here. It became a means of focusing the business decision as described in the following:

> To try to imagine its future by the collective efforts of the members of the organization, the firm needs some common lens which is shared by many members.[28]

In the enlightened plants the 'common lens' that helped to focus the plants' efforts tended to be through the role of the manufacturing strategy, which helped to bridge the gap between technology and market requirements. As I noted earlier, none of the enlightened plants had a technophilia bias, and manufacturing strategy served to provide explicit links between market requirements. This was aided by the closely integrated efforts between manufacturing and marketing staff within the enlightened plants linked to manufacturing/technological capability in-house. The main commonly shared task was to deal with the changes in market requirements.

The use of technology and process choice to manage change

The willingness to use technology and process choice to deal with ongoing changes demanded in the market was more of a problem for traditional than enlightened plants. For the enlightened plants, such change is seen as inevitable and appropriate technology is sought. For the traditional plants, such change is viewed as threatening and the process is one of adjustment around existing approaches rather than an opportunity for learning and change to accommodate a radically different set of market conditions.

The change from mass production to the current era was viewed differently by the two groups. The traditional plants struggle with the change required in markets and see their approach as one of adaptation from line to batch processes with a continued emphasis upon low-cost manufacture.

By contrast, the enlightened plants recognize that there is a major and distinct paradigm shift – although none of them used phrases such as mass customization or flexible specialization. While the enlightened plants used different phrases and descriptions for the current era, they shared the same underpinning set of beliefs. They recognized the need to improve every area of their manufacturing performance simultaneously, and that a range of competitive requirements must be met, not just low cost. In order to deal with this, FMS was a core feature of the enlightened plants. Investment was made to ensure that a range of variations of models could be achieved. Success was measured in terms of changeover times, and capability to produce a range and mix of volumes, delivery requirements and other competitive factors. The rationale behind the expenditure was clearly discernible between enlightened and traditional plants. Traditional plants spent in order to increase precision around limited ranges coupled with lower costs; enlightened plants used this investment to enhance their capability in areas such as speed and flexibility and downsizing was not part of the equation.

Examples of technology capability within the enlightened plants

We saw earlier that if wrong investment decisions are made a huge liability and financial millstone is in place. Inappropriate investment was evident in the traditional plants. For example, one of the traditional plants boasted of the remarkable precision of one of the robots, able to position panels to within fractions of millimetres. However, when asked about the lack of flexibility that the robot had for rapid changeovers, the manager replied: 'Well . . . we didn't buy it for that!'

By contrast, in one of the enlightened plants flexible, assembly systems were installed to improve process quality, increase factory output, and build different versions of cars. Their manufacturing director stated this was to assemble cars that could compete with models from Japan in price, quality, and in meeting ever-varying customer demands. Modular subassembly of components was in place and the powertrain assembly system was flexible enough to combine up to 12 different transmission and engine combinations, along with various accessory options, such as air-conditioning.

In another enlightened plant, robots were used for much of the required body work and numerous robots were used for spot-welding body side panels, the roof, and the rear end structure. However, the plant's main aim was to improve delivery speed and an extended integrated carousel assembly line enabled the cycle time for body build to be reduced from 7.5 to 4.5

minutes per body. The manufacturing strategy here followed on from an understanding of market requirements. This resulted in appropriate investment in technology. The rationale behind the investment was to be more efficient, and to increase speed of delivery, rather than to reduce costs.

Another enlightened manufacturing manager stated how the plant was part of an overall, company-wide to achieve a number of 'anys': any one of its models, at any of its plants, anywhere in the world, at any volume level, and at any time demanded by local market conditions. Its car models grew from 11 to 27 models and 54 body types within a four-year period in the mid-1990s. The ability to do so was dependent to some degree on the appropriate investment including an intelligent body assembly system (IBAS) which allowed the plant to weld at least ten car-model shells – rather than the previous limited capability of just two – in any manufacturing sequence. The plant can now make model changes simply by changing the computer software that controls the body assembly system. Again, the need for flexibility, and not just low cost, was the chief driving force here.

An enlightened computer plant had board assembly operations that were virtually error-free due to barcoding linked to robot technology. Barcoded components were placed in a predetermined order in a robot feeder; the robot, programmed to follow a board schematic, did the component insertion. The technology combined a non-contact laser scanner, a computer, keyboard and screen with a hand-held device used by trained operators. But the rationale for investing this was 'to free up personnel so that they can now be involved in more creative work rather than repetitive, monotonous tasks which could be done by robots.'

The plant was an interesting example where a number of robots were replaced by smaller, more flexible robots. The former approach, which had 43 individual robots on the line, was replaced by four robotic cells, each with three heads. As a result, line speed was enhanced and the new method eliminated a number of sequential steps and allowed more material to fit into the cell. This allowed aggregate volume to increase from 100,000 to 140,000 units per week, yielding a 40% gain in productivity.

Conclusions

It is clear that only with an understanding of the basic process choices available, together with a conviction for appropriate investment in process automation, can a company hope to compete in markets. Without these key areas of understanding in place a company or plant will be tied in with the wrong basic process choice and spend vast amounts of money on automation which does little to enhance the company in its competitive environment.

While it is clear that the management of technology is a profoundly difficult task, successful implementation of CIM in all forms is dependent, to some degree at least, upon the firm's clear and correct understanding of present and future market needs, and investing in the appropriate automation to support these needs. For the enlightened plants, investment came in stages as part of their continued but incremental improvement. Investment was made as an holistic decision, aided and enhanced by the role of manufacturing strategy with senior manufacturing personnel involved in the business of the plant, rather than as a result of the force of one particular group within the plant. Justification went beyond mere accounting criteria to a long-term commitment to satisfying customers in what are now erratic, volatile, dynamic and ever-changing markets – characteristics of all three industries. The strategic, focused and holistic approach of the enlightened plants is shown in Figure 4.5.

Figure 4.5   The enlightened approach to managing process technology

Strategic management of technology includes avoiding two disastrous strategies:
- Failing to invest in order to look good in terms of accounting rations, especially return on net assets and productivity, both of which can be made to look artificially impressive by not investing.
- Throwing money at technology in the hope that this will magically transform the firm overnight.

Justification for investment must be seen as a long-term but ongoing investment.

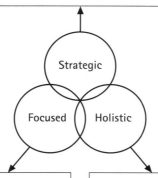

Focused technology means having a clear understanding of market requirements and then focusing the plant into specific focused areas. This can be done by customer, by process type, by product family, or other combinations. There is a need to see the plant as 'plants within plants' focused into cellular areas. Strategic resonance occurs between market requirements and plant capabilities.

Holistic technology means investing as a result of company-wide, market-driven decisions. This stops the technophilia problem. Investment is made in order to satisfy a range of customer requirements and not low cost only. The process ensures strategic resonance takes place.

The traditional plants saw technology as a quick-fix, but expensive, solution, once the often protracted financial justification had been made. Justification in terms of future manufacturing performance was undoubtedly centred on cost savings, rather than a wider set of competitive criteria that formed the central part of the enlightened plants' approach. The driving force behind the enlightened plants was in how ongoing investment would help to meet volatile market conditions. However, these attitudes were, themselves, the result of various factors. First, in enlightened plants, senior manufacturing personnel were involved in the decision-making process for investment within the plants; second, in the enlightened plants, these senior manufacturing personnel were using technology to support the business and could not be accused of technological myopia for its own sake; third, manufacturing strategies within the enlightened plants included technology as part of its overall content and these strategies ensured that other areas – such as training – were linked with investment in technology.

Managing technology can be a difficult, uncertain task, but having these three factors in place helps to ensure success, as was evident in the enlightened plants.

NOTES AND REFERENCES

1. These figures came from Standard & Poor's Industry Survey, June 1999. It should be kept in mind that some plants have much heavier investment than others within the same company. This does not necessarily ensure that they perform better than less automated plants and parallel investment (though less in amount) needs to be spent on ensuring that the workforce understands and utilizes the technology.
2. See, for example, Pine, B., Bart, V. and Boynton, A. (1993) 'Making mass customisation work', *Harvard Business Review*, September–October; Pine, B.J. II (1993) *Mass Customization: The New Frontier in Business Competition*, Harvard University Press, Cambridge, USA; Gilmour, J.H. and Pine, B.J. II (1997) 'The four faces of mass customization', *Harvard Business Review*, January–February, 91–101.
3. Piore, M. and Sabel, C. (1984) *The Second Industrial Divide: Possibilities for Prosperity*. Basic Books, New York.
4. Kidd, P. (1994) *Agile Manufacturing – Forging New Frontiers*. Addison Wesley, Reading, USA.
5. Hayes, R.H. and Wheelwright, S.C. (1984) *Restoring Our Competitive Edge: Competing through Manufacturing*. John Wiley & Sons, New York.
6. Keller, M. (1993) *Collision*. Currency Doubleday, New York.
7. *Fortune*, November 16, 1992.
8. Brown, S. (1996) *Strategic Manufacturing for Competitive Advantage*. Prentice Hall, Hemel Hempstead, UK.
9. *The Economist* (1995) 'Technology and unemployment: A world without jobs?', 11 February
10. *The Economist Manufacturing Technology Survey*, March 5, 1994.
11. Lei, D., Hitt, M.A. and Goldhar, J.D. (1996) 'Advanced manufacturing technology: organizational design and strategic flexibility', *Organization Studies*, **17**(3): 501.

12. Brown, S. (1996) *Strategic Manufacturing for Competitive Advantage*. Prentice Hall, Hemel Hempstead, UK.
13. Hill, T. (1995) *Manufacturing Strategy*. Macmillan, Basingstoke, UK.
14. *Industry Week*, June 8, 1998, **247**(11): 30.
15. *Forbes*, November 6, 1995, **156**(11): 124.
16. Honeycutt, E.D., Siguaw, J.A. and Harper, S.C. (1993) 'The impact of flexible manufacturing on competitive strategy', *Industrial Management*, November–December, **35**(6): 2.
17. Porter, M. (1980) *Competitive Strategy*. Free Press, New York.
18. Ettlie, J.E. (1996) 'Learning to launch new products', *Automotive Production*, **108**(4): 20.
19. *Fortune*, March 30, 1998, **137**(6): 158.
20. *The Economist*, December 17, 1994, **333**(7894): 63.
21. Mohsen, A. (1997) 'CIM: getting set for implementation', *Industrial Management & Data Systems*, **97**(1): 3.
22. *Fortune*, November 14, 1994, **130**(10): 92.
23. Teece, D.J., Pisano, G. and Shuen, A. (1997) 'Dynamic capabilities and strategic management', *Strategic Management Journal*, **18**(3): 62–74.
24. Leonard-Barton, D. (1993) 'Core capabilities and core rigidities: a paradox in managing new product development', *Strategic Management Journal*, **13**: 111–125.
25. See, for example, Womack, J., Jones, D. and Roos, D. (1990) *The Machine That Changed the World*. Rawson Associates, New York.
26. Bessant, J. (1993) 'The Lessons of Failure: Learning to Manage New Manufacturing Technology', *International Journal of Technology Management*, **8**(2/3/4): 197–215.
27. Prahalad, C. and Hamel, G. (1990) 'The Core Competence of the Corporation', *Harvard Business Review*, May–June: 79–91.
28. Itami, H. and Numagami, T. (1992) 'Dynamic Interaction Between Strategy and Technology', *Strategic Management Journal*, **13**: 119–135.

5

Quality within the plants

Introduction

Of all the different performance variables in this research, quality was the one that provided the single most distinctive insight in terms of both attitudes and capabilities within plants. There were strong opinions on both sides: those plants that remained committed to quality and their reasons for doing so, and those plants that did not.

Unlike other performance measurements, quality (though not necessarily total quality management (TQM), which as we will see is not the same thing) was one dimension most readily advertised and instantly visible to the visitor. It was interesting to visit various plants and divisions, many of which had ISO 9000 certificates and other awards staring down proudly. What was curious, though, was that in the reception areas of some of these plants proudly boasting their accreditation to these and other awards, there were no welcoming humans in sight – hardly the stuff that customer satisfaction is made of!

A curious range of quotes was forthcoming in the interviews I conducted for this book. I spoke with:

● Senior-level managers in plants who stated that they had 'done quality'. In other words, for them, quality was something that was somehow attained, had now been achieved once and for all, and then put away – especially, I discovered, after ISO 9000 had been attained. That's a little bit like saying, 'we had a wash sometime ago so we don't need to do it again!' That is the complete opposite of any notion of continuous improvement which is an integral feature of world-class quality. Some academics, too, can sometimes view quality as passé. Gary Hamel from

London Business School stated, rather dismissively: 'The challenge is no longer quality; nor is it globalization. You've been there, done that, got the ISO 9001 . . .'[1] He is being deliberately provocative, of course, but the reality is that the challenge of quality is still there and will be so for ever for any firm intent on competing into the twenty-first century. Moreover, wearing the badge of ISO 9000 does not mean that a firm can then sit back and relax.

- Other staff who saw quality as a waste of time because, they said – and here they echoed the sentiments of the original writers on business process re-engineering (BPR) – that TQM often meant trying endlessly to improve in activities which they should not be dealing with in the first place.

- Several managers who thought that TQM was something that had 'had its day' (to quote one of the plant managers) and had been replaced by BPR.

- Other managers who had the same evangelical zeal about quality that they had always had from the early days of their commitment, and who were keen to demonstrate achievements gained from TQM. For example, in response to the question, 'Why have your quality levels remained so high?', one of the plant managers replied, 'We just stick with it, day after day, getting better all the time' (deliberately alluding to a line from a Beatles song).

There were a number of major issues that needed to be tackled in greater depth, including:

- How is quality perceived within the plants – as product, process or both?
- Do plants still see quality as a key competitive factor, or as a management 'fad' of the 1980s?
- Has Japanese/world-class quality been transferred to Western plants?
- How important is TQM to the plants?
- How is ISO 9000 perceived in the wider aspect of TQM?
- How does BPR link to TQM?
- What is the importance of leadership – especially manufacturing personnel?

But the real insight would be gained from the answer to the question: Is there a difference between enlightened and traditional plants in terms of how the plants perform in process quality?

Defining quality

Quality is about providing customer satisfaction. Undoubtedly, this is not always easy – customers can be, among other things, annoying, fickle and frustrating. Often they may not even know what they want – which adds to the difficulty of the task of trying to provide customer satisfaction. But read any definition offered by the major gurus – Deming,[2] Feigenbaum,[3] Juran[4] and Crosby[5] – or the next generation of writers – e.g. Oakland[6] – and the same theme will pervade. Quality is about meeting and, if possible – with all the dangers that this may entail – exceeding customer expectations. In order to do this we must provide 'right-first-time processes' and 'conform to specification' but the specification is determined ultimately by the customer. This task is made even more difficult because the customer may not always be the end user – particularly in industrial markets. Defining and agreeing on the definition is difficult enough. Successfully providing quality to customers is even more difficult because firms do not fully understand the scope of the term 'quality'.

 ## The scope of quality

Quality is a comprehensive term that must include both process and product quality plus hard and soft factors – all four facets are dependent upon each other in terms of the overall quality offering, but each has a specific focus. A product can be a quality product which, if not supported by process enhancements (delivery speed, cost, various configurations, and any other customer requirements), will fail as a total quality offering. Conversely, a quality assurance system may well be in place whereby sophisticated process charts and other tools are being used to ensure process quality, but the product itself may not be perceived as providing satisfaction to the customer. If this is the case, there is a failure in product quality. There are many examples of product quality failures. For example, in Britain, the infamous Sinclair C5 failed not because of process quality failures but because nobody wanted that actual product. All conformance to in-house specifications of weight, height, width and so on counted for nothing.

The soft issues are vital in quality. If the culture does not support or understand the need for quality, then quality initiatives, however good intentioned, will fail miserably. By contrast, if quality is not measured via the hard side to quality, no improvements can be noted and fed back. All the customer courses in the world are pointless if the hard measurements in

Figure 5.1   The four linkages in the scope of quality

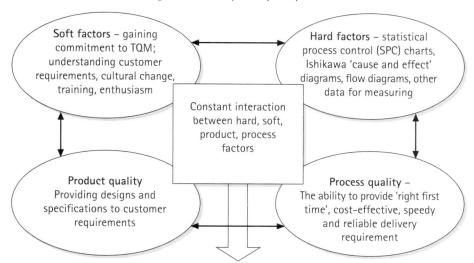

The total quality offering to customers

quality do not take place. The importance of these four factors in the overall scope of quality is illustrated in Figure 5.1.

The element of 'total' is crucial here because quality must pervade every area of the firm if the quality drive is to be successful. For the customer, a successful drive will result in better products and services – often produced at lower cost. Cost is not the only issue, though. The product must also be offered with no product quality failures. Delivery speed and reliability will often be improved, due to better in-house process quality capabilities. For the firm, the benefits of successful quality may include a range of factors: enhanced reputation, increased market share, lower cost production, and consequently better profit performance. However, it must be stressed that quality is not simply about improved financial performance – this improvement in profitability and other financial criteria is brought about as a result of strategic thinking toward quality. Cost reduction *per se* does not mean that quality is in place, and as we will see, this was an area that caused confusion for some plants.

Why quality has emerged as a strategic issue

We saw in Chapter 1 that one of the aims of strategic decisions is to create competitive advantage for the firm. Quality no longer necessarily means creating advantage but it is of strategic importance because it is a necessary feature to be able to compete at all in many markets. Quality emerged as a strategic issue because of two important, inter-related factors. First, the number and capabilities of new entrants into market. For example, the chief reason why quality became such a major issue for the 'Big Three' US car manufacturers in the 1980s was that it became clear that the Japanese plants' capabilities were vastly superior to their American competitors. The American car manufacturers had been too busy competing against each other, and by the beginning of the 1980s had still not paid sufficient attention to the massive threat posed by the new Japanese entrants. It was only when these capabilities became apparent that the US companies had to pay a great deal of attention to quality. As Tom Peters[7] stated succinctly in 1995, reflecting on the situation of the US auto industry at the beginning of the 1980s: 'Our cars were trash!' However, the distinction between American and Japanese capabilities in quality was not confined to the automobile industry. For example, David Garvin's investigation of American and Japanese air conditioners[8] showed that the worst-produced units (all of which happened to be American) had between 50 and 1,000 times the failure rate of the best-produced units (all of which were Japanese). Quality is now a major issue because there is far greater competition than ever before in most markets. The number and capabilities of new entrants into markets has raised competition between new and existing players, all of whom have to compete to world-class standards. This intense competition has helped to redefine the term 'world-class' when applied to quality. Rosbeth Kanter[9] argues rightly that the term has less to do with being better than competitors than with denoting the ability to compete at all in global competition. It may well be necessary to speak of 'world-class' quality capability as an order-qualifier,[10] in order to compete in markets. If TQM came to the fore with the emergence of globalization, how can managers see this as passé now that competition through globalization is more intense than ever before? The issue, then, is that quality is not a fad. It is a necessary core feature to attaining strategic resonance.

The second major factor is that directly as a result of fierce competition, customers now have far more choice. This is very clear in the computing, telecoms and automobile industries. For example, in the computing industry, the days when customers were locked in to one proprietary system with very little chance of switching to another supplier have long since gone. Now, because of the open, easy-to-use systems, without dependence on the installation science of a particular supplier, customers have far greater choice. This has had enormous benefits for customers but has placed even higher standards on manufacturing capabilities. Production/operations have to be able to respond to changes with great speed to meet the mix, range and volume of customer requirements. The challenge for firms, though, is that although they may know that these capabilities need to be in place, they fail to understand how to put them in place. This chapter provides some of the keys to achieving this – including the need to have senior-level manufacturing personnel in place, as well as plant-specific manufacturing strategies which include higher aspirations in quality as part of their content and aim.

Regardless of how a firm chooses to view quality, or even if it has experienced little or no perceived benefit in its aim of attaining it, quality is still a strategic issue. Walk around a plant that is intent on competing against the best, and quality pervades. This was clear when I walked around plants and saw quality circles taking place on a daily basis. It was also evident in the prolific display of various tools and techniques of measuring quality. And it was obvious when speaking to front-line operators who would speak in terms of customers when explaining their role in operations. Sadly, by contrast it was equally clear that a number of plants had simply abandoned their former enthusiasm with quality, seeing it as passé. As I mentioned earlier, the key question is this: if quality emerged as a strategic factor in the 1970s and 1980s because of increasing amounts of competition, then how can it be seen as passé now that competition is even greater than ever before due to increased globalization? The answer is that only the foolish would think that quality has lost its strategic importance.

Implementing total quality management

Quality has developed over time to total quality management (TQM). A working definition of the role and scope of TQM is:

> TQM is an integrative management philosophy aimed at continuously improving the quality of products and processes to achieve customer satisfaction (by) making quality a concern and responsibility for everyone in the business.[11]

This is a useful definition because it brings out several important interlinking factors:

- The need to integrate functions.
- Management philosophy.
- The importance of continuous improvement.
- The need to think in terms of both product and process quality.
- The importance of providing customer satisfaction.
- The issue of quality as a company-wide concern.

The reason for failure of TQM within plants includes the inability to have these and other pertinent areas in place, and I will discuss these later in the chapter. TQM involves all functions within the firm, together with other key stakeholders such as suppliers, and it is not suggested here that TQM is confined to production/operations personnel. But the performance of process quality within the manufacturing plant will fall essentially under the responsibility of manufacturing employees. Although the quality gurus, including Deming, Juran and Crosby, clearly agreed that there must be senior management commitment to quality within the firm/manufacturing plant, they did not specify that this commitment must include senior manufacturing personnel. The phrase 'top management' was the umbrella term used to denote this commitment from senior management and senior manufacturing management personnel was assumed. Take Juran's wonderfully honest account of his contribution to Japanese quality revolution.[12] As insightful as this is, he again did not specify that it was important to have senior ranking manufacturing personnel in place. What he did say, recounting his involvement in the process of spreading the quality message throughout Japanese firms was:

> The senior executives of Japanese companies took personal charge of managing for quality. The executives trained their entire managerial hierarchies in how to manage for quality.

This is an important issue because, as I mentioned in Chapter 1, sometimes there is no manufacturing presence at senior levels of the firm or even within a division or strategic business unit (SBU). Nor does it mean that a person with the title of director or vice president of manufacturing is necessarily knowledgeable about, or committed to excellence in, manufacturing. I found alarming cases where the term 'vice president of manufacturing' was very misleading. One vice president proudly boasted that he had never visited any plant under 'his control'. 'Besides,' he added, 'I'm really a finance guy!' The inclusion of senior-level manufacturing personnel who actually know about the strategic capabilities and opportunities in manufacturing was an important issue in the link between manufacturing personnel's role and subsequent plant performance in quality.

Successful TQM always embraces the following points:

- **Top management commitment** – there has not been one documented case of successful TQM without management commitment. Without this commitment, quality will erode in the organization. Managers have to set standards and lead by example. They also have to remain committed to areas such as training – one of many areas which, if managers are short-sighted, will be abandoned.

- **Continuous improvement** – the essence of quality is to improve in areas in which the firm already excels as well as attacking and improving upon those areas in which it is weak. The kaizen approach has to be in place. 'Kaizen' refers to small, incremental – but continuous – improvements in manufacturing. Individually, each improvement might not appear to be of any great use, but combined, the total contribution from these incremental changes can be huge.

- **All aspects of the business** – this includes all partners in the supply chain, as well as other alliances, in addition to all in-house employees at all levels of the firm who must be committed to quality.

- **Long-term commitment** – TQM is not a fad. For the reasons stated earlier in this chapter, TQM is of strategic importance. These reasons have not changed. As globalization impacts fully upon markets, the rate and intensity of competition will increase. This demands that all managers across all functions both understand the scope of, and remain committed to, quality. I stated in Chapter 1 that a necessary feature of a strategic decision is that it can have long-term repercussions. This is clearly the case with quality. A strategic commitment to quality will help to ensure strategic resonance; failing to commit over the long term will have catastrophic effects that may last for ever – and may include eventually the failure and ultimate collapse of the enterprise.

The human factor in implementing quality

A number of studies have shown the difficulties, and the enormity of the task involved, in the implementation of TQM in organizations.[13] A survey undertaken by *Fortune*[14] found that up to two-thirds of managers thought that TQM had failed in their companies. Comparisons between US and Japanese capabilities have often shown large differences in performance in Japan's favour.[15] However, a number of Japanese practices concerning quality have been transferred successfully to the West, particularly in Japanese transplants.[16] Although it is dangerous to be overly prescriptive in providing a list of ingredients that will ensure that successful quality will take place, some factors seem to be necessary. First, there is a major ongoing necessity to link TQM with the organization's strategic position. Unfortunately, TQM fails in some firms because it is launched as a programme that has a start and end date attached to it. As a result, TQM will be unconnected to business strategy, defined too rigidly and narrowly, and expected to bring about instant and 'miraculous transformations'.[17]

The second factor is the critical role of leadership in TQM. A number of reports[18] have stressed this factor but have ignored, or just simply glossed over, the vital role of senior manufacturing personnel in TQM. The critical role of leadership was made clear by the major quality gurus. For example, Feigenbaum stated:

'Quality-consciousness' in a company depends upon many intangibles, among which management's attitude toward quality is paramount . . . Basic quality responsibility rests in the hands of company top management . . . Getting quality results is not a short-term, instant-pudding way to improve competitiveness; implementing total quality management requires hands-on, continuous leadership.[19]

Similarly, Deming declared:

Actually, most of this book is involved with leadership. Nearly every page heretofore and hereafter states a principle of good leadership.[20]

And Juran writes:

Charting a new course [for TQM] requires extensive personal leadership and participation by managers.[21]

For many years, such advice was lost on many firms whose CEOs were fixated on quick-fix, bottom-line approaches. Quality was somehow assumed, but this cannot be so. Senior managers still have to remain committed to quality as a way of life, for ever. The role of leadership is an important feature of both the Malcolm Baldridge National Quality Award and the European Quality Award, though again neither award speaks specifically of senior manufacturing personnel in terms of their role and contribution to plant performance. Senior manufacturing personnel's role in the strategic leadership seems to have diminished over time in the transition from craft, to mass, through to the current era of manufacturing. An important development here was the emergence of a distinct and separate quality assurance or quality control department within the firm so that quality became essentially divorced from operational level responsibility and became, instead, the responsibility of 'managers of quality'.

Ensuring that quality commitment pervades the whole organization is a difficult one and calls for the very best of management skill and capability. However the benefits of TQM can be enormous.

The benefits of total quality management

Firms do not embark on quality just because they have to in order to satisfy customer and competitive demands. This is a major factor and it does explain why firms have to become serious about quality, but commitment to quality has an attraction that goes beyond satisfying the hurdles of competition. The promises of benefits to the firm itself were made by Juran and Deming. Crosby[22] stated how the cost of quality – the cost of not doing things right, first time, every time – would decrease over time and as a result the firm would gain tangible (including financial) benefits. Crosby defined quality simply as 'conformance to requirements' and advocated zero defects and prevention as a central philosophy in quality. He spoke of five stages of development and, in the first stage, the cost of quality was reckoned to be about 20% of sales. At this first stage, Crosby argued, management has no real comprehension of quality. However, by stage 5, the final stage, the cost of quality should fall to about 2.5%. Crosby estimated that an organization could reduce its cost of quality from 20% of sales to 2.5% within a five-year timeframe. Such promises make quality attractive to managers but is there recent evidence to support such claims? Apparently there is. In 1995, Gary Tooker, CEO of Motorola, discussed the company's success with quality. Motorola has an aim of achieving total customer satisfaction. So for them quality is wholly about customer satisfaction. In order to reach this goal, Motorola has five initiatives in place, covering both soft and hard issues in quality. These initiatives aim to:

1. Produce products and services to a six sigma standard (no more than 3.4 defects per million products or services).
2. Reduce total cycle time in all activities.
3. Lead in the areas of products, manufacturing and the environment.
4. Improve profitability.
5. Provide a creative, co-operative workplace in which employees are empowered.

Motorola's commitment to quality saved $6.5 billion in manufacturing costs between 1987 and 1995. Other success stories of quality provide good insight. For example, in 1996 a survey in *Automotive Engineering*[23] described a five-year study on the financial performance of 160 automobile parts suppliers in Japan, Europe and the USA. The results showed that commitment towards quality had a profound effect upon the profitability of suppliers. Companies that implemented quality management programmes were able to lower production costs, enhance productivity and innovate more effectively. Among the various suppliers, Japanese companies benefited the most from adhering to quality management. Also in 1996, an analysis of 359 firms that fully or partially implemented TQM revealed that even partial implementation of the concept produced positive results.[24] In 1998, a survey of 108 firms revealed that performance, measured by both accounting variables and stock returns, is improved for those firms adopting TQM.[25] A problem for some firms is that they sometimes do not possess the knowledge and wisdom required to maintain the commitment to quality and, because results haven't been quickly achieved, firms abandon this commitment. Clearly, there are good business reasons to remain committed to quality. For all the benefits cited above, though, there remains a major problem with quality which needs to be overcome.

Problems of total quality management

Quality is difficult to maintain for two reasons. First, if the firm enjoys success with quality efforts it can be tempted to sit back, convinced that quality is easy and that quality has been achieved. Second, if a firm does not enjoy instant results with quality efforts, there is a tendency to abandon it. The following summarizes the problems with TQM:

> The 1990s have not been good to TQM: a survey of 500 executives in US manufacturing and service firms indicated that 'only one-third believe that TQM made them more competitive' . . . a survey of 100 British firms that had implemented quality programs found that only one-fifth believed that their programs had 'a significant impact' . . . an American Electronics Association survey revealed that use of TQM by member firms dropped from 86 percent in 1988 to 73 percent in 1991 and that 63 percent of the firms reported that TQM failed to reduce defects by 10 percent or more, even though they had been in operation for almost two and one-half years on average . . . McKinsey & Company found that two-thirds of the TQM programs it examined had simply ground to a halt because they failed to produce expected results . . . At the same time, widely acclaimed TQM programs began to stumble: Florida Power and Light, winner of Japan's prestigious Deming Prize for Quality Management, slashed its quality department staff from 85 employees to three after group chairman James L. Broadbent found that many employees feared that the 'quality improvement process had become a tyrannical bureaucracy' . . . And the Wallace Company, a Malcolm Baldrige National Quality Award winner, filed for Chapter 11 bankruptcy protection.[26]

The main problem with quality is that it is neither easy to instil, nor easy to remain committed to over the long term. If quality were so easy, then all firms would remain committed to it. What becomes clear, though, is that many firms have become disillusioned and have given up on quality. Even those that talk of being committed to quality still suffer problems with product and process quality. Throughout the 1990s, there were massive numbers of product recalls in many industries. In 1997, *Ward's Auto World*[27] described how General Motors (GM) had recalled about two-thirds of the 11,000 Cavaliers it had sold in Japan. The report added that the recall could reinforce a widely held scepticism about the quality of American cars. Quality problems with GM cars were exemplified in 1992, when 1,100 Saturn cars had been shipped to customers with improper antifreeze, causing possible damage to the cooling system. To its credit, GM provided the customers with brand new cars. In 1993, the Saturn plant had to recall over 350,000 cars because of faulty generator problems (34 fires were reported due to this quality failure), and the cost of this was around $8 million. Also in 1993, GM had to repair half a million leaky gaskets on their Quad 4 engines – and the cost for this recall was estimated at $22 million.[28] In 1993, US car makers had to recall 11 million vehicles to fix a range of defects on cars.[29] However, this figure included Japanese transplants in the

USA – Honda, for example, recalled 900,000 vehicles in 1992 to repair gasoline leaks. In 1994, Chrysler recalled 15,000 Neon cars together with LH and LHS Sedans to repair faulty electrical wires. Similar problems were noted at Ford in the mid-1990s, and this impacted on new product innovation when Ford had to suspend temporarily production of the Mustang sports car because of bad welding on the wiring harness, which provides electrical power. However, Ford did commit, and has remained committed, to quality, not only in its own plants but also in plants that it has purchased. An example is shown in Box 5.1.

Box 5.1

Strategic quality at Jaguar

Jaguars – the automotive variety – have traditionally been known as beautiful but temperamental beasts. In the 1970s, people joked that to keep one Jag on the road, a driver needed to own two. Then, in 1989, the storied British luxury brand got the ultimate wake-up call: it clocked more defects per car than the hapless Yugo in a J.D. Power & Associates Inc. survey . . . After 10 years and billions of dollars in new quality and manufacturing programs under parent Ford Motor Co., however, Jaguar has risen to the top in the US quality ratings. In the latest J.D. Power Initial Quality Study, released May 5, Jaguar placed No. 1, ahead of brands such as BMW, Mercedes-Benz, and Lexus. How did Jaguar do it? 'Ford procedures, without a doubt . . . Ford has been extraordinarily patient and intelligent in helping Jaguar where it wanted it (in quality) and leaving Jaguar alone where it needed to be left alone (in styling)'. Since 1989, when Ford paid $2.6 billion for Jaguar, the auto giant has pumped as much as $6 billion into the luxury carmaker . . . But better management was only part of the process. In 1993, the 50-year-old Browns Lane factory in Coventry was totally overhauled. A modern assembly line was installed, and the plant was expanded. The efforts have paid off. Michael Beasley, Jag's executive director, says productivity at the plant has quadrupled. And this year, Browns Lane ranked second in J.D. Power's quality listing of European factories, just behind a BMW plant.

Source: Business Week, 'How Jaguar Stopped Being A Punch Line', June 7, 1999.

Insight into the colossal amounts of recalls that have taken place in the car industry is shown in Table 5.1.

General Motors alone had over 29 million recalls between 1970 and 1999. Just imagine that the costs of repair were a mere $10 per vehicle – you soon get a sense of the real 'cost of quality'! However, the problem with quality

Table 5.1   Largest automobile recalls

Manufacturer	Number of vehicles	Date	Reason
Ford	7,900,000	June 1996	Ignition switch
General Motors	6,682,084	December 1971	Engine mounts
General Motors	5,821,160	February 1981	Rear axle
Chrysler	4,300,000	March 1995	Minivan latches
Ford	4,072,000	June 1972	Shoulder belts
General Motors	3,707,064	January 1973	Power brake
Volkswagen	3,700,000	October 1972	Windshield wiper
Honda	3,700,000	April 1995	Seat belts
Ford	3,600,000	September 1987	Fuel line coupling
General Motors	3,100,000	December 1984	Axleshaft separation
General Motors	2,966,979	March 1969	Throttle linkage
Nissan	2,730,462	April 1995	Seat belts
General Motors	2,570,914	March 1969	Exhaust system
General Motors	2,216,325	September 1995	Seat belt anchorage
General Motors	2,200,000	April 1997	Hydraulic power

Source: National Highway Traffic Safety Administration.[30]

was not just about recalls but went deeper than that. By the mid-1990s, a number of factors indicated an end of an era. *The Economist*[31] noted how, by 1995, Deming was dead and Joseph Juran, the co-founder of the quality movement, had given his farewell lecture in 1994. Moreover, the American Quality Foundation has been disbanded and applications for the Baldridge award, America's prestigious prize for quality, has slumped.

Another problem was that success with quality had its own downside: the loss of jobs. This flies in the face of Deming's statement that companies must 'drive out fear, so that everyone may work effectively'. As *The Economist* pointed out, even those firms committed to quality and aware of the importance of their workforce seem intent on downsizing:

Hector Motroni, head of quality at Xerox, says the firm has been through '11 years of wrenching change' since it adopted TQM in 1983. And although Mr Motroni credits total quality with reinvigorating the firm, he concedes that job cuts and the loss of management layers – Xerox is in the process of cutting its workforce by another 12%, to 85,000 – has damaged motivation and made it harder to sell the TQM message.[32]

In spite of the reductions in applications for the Baldridge Award in the USA, many firms seem intent on pursuing awards in order to demonstrate their commitment to quality. Even those who have abandoned TQM still wish to show that they have achieved some level of quality. Possibly the most important award has been the emergence of ISO 9000.

ISO and quality

As mentioned earlier, a number of plants proudly boasted of their accreditation to ISO 9000. Some of these plants saw ISO 9000 and quality as interchangeable, almost synonymous terms, but we will see that this is clearly not the case. The interest in the ISO series standard is pervasive in many countries, and ISO 9000 certification is used extensively by companies in the European Union. For example, firms that manufacture products for the health, safety or environmental sectors often cannot be considered as suppliers without having ISO 9000 in place. But this says more about how companies are desperate to be seen to have standards in place, and to display some sort of badge, than it says about world-class capabilities in quality. Moreover, I saw a number of Japanese transplants that were rather dismissive of ISO 9000 and who clearly outperformed their ISO 9000 registered rivals. In the West, too, I saw evidence that ISO 9000 was seen as insufficient to demonstrate quality. For example, Ford, Chrysler and General Motors include the complete ISO 9000 standard in their supplier quality systems requirements, but have also expanded this. As a result, Quality System (QS) 9000 was introduced in North America in 1994; the standard was devised specifically for automotive manufacturers and suppliers to replace the old, preferred supplier, quality assurance programmes. Ford, Chrysler and General Motors saw the need to develop elements of, but to go beyond, the ISO 9000 system. It is clear, therefore, that ISO 9000 and TQM are not one and the same thing. Some firms will use it as part of other, wider systems. However, it is too easy to be wholly dismissive of ISO 9000 – although I met many managers who are – because ISO 9000:

- is often a necessary part of the entrance criteria in order to compete in particular industries;
- can be a good starting point when trying to reach other more demanding awards, such as the criteria for the Malcolm Baldridge National Quality Award;

- can offer a framework for showing customers how products are tested, employees trained, documentation assured, and defects corrected;

- can provide good discipline in education, registration and gap analysis, registrar selection, action plans, internal audits, and registrar audits; documentation by itself can be an important element provided that it does not become too bureaucratic (and therein lies the big problem with ISO 9000 and other quality standards: it can lead to voluminous amounts of unnecessary documentation);

- can become a key ingredient in the hard side of quality – measurement; the problem is it is easy to be obsessive about, and to concentrate on, measuring the wrong things – and to measure in great, and unnecessary, detail.

The ability to demonstrate that such systems are in place does not mean that customer satisfaction has been achieved. ISO 9000 almost assumes that customers needs are known and being satisfied and that is a big assumption. In addition, I have seen many occasions when companies have achieved ISO certification and then sat back, believing that the pursuit of quality is now over – the fatal flaw in any firm when it comes to quality.

So ISO 9000 has created both benefits and problems for firms intent on pursuing quality. It can be useful – vital even – in some industries. But it is not enough and it certainly cannot be seen as synonymous with TQM.

An even bigger area of confusion lies in the link between TQM and business process re-engineering (BPR).

Re-engineering and TQM

Business process re-engineering (BPR) is not meant to be the same as, or a replacement for, TQM. Clearly, BPR goes beyond TQM in its overall scope. While both TQM and BPR are strategic in scope, BPR has more fundamental consequences in terms of immediate – and sometimes radical – outcomes. However, BPR is mentioned here because of the perceived confusion within plants and how, for some managers, BPR was viewed as a replacement for TQM. Major advocates of BPR, Hammer and Champy,[33] define BPR as 'the fundamental rethinking and radical redesign of business processes to achieve dramatic improvements in critical, contemporary measures of performance such as cost, quality, service and speed'.

These are important issues and the words are dramatic: 'fundamental rethinking', 'radical redesign' and 'dramatic improvements'. As stated earlier, many firms have failed with TQM. I found instances of firms who readily embraced BPR because they had failed in, or had become disillusioned with, TQM. Whether BPR was meant to be a replacement is not the issue –

the issue is that a number of managers had embraced BPR as the replacement.

BPR took over TQM as the most popular topic in the business press from early 1993.[34] Bearing in mind that the first major article on BPR appeared in 1990, probably no other single managerial innovation has acquired quite so much attention in such a short period. For example, in a 1993 survey of 224 North American senior business executives, BPR was listed as the most important management issue, and 72% of those surveyed had committed to BPR in their organization.[35] A 1994 survey of British organizations showed that 59% of these were either already involved, or planned to be involved, in BPR activity.[36] A large survey published in 1997[37] found that 782 companies would remain committed to, and would continue to invest in, BPR initiatives in spite of the negative reactions against BPR that had begun to appear in the business press. In fact, 70% of the companies that had already undergone re-engineering fully expected to maintain or add still further to their present re-engineering budgets. However, only 47% of the respondents reported revenue growth and only 37% succeeding in increasing their market share.

BPR attempts to concentrate the firm on what it does best. In that sense, it has links with the profoundly important notions of focus, core competencies and resource-based approaches to strategy. But this can be overdone as the following points out:

> The dominant strategic modality of business practice in the first half of the 1990s has been corporate re-engineering. Businesses have been downsized and rightsized and new processes have been designed to enhance productivity. Portfolios have been rationalised with a renewed emphasis on core businesses, such as General Motors' spinoff of its EDS subsidiary or SAS's exit from Intercontinental Hotels . . . Yet, for many companies that are re-engineering, their sales are falling faster than their cost structures. So too is their ability to stay at the leading edge of innovation. The danger is that even if re-engineering has short-term cost benefits, it does not necessarily provide a vision for the future. Nor does it necessarily deliver the highest long-run benefit to shareholders.[38]

However, the problem can be that in the name of rightsizing, the brain of the firm – the essential expertise and know-how upon which core competencies must depend – can undergo a corporate lobotomy. *The Economist*[39] picked out some of the dangers with this when it stated:

> In the end, even the re-engineers are re-engineered. At a recent conference held by Arthur D. Little, a consultancy, representatives from 20 of America's most successful companies all agreed that re-engineering, which has been tried by two-thirds of America's biggest companies and most of Europe's, needs a little re-engineering of its own . . . As well as destroying morale, this approach leads to 'corporate anorexia', with firms too thin to take advantage of economic upturns.

Can TQM and BPR be combined? Some think so:

> In today's challenging economic climate, many organizations have come to realize that improved quality is an essential entry ingredient for successful global competition. Total quality management (TQM) is based on a broad organizational commitment to make continuous quality enhancements in products and services for customers over a long term. Business process re-engineering (BPR) allows for radical changes in organizational processes intended to make quantum leaps in performance by taking advantage of the advances in the information and telecommunication technology. While they seem to be two completely opposite approaches, TQM and BPR can well be combined into the 'endless quality improvement' concept.[40]

However, it is mighty difficult for firms who have promised empowerment and involvement from the workforce in TQM to then cut out large numbers within the firm, in the name of re-engineering, and then expect wonderful commitment from the workforce.

Evidence from the plants

The question is: 'How did enlightened and traditional plants perform in quality?' In particular:

- Is TQM currently an explicit feature of the plant?
- Has TQM been abandoned and, if so, has it been replaced by some other approach?
- What was the rate of failures/defects within the plants?
- What percentage of employees within the plants are involved in quality circles or continuous improvement (CI) groups?
- What is the number of suggestions per employee within plants? Although this may be seen initially as an input of quality, the number is actually an output measure of the effectiveness of quality circles.

The key findings

The differences between traditional and enlightened plants lent themselves to two key categories: soft factors (management and commitment of human resources) and hard factors (statistical, measurement areas) in quality. As we will see, there were clear links between the importance given to human resource management and the subsequent commitment to, and capabilities in, process quality within the plants.

The main distinctions between traditional and enlightened plants include:

- All of the enlightened plants remain committed to TQM; traditional plants had either not been involved at all or had abandoned TQM in the past. What became substituted in its place are a number of hybrid approaches often, in the name of 're-engineering', together with various in-house cost-cutting initiatives, not necessarily related to quality.

- The frequency of meetings for staff ranged between zero and four meetings per month for the traditional plants and from eight meetings per month to daily meetings for the enlightened plants. All of the Japanese transplants had manufacturing meetings on a daily basis, mainly within CI groups.

- The annual suggestions per employee ranged from 5 to 12 in the traditional plants, and from 17 to 27 for enlightened plants.

- All of the enlightened plants involve at least 95% of their manufacturing staff in quality circles or CI groups within their plant; the greatest number of employees involved in traditional plants was 50%; some of the traditional plants had no manufacturing involvement in quality initiatives.

Clearly, there are major distinctions between the two groups in terms of the role and importance given to employees in TQM (*see* Figure 5.2).

But it isn't only the soft, human resource aspects that make the difference between traditional and enlightened approaches to quality, important as these are. The hard side to quality – measuring quality processes – was equally important. Enlightened plants remain committed to measuring quality and employ a number of different tools and techniques to do so. Measuring quality is an ongoing pursuit, with results constantly monitored and fed back within manufacturing cells, CI groups, and other focused teams. Enlightened plants used tools and techniques including work study, statistical process control (SPC) charts, and cause and effect or Ishikawa

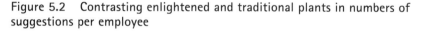

Figure 5.2   Contrasting enlightened and traditional plants in numbers of suggestions per employee

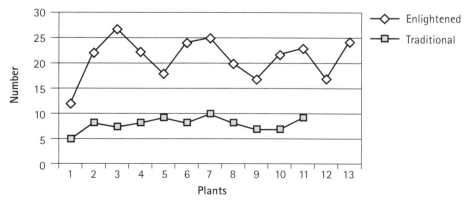

diagrams. Work study was an interesting factor behind the enlightened plants' approaches to quality. If ever a technique might be associated with the traditional, 'bad old days' of manufacturing, it would be work study. Then, surreptitious stop-watch specialists or supervisors would stand over fearful workers and try to squeeze the last drop of productivity possible from them. Such tactics created a range of industrial disputes and caused poor industrial relations between workers and managers. But be aware that it is the motive behind the use of work study rather than the tools and techniques themselves that is often the problem. In fact, work study can be an integral part of world-class practice.[41]

Perhaps the most telling distinction between enlightened and traditional plants is in process quality performance. Here, the distinctions between enlightened and traditional plants became prominent. The percentage failure rate at final inspection ranged from 0.58% to 1.6% in the enlightened plants, compared to 3% to 5.8% in the traditional group (*see* Figure 5.3).

Although some managers may be suspicious of the value of measuring the percentage of defects at the final inspection stage, there are good reasons for using this measurement. First, it is a common measure that can be used across all high-volume manufacturing and is, therefore, applicable to both computer products and cars. Second, although quality problems should have been dealt with before final inspection, the measurement at this final stage indicates just how good, or otherwise, process quality has been at these earlier stages. Third, it can be a means of creating urgency by focusing on the costs of quality. For example, at one stage it took Volkswagen more time of rectification effort at this final inspection stage to deliver a quality car than it took Toyota to make a car in the first place.[42] Fourth, final

Figure 5.3 Comparing enlightened and traditional plants in percentage of defects at final inspections stage

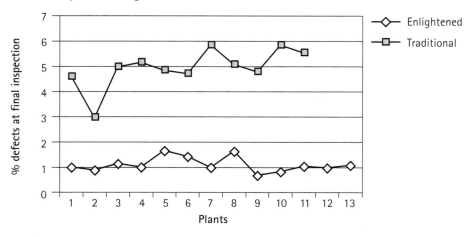

inspection in-house is a critical measurement because it becomes the last opportunity to rectify mistakes before shipping to customers. Thus, although plants should be dedicated to preventing problems occurring in the first place, it is far better to deal with internal quality problems than rectify returned products from customers.

Further evidence within the plants

As well as the quantitative data that I unravelled, further insight was gained by getting behind the numbers and discussing issues with key senior personnel within the plants. It would be misleading to say that traditional plants were not aware of the importance of quality – quality was seen as essential for both groups. However, four points came to light in distinguishing enlightened and traditional plants.

Differences in the language of quality

The enlightened plants' approach is much more customer-focused, both in terms of practice and in-house terminology, than that of the traditional plants. For example, in enlightened plants, operators tend to speak of customers when asked about quality, and manufacturing managers speak in terms of meeting customer needs. This attitude was also evident in company documents. For example, one of the enlightened plants define quality as 'a set of product or process attributes that provide a value to customers that meets or exceeds their expectations. The company recognizes two kinds of customers: external and internal. External customers are companies and individuals who purchase goods and services; internal customers are people and departments inside whose performance is directly affected by the performance of co-workers.' The importance of quality is mentioned in the mission statements of some of the plants. One of the enlightened plant's mission statements included the following:

> Our operating philosophy is to meet customer needs and expectations by establishing and maintaining an environment which encourages all employees to pursue never-ending improvement in the quality and productivity of products and services throughout the corporation, its supply base, and its dealer organizations.

And an enlightened Japanese transplant's quality manual stated:

> Satisfied customers assure our future. Our number 1 target is Customer Satisfaction. We are always open to customers' voices. They enable us to better our ways of operation.

This serves not merely as a message to customers, but also as a catalyst for company-wide purpose and commitment to quality within the plants. This is particularly important to production/operations who are charged with the responsibility of constantly measuring process quality.

Internal cost reduction versus external competitive concerns

For the traditional plants, there was an association of quality with 'getting better all the time' with processes purely as a means to reducing costs. Although essential, this represents only one aspect of quality. The traditional plants' approach was focused essentially on low-cost production. In some of the traditional plants, a reversed logic seemed to be in place, namely that if costs had come down then quality had somehow taken place. One manufacturing director even stated:

> We have made great improvements . . . our costs have come down by 22% over three years so our quality is good.

What strange, reversed logic! A senior manager asserts that costs have come down and so quality is good. It's exactly the wrong way round! By contrast to this traditional mindset, enlightened plants achieve costs reductions as a result of, rather than the sole reason behind, quality drives. For example, one enlightened plant saved $700 million between 1993 and 1997 in manufacturing costs. It did so without any downsizing but by being committed to continuous improvement, which was measured in all manufacturing operations. Another enlightened plant made a series of aggressive changes in order to regain its competitive position. It reduced product cost by redesigning the entire product line for improved manufacturability and flexibility. Senior manufacturing personnel were vital to these changes. As a result, this plant was able to announce that it offered the industry's lowest-priced, highest-quality terminals with off-the-shelf availability. But, again, let's be clear: the aim was not to reduce costs; the aim was to link manufacturing capability with market requirements. Added technology was used to track quality through each process and, as a result, costs reduced by 18%.

The role of manufacturing personnel

A theme throughout this book is that manufacturing personnel in enlightened plants are involved in business areas, and not employed merely for their technical input. This carried over to quality within the plants. All of the enlightened plants had senior personnel (across all functions, including manufacturing) who remained committed to quality. The role and involvement of senior level manufacturing personnel was an important factor in the enlightened plants for three reasons:

- They helped to 'champion' the quality drives within the manufacturing function particularly in the area of measuring and improving process quality.
- They provided guidelines and direction in areas such as training and quality manuals.
- Because of their involvement in the business of the plant, they were instrumental in translating customer requirements into operational capabilities throughout the plant.

Plant-specific manufacturing strategies were the central means of doing so. Benchmarking against competitive product offerings is a central feature to ensuring that products are quality products in the enlightened plants. This is a means of focusing the plant away from being excellent in process quality in the wrong areas, which actually added no value for customers. As one of the plant manufacturing managers explained:

> There's not a great deal of point in being a low-cost producer if your customers want delivery competence from you and they're prepared to pay for it.

In enlightened plants, manufacturing strategy is used to satisfy a wide range of customer needs (in the above case, delivery speed was vital) and is not concerned with costs only.

Differences in attitudes to total quality management

In the traditional plants, TQM had largely been abandoned and was replaced, in some instances, by initiatives such as BPR. Perhaps BPR and TQM can complement each other in practice. But what comes out in this research is the perception within traditional plants of BPR as a means of replacing TQM. For example, one manufacturing manager at a traditional plant explained: 'TQM feels old now . . . to hell with all that . . . we've got to get our costs down.' BPR was seen as licence to do this: the first fruits of their BPR efforts was in firing over 600 staff who had formerly been sold the idea of TQM at the plant. Cynicism was evident at one of the plants, who claimed they had 'done quality'. The sentiment was expressed by a senior marketing manager:

> We've had all the buzz words here . . . we're an American company and so as soon as some sort of guru-speak comes out from over there we've had to latch onto it over here . . . Management By Walking About, CI, TQM, we've done them all . . .

Not surprisingly, TQM had been abandoned in favour of cost-cutting initiatives in the name of quality. By contrast, the long-term vision and commitment to quality became a central part of the language and culture within the enlightened plants.

The important fact to bear in mind with the enlightened plants' commitment to quality is that it was both comprehensive in scope and demanding in application. For example, manufacturing managers working alongside other key functions set very demanding goals for front-line staff. Training was ongoing and rigorous for employees and focused on a number of key areas including:

- An emphasis on prevention in quality.

- Ongoing commitment to the idea of co-workers being the 'internal customer' within plants.

- Problem solving via continuous improvement initiatives – these meetings often take place on a daily basis within the enlightened plants.

- Empowerment of front-line operators – I often saw instances of work cells whose responsibility in process quality included hiring, firing and disciplinary measures. This is made possible because all of the enlightened plants have much flatter organizational structures than their traditional counterparts.

- An emphasis on simplicity in operations so that quality issues emerge and are dealt with quickly. Enlightened plants keep things simple, focusing on the few key concepts and core processes that meet their customers' needs.

Conclusions

World-class enlightened quality capability is not confined to the Japanese. In plant tours, I saw that a great deal of manufacturing learning – admittedly from the Japanese – had taken place and was ongoing. I saw much evidence of Japanese practices taking place within these plants. These practices included the use of small work teams, quality circles and kaizen (ongoing, incremental improvement) practices. For the enlightened plants, the tools and techniques of quality – as important as these are for measuring process quality – are not sufficient by themselves. Instead, a strategic view, often involving cultural change within the plant, was in place. In fact a strategic, focused and holistic view was at the centre of enlightened approaches to quality, as illustrated in Figure 5.4.

The enlightened plants see quality as a long-term competitive requirement, an ongoing, never-ending means of out-performing competitors. This long-term vision and commitment to quality became a central part of the

Figure 5.4   Being strategic, focused and holistic in quality

Strategic quality means that the organization remains fully committed to quality and sees it as a necessary and central feature of its competitive position. TQM is not a fad. This commitment requires ongoing investment, especially in training. The firm ensures that it benchmarks against competitors as well as 'best practice' in other industries in order to enhance its quality offering to customers.

The firm focuses on, and continually reviews, customer requirements to ensure that it knows what these are. It then focuses its efforts on meeting these requirements through its operations capabilities. This may mean that specific areas are dedicated to particular customers.

The firm understands that total quality pervades entire supply and distribution networks, as well as its own employees. The firm recognizes the importance and contribution of key stakeholders and works with them on a partnership basis dedicated to ensuring quality.

language and culture within the enlightened plants. One transplant manager stated that: 'Our philosophy with quality is very simple: stick with it and keep doing it . . . that doesn't sound very academic for you, does it? But it's our approach and it works.'

Various researchers have reported on quality in Western plants, including studies of lean manufacturing. But what distinguishes the research in this chapter on quality performance from other research is whereas the measurements of process quality of an enlightened plant would be similar to world-class or lean plants, it is the reasons behind the results that are of interest to this chapter. Often, quality capability is seen purely at the operational level and very little is said about senior manufacturing personnel's contribution other than in measuring and monitoring process capability. For the enlightened plants, senior manufacturing personnel's involvement went much further than this because:

- they champion – and remain committed to – quality;
- they see quality in terms of a wide range of capabilities and not just prevention of defects; and

- manufacturing strategies help to define the in-house, process-quality standard, once the external market requirements for quality are understood and agreed by senior marketing, manufacturing and other key personnel within the plant.

While it is naive to prescribe a panacea for ensuring quality, the above evidence provides insight into identifiable links between management commitment, strategy and plant performance. Clearly, in the enlightened plants TQM is not seen as a programme but as a way of life. The biggest challenge for the traditional plants is to see quality as a strategic issue, rather than as a quick-fix, cost-cutting solution (which clearly pervades in some of the traditional plants). For the enlightened plants, time horizons are long-term, combined with a sense of urgency to improve every day in all areas of the business. This includes improving on those areas in which the firm or plant already excels as well as those areas in which the need to improve might seem more obvious. Such an approach is aided by senior manufacturing personnel who use manufacturing strategies to translate information about customer requirements and ongoing competitive analysis in order to enhance performance to world-class, operational capability within their plants.

NOTES AND REFERENCES

1. Hamel, G. (1998) 'The challenge today: changing the rules of the game (importance of non-linear innovation)', *Business Strategy Review*, Summer.
2. Deming, W.E. (1986) *Out of the Crisis*. MIT Press, Cambridge, USA.
3. Feigenbaum, A.V. (1951) *Total Quality Control: Engineering and Management*. McGraw-Hill, New York.
4. Juran, J. (1988) *Juran on Planning for Quality*. Free Press, New York.
5. Crosby, P. (1979) *Quality Is Free*. McGraw-Hill, New York.
6. Oakland, J. (1994) *Total Quality Management*. Butterworth-Heinemann, Oxford.
7. Quote taken from Tom Peters in conversation in *The Money Programme*, BBC TV, October 29, 1995.
8. Garvin, D. (1983) 'Quality on the Line', *Harvard Business Review,* September–October, 65–75.
9. Kanter, R. (1996) *World Class*. Simon & Schuster, New York.
10. Hill, T. (1995) *Manufacturing Strategy*. Macmillan, Basingstoke.
11. Ahire, S., Waller, M. and Golhar, D. (1996) 'Quality management in TQM versus non-TQM firms: an empirical investigation (total quality management)', *International Journal of Quality & Reliability Management*, November, **13**(8): 8.
12. Juran, J. (1993) 'Made in the USA: A Renaissance in Quality', *Harvard Business Review*, July–August: 42–50.
13. See, for example: Garvin, D. (1986) 'Quality Problems, Policies and Attitudes in the United States and Japan: An Exploratory Study', *Academy of Management Journal,* **29**(4); Garvin, D.A. (1991) 'How the Baldridge Award Really Works', *Harvard Business Review*, November–December: 88–93; Schroeder, R., Sakakibara, S., Flynn, E. and Flynn, B. (1992)

'Japanese Plants in the US: How Good Are They?', *Business Horizons,* **35**(4): 66–72; Harber, D., Marriott, F. and Indrus, N. (1991) 'Employee Participation in TQC: An Integrative Review', *International Journal of Quality and Reliability Management,* **10**(6): 17–27.

14. *Fortune,* October 18, 1993.

15. See, for example: Garvin, D. (1983) 'Quality on the Line', *Harvard Business Review,* September–October: 65–75; Handfield, R. (1989) 'Quality Management in Japan Versus the United States: An Overview', *Production and Inventory Management Journal,* **30**(2): 79–85; Flynn, B. (1992) 'Managing for Quality in the US and in Japan', *Interfaces,* **22**(5): 69–80.

16. Kenney, M. and Florida, R. (1993) *Beyond Mass Production.* Oxford University Press, New York.

17. Kanter provides insight here in Romano, C. (1994) 'Report Card on TQM', *Management Review,* **83**: 22.

18. See, for example: Choi, T. and Behling, O. (1998) 'Top managers and TQM success: one more look after all these years', *Organizational Dynamics,* **26**(3).

19. Feigenbaum, A.V. (1951) *Total Quality Control: Engineering and Management.* McGraw-Hill, New York.

20. Deming, W.E. (1986) *Out of the Crisis.* MIT Press, Cambridge, USA.

21. Juran, J.M. (1994) 'The Quality Trilogy: A Universal Approach for Managing for Quality', in H. Costin (ed.) *Total Quality Management.* Dryden, New York.

22. Crosby, P. (1979) *Quality is Free.* McGraw-Hill, New York.

23. *Automotive Engineering* (1996) 'How quality pays; global automobile supplier survey reveals quality's impact on the bottom line', *Automotive Engineering,* April.

24. Ahire, S., Waller, M. and Golhar, D. (1996) 'Quality management in TQM versus non-TQM firms: an empirical investigation (total quality management)', *International Journal of Quality & Reliability Management,* **13**(8): 8.

25. Easton, G.S. and Jarrell, S.L. (1998) 'The effects of total quality management on corporate performance: an empirical investigation', *The Journal of Business,* **71**(2).

26. McAbe, D. and Wilkison, A. (1998) 'The rise and the fall of TQM: the vision, meaning and operation of change', *Industrial Relations Journal,* **29**(1).

27. *Ward's Auto World,* January 1997, pp. 25–26.

28. *Wall Street Journal,* February 16, 1993, **B**: 9.

29. *Auto Service Monitor inc.* (1994).

30. Details of these recalls come from National Highway Traffic Safety Administration.

31. *The Economist,* January 14, 1995.

32. Ibid.

33. Hammer, M. and Champy, J. (1993) *Reengineering the Corporation.* Harper Business, New York.

34. De Cock, C. and Hipkin, I. (1997) 'TQM and BPR: beyond the beyond myth', *Journal of Management Studies,* **34**(5).

35. Conti, R.F. and Warner, M. (1994) 'Taylorism, teams and technology in "reengineering" work-organization', *New Technology, Work, and Employment,* **9**(4): 48.

36. Grint, K. and Willcocks, L. (1995) 'Business process re-engineering in theory and practice: business paradise regained?', *New Technology, Work, and Employment,* **10**(3): 61.

37. This was a report from Gemini Consulting Inc.'s survey of 782 companies which was cited in *Journal of Business Strategy,* May–June 1997, **18**(3).

38. Robertson, T. (1995) 'In praise of revitalisation – Re-engineering is not everything: Companies also have to rediscover growth', *Mastering Management* – Part **8**(9): *Financial Times,* December 15.

39. *The Economist*, September 9, 1995.
40. Lee, S. and Asllani, A. (1997) 'TQM and BPR: symbiosis and a new approach for integration', *Management Decision*, May–June, **35**(5–6).
41. Adler, P. (1993) 'Time and Motion regained', *Harvard Business Review*, January–February.
42. This was mentioned by Professor Dan Jones during a TV programme, *Car Wars*, shown on the UK's Channel 4 station in January 1994.

6

Inventory and buyer–supplier relationships

 ## Introduction

We saw in Chapter 2 how the major players in the computer industry have had to reconfigure entire supply networks in order to remain competitive. We also saw how, particularly in Compaq's case, the failure to do so can cost a company dearly, and how, by contrast, Apple's turnaround at the end of the 1990s owed a great deal to expert inventory management. Clearly, inventory management within the plant and relationships with suppliers are vitally important areas for manufacturing management, and so I sought answers to the following questions:

- How is materials management perceived within the plant: as functional or strategic?

- How do the plants perform in key areas such as stock-holding and finished goods inventory?

- How well is just in time implemented in the plants?

- How do plants manage their relationships with their suppliers – do partnerships exist and, if so, what is the nature of the relationship?

Materials or inventory management has been one of the greatest areas of contrast between much of Western and Japanese manufacturing. In recent years, many Western firms have tried to emulate some of the Japanese practices that have underpinned Japan's success in many industries. In essence, many Western manufacturing firms have tended to view materials management as a tactical activity and purchasing/materials management has been relegated to a reactive function, much like manufacturing itself. Often in the West, this has meant that purchasing has been viewed as a buying function, one that responds to production requirements – after they, in turn, have been determined by marketing. In Japan, by contrast, inventory management has been seen as strategic, an essential part of the complete range of capabilities that will enable the firm to out-compete other players in the market. The importance of inventory management is exemplified in the UK's Best Factory Awards, reported in the Institute of Management's publication, *Management Today,* in which Colin New from Cranfield's School of Management stated:

> Repeatedly, the Best Factory Awards process has highlighted the fact that one of the strongest drivers of excellence in inventory management is the market discipline imposed by harsh, demanding customers . . . look no further than the supplier base of the UK's large supermarket groups, or the first-tier suppliers of the automotive giants: you either get good, or you get out.[1]

A distinction between past and present approaches to inventory management is that in the past, materials/inventories would be viewed as an asset – one that could be shown on the balance sheet and could therefore be seen as part of the firm or plant's worth or value. This is now seen by more enlightened approaches as accounting nonsense. Instead, materials/inventory should be seen as a liability, one that will ruin cashflow and eat into capital that can be better used elsewhere. Furthermore, there are major dangers with certain types of inventory due to factors such as obsolescence and seasonal demands. Take computers for example: around 80% of the cost of a PC is made up of components such as the processor chip, which, during the 1990s, fell in price by an average of 30% per annum. The danger of obsolete inventory increases each day that PC parts are stored as inventory. Poor inventory management leaves a PC manufacturer with products that are priced higher than other competitors. The critical scenario is that when a manufacturer is caught in the middle of a big-step change in technology, such as the transition from the 486 chip to the Pentium, it can be left with millions of dollars of outdated PCs. We saw the important role and contribution that inventory makes to innovation in Chapter 3. Poor inventory management can have a devastating effect on new product development. When a firm has a problem with excess outdated inventory, it has to frantically sell products as cheaply as possible, often below cost, just to gain some income. Inventory management was an ongoing challenge for PC manufacturers throughout the 1990s. For example, *Fortune* noted that:

> Compaq, HP, Intel and Dell are facing inventory problems due to steadily declining PC desktop prices. The Compaq strategy of moving excess profit into its distribution channels worked in the 4th qtr 1997, but it has misfired in 1998. Inventory stands at an estimated 8 to 10 weeks because corporate buyers were attracted to IBM's price cuts in Feb 1998. HP faces a dilemma when confronting its three to five weeks of inventory.[2]

So, far from being an asset, excess inventory of all kinds – raw materials, components, subassemblies and finished goods – will result in delays, increased costs and poor responsiveness to changing customer needs, all of which combine to be a huge liability. Expert management of inventory will enable the firm to provide lower costs, rapid response and flexibility for its customers.

Materials management will undoubtedly be influenced by, and impact upon, other major areas of manufacturing management – in particular, process technology, quality management, product design, process design and scheduling. Tactical quick-fix methods such as the economic order quantity (EOQ) formula fail to deal with the strategic issues of inventory. Materials management impacts on all stages of the supply chain and this very fact demands a strategic approach so that the firm will determine where it will be involved in activities within the supply chain. Focusing the firm's efforts in terms of how it lines up within the supply chain will then provide insight into the crucial business question for the firm, namely 'What business are we in?'

Materials requirement planning and just–in–time

A number of approaches to managing inventory emerged from the 1960s, particularly materials requirement planning (MRP), manufacturing resource planning (MRPII), and, more recently, enterprise resource planning (ERP) has gained popularity. But these approaches can depend too heavily on software packages as some sort of panacea for manufacturing. Too often the very fact that software is involved means that justification for investing in it in the first place can be down to how smart or clever the software is, rather than what it can really do for the business. As a result, an emphasis on software as a solution to inventory problems will typically be championed by a small (and often technologically myopic) power group within the firm and will leave others feeling alienated from the process simply because they do not understand it and are not convinced of its contribution.

However, with the emergence of just-in-time (JIT) management, and its dependence upon strategic buyer–supplier relationships, the real strategic importance of inventory came to light. As mentioned earlier, MRP is linked to computing and a plant can spend large amounts of money on elaborate software packages. There is no doubt that MRP can be a powerful means of focusing the plant's efforts. For example, the basic questions that MRP asks are those that every manufacturing firm should ask, regardless of investment in particular software solutions such as MRP:

- How many products are to be made?
- When do these products need to be made?
- What is the finished product composition in terms of materials and components?
- What are the numbers and types of components and materials currently in stock?
- How many items have to be ordered from suppliers?
- What is the lead time for suppliers and, consequently, when do orders have to be placed?

The apparent simplicity of these questions camouflages the huge complexity of running MRP and MRPII. In many markets, in particular with automobiles and computing/telecommunications products, the product variations for models will be extremely wide. This in turn means that the calculations to determine all of these variations will be a massive task. The data integrity for MRP has to be faultless to avoid the dreaded 'garbage-in–garbage-out' scenario. The data includes specific bills of materials per product and the volume/variety mix of all products in a particular time period.

MRP can be used as an exhaustive management tool whereby the numbers of products and subcomponents can be determined and tracked throughout the process. However, MRP should not be used to push components or materials on to a particular workstation before they are required. If this happens, it becomes a nightmare trying to manage operations when stacks of inventory clog up what should be a balanced and smooth process. So a major concern is that, ironically, using MRP might create work-in-process inventory. Materials or components that have been ordered in due to the MRP calculations might then be pushed on to a particular workstation before they are required. The indicative problems with MRP are:[3]

- Planning and implementing MRP can take years – although off-the-shelf software packages are available, in reality each firm must have an individually tailored approach if the system is to be successful.
- Data entry and maintenance take up much time – even if the reports are exception reports detailing changes from the last MRP run.
- Data integrity is essential – this calls for an holistic approach that involves all major functions within a firm to agree on the sales, purchasing and inventory figures. This should present an opportunity, but often it will be the cause of failure brought about by the inability to provide accurate forecasts of supplies and sales, incorrect engineering data, etc.

The MRP system is very dependent upon the master production schedule (MPS) which summarizes all products to be built within a given time period. Toyota, for example, tends to have a monthly fixed time period – or 'bucket' – which will then serve as a build requirement both within its plants and for suppliers who are provided with this fixed monthly plan. Toyota states:

> We can handle detailed specifications on a 10-day basis for domestic shipments. We can even handle some modifications in specifications on a daily basis. Monthly planning enables us to respond to orders quickly while maintaining a steady level of production throughout the month.[4]

Nissan UK has the same approach: they provide a five-month forecast and then fix a one-month period which is the commitment to suppliers.

But an MPS can only be made possible by close relationships between manufacturing, marketing and purchasing personnel. If this does not take place the MPS will be meaningless – and will result in stock-outs of materials and components and problems with delivery capabilities. Some firms will choose either MRP or JIT. But this is nonsense because a firm can have both. Even if a firm chooses not to invest in MRP, it must have alternative computerized systems in place in order to deal with the huge complexity of volumes and varieties of products manufactured in a given period.

JIT is one of the most misunderstood management terms. Firms that see JIT as a magical alternative to avoid detailed computerized planning, and that will allow them to demand that the exact numbers of components are delivered at exactly the right time, are deluding themselves. A big problem is that some firms will view JIT merely as some sort of cost-cutting exercise in reducing inventories. Such a view is profoundly wrong and does not do justice to the major requirements of JIT. JIT is dependent upon both the excellence of internal manufacturing capabilities and the development and management of strategic relationships with suppliers. For example, Toyota's assembly plant in Georgetown, Kentucky, produces around 1,000 Camrys a day. The plant is fed by a JIT inventory system delivering components from both Japan and the USA five times a week. The parts are scheduled precisely to the minute they will be used. But in order for firms to emulate this sort of capability with JIT, they need to move away from short-term cost-cutting ideas to a long-term view of continuous, ongoing improvements. Of course, this sounds like TQM as we saw in Chapter 5. In fact TQM is indeed an integral feature for JIT to be successful in manufacturing plants. JIT management is, therefore, not simply an inventory reduction exercise but is a complete shift away from traditional Western manufacturing. The following should be plastered on the plant walls of those firms that commit to JIT:

JIT is part of a fundamentally different approach to management which when fully developed will help to create a totally new industrial culture.[5]

Japanese manufacturing plants have insisted that in their manufacturing operations there should not be idle time, waiting or buffers. The Japanese use the terms *muda* (waste), *mura* (inconsistency by machines or workers), and *muri* (excessive demands upon workers or machines). These three factors have to be dealt with when a plant tries to implement JIT. The antithesis of JIT is *just-in-case*, whereby a plant's problems become hidden by holding vast amounts of inventory. Holding inventory at any stage of the manufacturing process can serve to cover poor operational performance. However, when there is little buffer inventory, *muda*, *mura* and *muri* become prominent. Reducing inventory will, in the first instance, cause problems to surface – problems that have previously been covered by excess inventory. The plant then has a simple decision: whether to stay with excess inventory and hide the problems, or to deal with problems as they arise in the name of continuous improvement within the plant. Unfortunately, I saw many plants that have given up on JIT and reverted back to just-in-case inventory management, because either their internal quality problems revealed that major changes had to take place, or they were incapable of forming sufficiently strong relationships with suppliers. On some occasions both of these reasons came into play but the plants would still insist on saying that they were 'world-class'.

Interestingly, when these problems appear, the strategic importance of inventory is revealed. Instead of a quick-fix tactical approach – buying more stock to cover problems – the firm must take strategic measures: continuous and ongoing improvements in-house to reduce stock levels, coupled with strategic alliances with suppliers to enhance delivery and innovations and reduce total costs.

The firm within the supply chain

A basic supply chain is illustrated in Figure 6.1.

The contrast between past and present approaches to the supply chain is important. In the past, the perceived wisdom for large firms was that the goal was to own as much of the supply chain as possible. The rationale for this was to gain control of activities involved in the chain and supposedly to reduce costs due to ownership. The problem, however, was that the firm would then be pulled into different activities in which it had little or no experience or expertise. The recent era has seen firms placing greater attention on focusing on what they do best and then outsourcing or

Figure 6.1   The supply chain

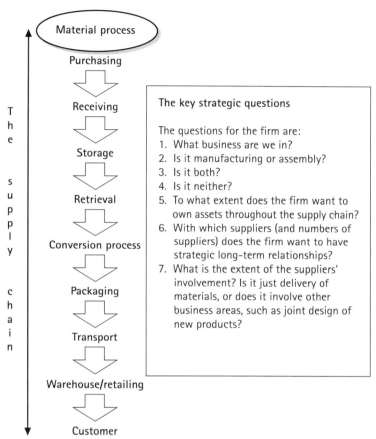

subcontracting all other activities. Such a strategy is at the core of the principles of re-engineering – although as we saw in Chapter 5, re-engineering has often been confused with downsizing. The result of such outsourcing activities is sometimes that the linear, logical model that we use to describe the supply chain is replaced by a series of activities, as represented in Figure 6.2.

Such outsourcing can become quite circular in effect. One example involves Octel Network Services, Electronic Data Systems (EDS), Xerox and Motorola. A major client of Octel Network Services, a firm in Dallas that operates more than one million electronic voice mailboxes, is EDS. EDS in turn has a $3.2 billion contract to run Xerox's computer and telecoms networks, a deal that involves around 1,700 of Xerox's employees transferring to EDS. Xerox itself provides invoicing and billing services for Motorola,

Figure 6.2   Outsourcing and the effect on the supply chain

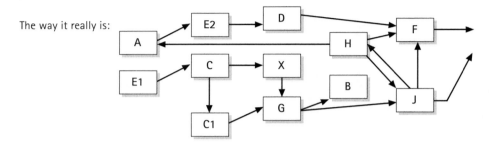

Source: Brown et al.[6]

which in turn designs and makes parts of Octel's voice-messaging systems and thus the circle is complete.[7]

Focus

The essential point of focusing on core areas and forming buyer–supplier relationships for other business activities has been the increasing attention of the firm to concentrate on what it does best, rather than being responsible for all activities in the supply chain. In this way, a company can concentrate on its core strength or competence. What this means, however, is that greater dependence upon suppliers is then a requirement for the firm or plant.

Focus can also mean completely divesting business areas in which the organization had previously invested. Sometimes such investment might have been made in the name of diversification and, therefore, spreading risk. For example, as we saw in Chapter 1, General Motors (GM) acquired Electronic Data Systems (EDS), a large computer-services company, and Hughes Electronics, the defence group, in the 1980s. These acquisitions were part of an expensive diversification strategy masterminded by Roger Smith, GM's chairman during most of the 1980s. The aim was to reduce the group's dependence on the highly cyclical US car market and exploit potential synergies with other industries. However, the expected outcomes did not materialize and the acquisitions diverted GM away from its core business depriving the firm of considerable amounts of cash.

Focus can mean that the firm becomes a virtual organization, employing far fewer people than before but achieving similar business goals. For example, TopsyTail, a small Texan company, sold $100 million worth of its hair-styling equipment between 1991 and 1997, although it had virtually no permanent employees of its own. Subcontractors handled almost all of the organization's activities – design, manufacturing, marketing, distribution and packaging. However, focus does not necessarily have to mean drastic reconfiguring and downsizing in the name of re-engineering, and will often mean, instead, focusing activities away from areas in which the firm does not want to continue to operate.

Outsourcing

Whereas focus can include divesting business assets that were once part of the firm's attempts to diversify, outsourcing is more often associated with the configuration in which the firm finds itself within the supply chain. As I noted earlier, the perceived wisdom was formerly that a firm should own all activities within the supply chain. At one time, Ford made almost everything that went into its cars, including the steel and glass. In 1980, it made about 87% of a car itself. Now it only makes 30–40%. Ford's strategy is to form close relationships with a smaller number of suppliers than before. Ford aims to cut its direct suppliers to 5,000 globally, from 50,000 a few years ago.

Similarly, in the past IBM produced the silicon as well as the software and hard drives for its computers. This approach – one of vast amounts of vertical integration – has been replaced by outsourcing strategies. As a result, a new group of contract manufacturers has emerged in the PC industry – companies such as SCI Systems, Solectron, Merix, Flextronics, Smartflex and Sanmina – who manufacture products for major PC players including IBM and Hewlett-Packard. In 1996, ICL sold its manufacturing company, D2D (itself derived from the manufacturing arms of ICL divisions), to Solectron, who also bought one of Hewlett-Packard's printed-circuit plants in Germany, another in Colorado going to Merix. All of these actions by the various PC firms served to focus them on areas in which they could excel, leaving other firms to take over other specifically outsourced operations. In the USA, such outsourcing has seen a remarkable growth of small manufacturing enterprises – companies with fewer than 100 employees comprised some 85% of the USA's 370,000 manufacturing firms.[8] However, outsourcing strategies can have major reactions from what were once seen as core employees. In 1996, there was a major strike at General Motors:

> ... when GM workers went on strike, the term 'outsourcing' became a dirty word. Widely used when describing GM's tactic of contracting out for the manufacture of certain automobile components that it had been manufacturing in house, 'outsourcing' in this context meant knocking yet another raft of auto workers off GM's assembly lines.[9]

> The United Auto Workers Union used the 17–day strike to complain that jobs were being threatened and technological leadership put at risk by the increased shift towards outside suppliers.[10]

So although the decision to outsource has become a popular one it can cause unrest. But simply divesting part of what was previously an owned asset is only one part of the puzzle. For such outsourcing to be successful, strategic buyer–supplier relationships need to be in place.

Buyer–supplier relationships

Firms often have enough problems trusting their own employees. Forming strategic relationships based on trust with other firms is even more of a problem for old-fashioned managers who might be wary of such relationships. The task is summarized in the following:

> Managing suppliers is thus no longer a task for old-style purchasing managers. Strategic purchasing is becoming a partnership between the big corporations that preside over design, assembly, and marketing of finished products, and fewer, smaller, smarter suppliers – often single-source suppliers.[11]

Chapter 7 explains how vital human resource management is to achieving enlightened capabilities. This has an impact upon inventory management. I found direct links between the amount of trust that a firm could provide in-house and the trust that it could demonstrate to its outside suppliers. Other firms have identified this link. An example from Kodak supports this assertion. George Fisher, Kodak's CEO, identified five key operating values for Kodak employees:

1. Respect for the dignity of the individual.
2. Uncompromising integrity.
3. Trust.
4. Credibility.
5. Continuous improvement and personal renewal.

Although these were initially set for internal employees, Kodak was clear that this would be extended to all other firms with which it would form strategic partnerships:

> With such values, it is not surprising that when Kodak wanted to improve several key dimensions of its relationships with suppliers, it chose the partnering approach ... A Kodak team took the partnering concept from idea to implementation on a global scale.

How did they do this?

> First, top management support and commitment is needed at each step of the way. Management must agree with and commit to the partnering concept, and fully empower the partnering development team.[12]

But getting senior managers to commit and to stay committed is a difficult task. Trust does not necessarily come easily to senior managers. M. Sako gives an insight into the nature of trust when she suggests that three types of trust need to be in place:[13]

- *Contractual trust* – which is the adherence to formal, legal promises.
- *Competence trust* – that either side is capable of providing what has been promised.
- *Goodwill trust* – which borders on ethics: trusting that appropriate behaviour will ensue.

Trust was a distinguishing feature between traditional and enlightened plants. The former maintained a threatening stance with suppliers, while the latter sought, after careful initial choice and selection of suppliers, to maintain close relationships with them, without any threats of price and delivery pressures. In the past, both academics and practitioners alike were suspicious of buyer–supplier relationships. Harvard's Michael Porter, in his book *Competitive Strategy*,[14] pitched the buyer–supplier relationship in largely adversarial terms. He suggested that the buyer should pursue the 'threat of backward integration' and threaten the 'use of tapered integration' – hardly the stuff of relationships based upon trust. The management of suppliers by GM's former chief purchasing director, Lopez, was well documented. He forced suppliers to reduce prices by renegotiating contracts and opening up parts to competitive bidding – sometimes going through several rounds of bidding. Lopez is credited with saving GM $3–4 billion as a result of these tough supplier management practices but the cost of doing so may be even greater than this short-term financial benefit. A key issue in choosing and maintaining a relationship with a supplier is in the supplier's willingness to be involved in new product development. Two telling quotes from GM's suppliers may yet come back to haunt GM in its development of new products where, increasingly, speed (as well as quality) are key factors:

> Why should we risk telling them our good ideas ... At GM there is no certainty.[15]

> GM's relations with its suppliers remain the worst in Detroit ... An electronics supplier tells of a $30 part he developed jointly with GM. He says that after he slashed the price

to $15, the GM purchasing agent demanded more cuts, citing a $9 bid from a Chinese company that had never made the part in question ... One parts maker that does $600 million in business with car makers says it is focusing its efforts on selling to GM's rivals.[16]

In the car industry, there has been a vast move away from the need for the manufacturer to own all areas of the supply chain. The pioneers of this were Japanese manufacturers and the effect has been profound:

In Japan, the actual contract between motor manufacturer and supplier is based on co-operation, a full exchange of information, a commitment to improve quality, and a recognition ... that prices can (and will) be reduced each year ... bargaining is not simply focused on price per se but on how to reach the target price while maintaining a reasonable level of profit for the supplier.[17]

At the beginning of the twenty-first century, Toyota produced only 20% of the value of its cars, whereas GM produced 70%, Ford 40% and Chrysler 30%. Of the big three in the USA, Chrysler is often cited as having the best buyer–supplier relationships. Chrysler purchases 60,000 different items from 1,140 different suppliers.[18] The total supplier base was reduced by 36% in a five-year period in the 1990s, and was envisaged to be reduced by another 25% by 2002. Chrysler has also been rigorously pruning its family of suppliers. For example, the number of vendors that supply fasteners was cut from 350 to 92, with the goal being 42 by 2001. The merger between Daimler and Chrysler means that the reduction in the number of suppliers will be even greater.

The same sort of rationalization has been taking place at Ford. Ford cut its direct suppliers to 5,000 globally from 50,000 a few years ago. But for those who remain in Ford's chain, 'the opportunities are limitless', according to the purchasing director for Ford's Europe-based global small- and medium-car centre.[19]

Managing the actual nature of the relationship is a strategic challenge. For example, Ford regards its engines and transmission systems to be its most important manufactured car components. As a result, Ford owns the design rights for these and manufactures them within its own factories. Other key items are also manufactured when they are seen as central to Ford's brand identity. Electronic parts, plastics, trims, and climate controls are produced at Ford's own plants.

Of the outsourced materials, Ford divides these into two groups. The first is 'certified full service suppliers'. These are suppliers who own the designs. The second group consists of suppliers who manufacture to a Ford design. Managing its supply base is made more complicated because Ford some-times acts as a subcontractor, producing and selling its proprietary designs to other manufacturers. Ford created a separate unit for its $16 billion a year car parts business called Visteon. The aim was to increase Visteon's non-Ford customers' base from 5% to 20% within five years.[20]

In the PC industry, managing supplier relationships is an integral part of the business. However, this too can be difficult. Hewlett-Packard linked with Canon to produce inkjet and laser printers. Together they captured 70% of the $3 billion a year market for monochrome printers in the USA. But although they jointly developed the inkjet, they now compete against each other for this product. *Fortune* summarized the position:

> In 1996, they got into a nasty price war that all but wiped out their margins. Each side blamed the other for starting it. And Canon surprised Hewlett-Packard by introducing its own, impressive printer software package that helped it grab a big chunk of the US market ... So, can the laser printer partnership last? Analysts wondered when HP chose Konica a few years ago to make the motors for its color laser printers because Canon's color motors weren't ready in time. Canon executives play down any friction. Says one: 'We're like a typical married couple. We rely on each other, and there is no prospect of divorce. But the husband likes to go downtown once in a while to watch pretty girls.'[21]

So the buyer–supplier relationship can be complicated because of its changing nature: what were once joint-developers can become out and out competitors. Another complication is that in recent years a number of mega-sized suppliers have emerged due to a range of mergers and acquisitions. For example, the merger of Lucas Industries of the UK and Varity of the USA put the group into the world's top 10 suppliers. The merger created a powerful new international force in braking, diesel engines, fuel systems and electronics. Similarly, the £1 billion acquisition by Bosch of AlliedSignal's global brakes business, and Johnson Controls' £863 million purchase of Prince Automotive, the vehicles interior company, exemplify the mega-deals 'helping to reshape the world automotive components business into one where a predicted 25–30 'mega-suppliers' will dominate the business by early next century.[22]

A similar trend took place in the PC industry. For example, NCR sold its manufacturing operations for $100 million to Solectron. Solectron is an example of the new group of contract manufacturers, which emerged in the industry. As I noted earlier, SCI Systems, Solectron, Merix, Flextronics, Smartflex and Sanmina manufactured for the likes of IBM and Hewlett-Packard. The two largest, SCI Systems and Solectron, each now have annual sales exceeding $2 billion.

Benefits of buyer–supplier relationships

Firms do not form relationships in order to be nice or to demonstrate they are capable of trusting another firm. They form partnerships because they provide benefits. These benefits can be tangible – in terms of enhanced quality, improved innovation etc. as well as more subtle benefits such as learning and know-how, which can be gained in a partnership. The major car firms depend on suppliers for innovation, especially where there are intentions to increase global efforts. The major suppliers – Bosch of Germany, Magneti Marelli of Italy, and LucasVarity of the UK – will partner the large vehicle makers into whichever region of the world they wish to make or sell cars.

The buyer–supplier relationship is vital to innovation. The partnering strategy played a major role in Chrysler's new line of cars in the 1990s. The strategy worked with the Chrysler Concorde and the Dodge Intrepid, and was then used as the basis for the innovation of the Neon. This approach enabled Chrysler to be the most innovative of the Big Three manufacturers in the USA. Chrysler's cutting-edge supply-chain management techniques came together in the late 1990s with the Plymouth Prowler. For example, thanks to a new, sturdier alloy developed by Alcoa, one of Chrysler's suppliers, the Prowler became the first car built in North America with an all-aluminium body. GM followed suit with its link with another supplier, Alcan, the world's second-largest aluminium group. Alcan spent $200 million over ten years in developing technology and partnerships with car makers. In 1998 it revealed a multi-billion dollar, ten-year supply deal for aluminium with General Motors. The two groups will 'explore new and expanding uses for aluminium, including aluminium intensive vehicles.'[23]

But innovation of products was not the only benefit from such close relationships with suppliers. Continuous improvement was also a feature. Chrysler's purchasing department has received thousands of cost-saving ideas since launching its SCORE (supplier cost reduction effort) supplier programme. In 1997, Chrysler announced that SCORE had reduced operating costs by $325 million with supplier participation up from 13% in 1994 to 26.6% in 1996.[24] Chrysler does not want to jeopardize quality in the name of cost-cutting and so it asks its suppliers to submit ideas for approval first. The aim is for each supplier to identify cost-cutting opportunities equal to 5% of its annual billings to Chrysler. SCORE has seen total savings of $2.5 billion for Chrysler.

Not surprisingly, Japanese transplants have seen enormous benefits in their relationships with suppliers. The quality goal for Honda of America's suppliers is to have a zero parts per million (ppm) defect rate. While that may seem hard to accomplish, 200 of Honda's 322 suppliers already ship defect-free parts each month. The remaining one-third accounts for an overall defect rate of 100 ppm. This is a dramatic improvement since 1986 when Honda began using more US-based suppliers. In 1986, Honda received 6,000 ppm defects from suppliers. There are many reasons for the dramatic improvement. Honda's designers work closely with suppliers to ensure that parts are manufacturable. Honda also has a 200-member department that works closely with suppliers to help them improve quality.[25] Clearly, for Honda, suppliers are an integral part of world-class, enlightened practice. Honda has a list of what it calls 'BPs': *best position, best productivity, best product, best process* and *best partners*. Suppliers do not feature within best practice only – they also appear as an important part of best position: 'For Honda to be the best, our suppliers must be the best.'[26]

 ## Distribution

One of the key issues facing manufacturers is how to distribute finished goods to customers. In the PC industry, Dell cut out the retail involvement to a large extent by selling direct to customers. Around 500,000 customers call Dell's operators each week.[27] This enables Dell to gauge trends in demand more quickly and to plan manufacturing flexibility. Dell has superb manufacturing operations and its inventory turnover was far in excess of Compaq. In the mid-1990s, Dell grew by nearly 50% a year in a market that was expanding at around 20%. Other PC manufacturers rethought their entire distribution and manufacturing strategies and inventory was central to both strategies. But making massive changes is easier said than done. As we saw in Chapter 2, although Compaq launched its three-pronged hybrid distribution programme – build-to-order, channel configuration and configure-to-order processes – in 1997, it had still not been successful by the end of 1999.

 ## Data from the plants

So far I have discussed the critical role that inventory can play. Now I will examine a number of capabilities within plants. As with the other findings in this book, I wanted to get behind the numbers to discover why some plants performed better than others. One of the issues was Class A inventory. This is inventory that accounts for something in the region of 70–80% of costs. The overly simplistic – but still useful – principle is the pareto, or 20/80 rule, i.e. 20% of the number of inventory items in the plant will account for 80% of the total costs. This is important because these Class A items demand good supplier relationships to deal with competitive factors such as cost and delivery. The contrast between enlightened and traditional plants was telling:

Figure 6.3   Contrasting enlightened and traditional plants in finished goods inventory

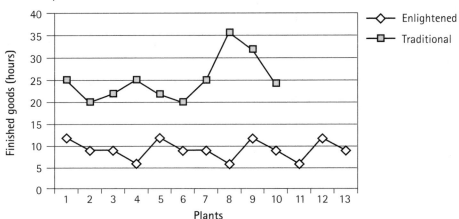

- The range of Class A components' work-in-process for enlightened plants was 3–18 hours; in the traditional plants, this went from 22–40 hours.

- Finished goods inventory ranged between 6 and 12 hours for enlightened plants, and between 20 and 36 for the traditional plants.

- All enlightened plants have electronic data interchange (EDI) links with all of their class A suppliers; none of the traditional plants had more than 50% of their suppliers linked by EDI.

- In the enlightened plants, the percentage of Class A suppliers whose contracts were at least three years in duration with the plants ranged between 80% and 95%; this was in contrast to the traditional plants, where no more than 50% of Class A suppliers had contracts in excess of three years with any of the plants.

- Perhaps the most interesting data came from the rationale in selecting suppliers. In traditional plants, price always scored the highest; price was the lowest factor in the enlightened plants, whose primary reason for choosing suppliers was quality.

This information is illustrated in Figures 6.3 and 6.4.

Further findings within the plants

The above data provided powerful insight into the differing performance characteristics between enlightened and traditional plants. But the question is: Why did enlightened plants perform better? The following provides some of the answers.

The extent of integration of functions

In the enlightened plants, an integrated, holistic approach was clearly evident in the creation of the master production schedule (MPS). As we saw earlier, this is an important precursor for successful MRP/MRPII. For these plants, this was a dynamic process agreed by all concerned parties – helped specifically by strong links between marketing and production. In addition, there were close links with suppliers, made possible by the joint efforts of manufacturing and purchasing staff.

In the enlightened plants, materials requirement planning (MRP) and just-in-time (JIT) worked well together: MRP was used for the MPS and was also central in ensuring the success of engineering design changes via the bill of materials file in MRP. The MRP system was used by the enlightened plants as a planning tool for projected capacity and scheduling and in order to advise the suppliers of forthcoming requirements. Materials would then be pulled from the suppliers on a daily basis by the plants. In the enlightened plants, planning (push) and JIT (pull) created a good fit. In the traditional plants, push and pull systems clashed and were confusing for both internal operations and in the relationship with the suppliers. Enlightened plants were noticeable for the simplicity of their planning – in particular in terms of master schedules that were fixed for a specific time period – thus creating greater clarity both in-house and with their suppliers than was the case in the traditional plants.

The traditional plants were noticeable for their technophilia problem[28] using elaborate computerized systems to manage inventories. However, in some of the traditional plants, the computer systems failed miserably and became a source and focal point of conflict between departments.

Figure 6.4   Contrasting enlightened and traditional plants in work-in-process levels (hours)

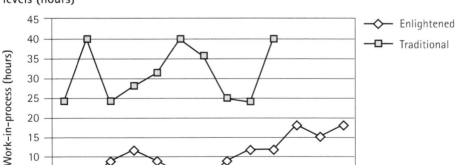

The role of electronic data interchange

Electronic data interchange (EDI) became an important means of exchange between enlightened plants and their suppliers, although it is important to note that technology did not detract from the close personal relations that tended to exist between these plants and their suppliers.

The success of just-in-time within the plants

Traditional plants struggled with JIT processes due to two key factors: an inability to perform to high process quality levels in-house, and to form strategic partnerships with suppliers.

There were major differences in terms of the use and meaning of JIT within some of the plants. Traditional plants clearly saw JIT as a cost-cutting exercise to reduce inventory costs in-house. Enlightened plants saw JIT as a complete shift away from how they used to manufacture and was part of a wider learning process for these plants. This learning process included failure as they experimented with JIT. Reduction of waste, through continuous improvement and learning, played an important part in enlightened plants. For example, in one of the enlightened manufacturing plants – a \$200 million products division – inventory levels declined by 30% and manufacturing cycle times by 50% in a two-year period.

Eight of the enlightened plants used a pilot area within their existing plant – a JIT cell – in order to learn by doing, a key factor of learning. As one of the enlightened manufacturing directors revealed:

> I can tell you, JIT was a nightmare when we first tried to do it . . . everything went wrong – machines, and problems with quality both here and with our suppliers . . . still gives me a nightmare thinking about it. The problem was we tried to do it too quickly – Friday night was one system, the following Monday we were on just-in-time. But we were committed to it and we stuck with it. We just kept going and we learnt as we went along.

JIT had rewards for the enlightened plants who out-performed their traditional rivals. In the traditional plants, materials were bought in batches and then pushed on to workstations regardless of whether the particular station was ready for the components – this in spite of the pretence of running JIT in some of the plants. Two key factors emerged as reasons for this: lack of training, and the fear factor. In keeping with much of the mentality of the traditional plants, JIT was seen as a quick-fix solution based around reductions in inventory, which would then keep down costs. Of course this is not the basis of JIT and, consequently, problems occurred. In all of the traditional plants, there was no evidence that any training was being provided either for in-house operators or for their suppliers. This was in direct contrast to the enlightened plants where training was a central and specific feature provided to help in the implementation of JIT.

A major tenet of JIT is that production occurs only to meet customer requirements for a specific time period. In the enlightened plants, particularly in computing and telecommunications plants, one common feature was that actual production was not always taking place. If the day's or week's quota had been met then operations staff turned their attention via quality circles, or other similar group approaches, to enhance other performance areas within the plant (preventative maintenance was a typical active area in these plants). Fear was a factor within traditional plants when it came to JIT. One of the features of the enlightened plants was that they did not always appear to be busy – the reason being that they were far more efficient. However, in the traditional plants, the operators' need to be seen to be busy was central. In fact the entire culture and approach were based, essentially, on fear. This was summarized succinctly by one of the traditional plant managers:

> I've been brought up on hard work and I don't want to lose my job . . . I can't stand around doing nothing, I like to keep going all the time . . . that's why you come to work anyway, isn't it?

When advised of other plants who were not always busy he added:

> I don't come to work to sit in groups discussing things all day – we haven't got the time . . . I've heard that this goes on but it doesn't go on here . . . as you can see we're too busy.

For the traditional plants, the attempted transformation from traditional to JIT approaches was pushed through as a dramatic drive, driven by cost reductions and often abandoned when frustrations arose, either in-house or with their suppliers. Again, lack of strategic vision was often the cause here. This was not the case in enlightened plants where senior manufacturing personnel championed the transformation to JIT in the same way that they did with sustainable quality drives. For the enlightened plants, quality and JIT went together. With both quality and JIT, relationships with suppliers are vital. As we will see, enlightened plants encouraged strong supplier relationships; traditional plants did not.

The nature of buyer–supplier relationships

In a sentence, the difference between enlightened and traditional approaches was that enlightened plants managed the relationship with their suppliers, while traditional plants thought that they were managing the suppliers themselves. Specifically, what distinguished enlightened from traditional plants in terms of supplier relationships included the following:

- Enlightened plants took longer in the selection process than the traditional plants. The criterion was not merely low price, which tended to dominate traditional plants' selection process.

- Once suppliers had been chosen by enlightened plants, the relationship was seen as long-term and strategic in nature. Relationships between traditional plants and their suppliers tended to be volatile and could be terminated easily.

- Enlightened plants tended to work more closely with suppliers in the development of new products in contrast to traditional plants who brought suppliers in far later into the development process.

For example, one of the enlightened plants involved key suppliers in the development of its sub notebook computer. The plants evaluated suppliers, rating them on technology, quality, responsiveness, delivery, cost, environment and business condition. The plants saw cost as only one factor among many, rather than as the sole factor, which still pervades in many other firms' supplier selection.

The enlightened plants were careful and took time before choosing suppliers, but once suppliers' contracts had been awarded the relationships tended to be viewed as strategic partnerships, formed as a means of out-competing other such partnerships within the same industry.

Price remained the essential factor for traditional plants in selecting suppliers. Quality – followed closely by other competitive factors – was the key ingredient for enlightened plants; price was the least important factor. The role of the supplier in enlightened plants was more of an overall business involvement, including early involvement in the design process, than was the case in traditional plants whose focus remained on low-cost endeavours from their suppliers.

For one of the enlightened plants, which happened to be a Japanese transplant, the closeness of buyer–suppler relationships is not confined to their plants in Japan:

> Scores of suppliers throughout Europe have contracted to supply parts and materials to our new passenger car plant in England and to [our] engine plant in Wales. We are working with many of those companies and with other prospective suppliers to develop and implement European versions of [our] Production System.

Insight into the nature of the relationship between this plant and its suppliers was provided in the following:

> Once you become our supplier, you're our supplier of that component forever, unless you perform so badly we can't do anything to help you.

Another enlightened plant's senior manufacturing manager stated that:

We always work closely with our suppliers, although we take a lot of time and effort in choosing the right ones in the first place. We help them achieve ongoing gains in quality and costs. That way we both benefit but, let me emphasise, that we do this because we are confident of their basic abilities in the first place.

The role of senior manufacturing personnel

It would be inaccurate to attribute the success of JIT within the enlightened plants to manufacturing personnel only. It is more accurate to say that it was due to a cross-functional approach, dependent on close in-house co-operation and communication between marketing, purchasing and manufacturing personnel together with close relationships with external suppliers. However, it would be fair to say that manufacturing's role was central to plants who were successful in implementing JIT. Their role was important for reasons similar to those cited in earlier chapters. First, they remained committed to JIT (in the same way that they were committed to quality, with which JIT is linked) in spite of initial failures. Second, they took time to learn from a range of sources (including conferences, external consultants and, where possible, other plants) in order to introduce JIT into their plants. Third, they monitored the success, or otherwise, of JIT within the plants and were responsible for reporting progress to other key functions, especially marketing and purchasing. And fourth, they were involved in choosing suppliers. This was an important issue because the importance of the buyer–supplier relationship is often stressed, without saying who the key personalities are, who are involved in the relationship, or the seniority of those people.

For the enlightened plants, seniority signalled the strategic emphasis given by them to materials management. Moreover, senior manufacturing personnel in enlightened plants were very clear that low cost was only one of a range of criteria for choosing suppliers. As we saw, other factors such as delivery speed and reliability were seen as more important in enlightened plants than in the traditional plants where low-cost criteria pervaded in choosing suppliers.

Conclusions

We have seen that inventory management is a key management issue for the plants. It is of strategic importance, rather than a mere buying function performed at lower levels of the organization, as has been the case in the past. In particular, JIT is far from being a simple short-term cost-reduction exercise: instead it is a massive challenge to many Western manufacturing firms

Figure 6.5   The strategic, focused, holistic approach to management

Strategic inventory management means that the firm moves away from tactical, quick-fix approaches, including mathematical formulas to manage inventory. Instead, the firm sees inventory as part of a range of crucial manufacturing capabilities that will determine whether the firm can compete against other players. Inventory will impact directly upon delivery speed and reliability, cost, quality and other key competitive factors.

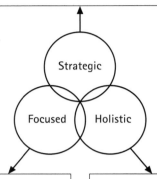

Focused means that the firm will home in on a smaller, more closely linked supplier base. As a result, there will be a concentrated effort between supplier and buyer to focus jointly on competitive factors.

The holistic approach means that the firm sees itself as part of an extended enterprise with other firms within the supply network. There is now a win–win attitude, although suppliers and buyers continue to place high demands on each other but do so in order to compete against other, similar partnerships.

in terms of how these firms will conduct business both internally – through its production/operations capability – and externally – in the firms' relationships with suppliers. Partnerships in the supply chain are strategic issues for world-class firms in the car, computer and telecommunications industries. The approach has to be simultaneously strategic, focused and holistic, as shown in Figure 6.5.

For the traditional plants, there is still a reluctance to form strategic buyer–supplier relationships. Relationships, if they exist at all, are cautious and sometimes volatile. It is clear from the turnaround of fortunes at Chrysler that there are massive benefits to be gained in forming technological partnerships with suppliers, in order to help ensure speedy and successful innovation. For the enlightened plants, the presence of senior manufacturing personnel, linked closely with purchasing, was vital in choosing appropriate suppliers. Part of the senior-level manufacturing role was to nurture the relationship with suppliers. Senior manufacturing personnel in enlightened plants were also important in terms of ensuring high quality levels as a requirement for JIT within plants. The link between the role of senior manufacturing personnel in making business decisions (e.g. choosing partners) and success of JIT is not explored to any depth in the literature. In this research, such a link was clear and, as we saw in the data, the enlightened plants clearly out-performed their traditional counterparts.

NOTES AND REFERENCES

1. *Management Today*, February 1998, p. 68.
2. *Fortune*, April 13, 1998.
3. Taken from Brown, S. (1996) *Strategic Manufacturing for Competitive Advantage*. Prentice Hall, Hemel Hempstead, UK.
4. Taken from a Toyota Motor Company brochure: *Just-in-Time Production*.
5. Hutchins, D. (1988) *Just in Time*. Gower Books, London.
6. Taken from Brown, S., Lamming, R., Bessant, J. and Jones, P. (2000) *Strategic Operations Management*. Butterworth-Heinemann, Oxford.
7. *The Economist*, November 25, 1995.
8. *The Economist*, January 27, 1996.
9. Leslie, W. (1996) 'High order strategy for manufacturing', *Journal of Business Strategy*, **17**(4).
10. *Financial Times*, June 26, 1996.
11. Burt, D. (1989) 'Managing Suppliers Up to Speed', *Harvard Business Review*, July–August: 127–135.
12. Ellram, L. and Edis, O. (1996) 'A case study of successful partnering implementation', *International Journal of Purchasing and Materials Management*, **32**(4): 20.
13. Sako, M. (1992) *Prices Quality and Trust: Inter-firm Relations in Britain and Japan*. Cambridge University Press, Cambridge.
14. Porter, M. (1980) *Competitive Strategy*. Free Press, New York.
15. *The Wall Street Journal*, July 29, 1994, p. 26.
16. *Business Week*, August 8, 1994, p. 26.
17. Turnbull, P., Delbridge, R., Oliver, N. and Wilkinson, B. (1993) 'Winners and Losers – The "Tiering" of Component Suppliers in the UK Automotive Industry', *Journal of General Management*, **19**: 48–63.
18. Dyer, J.H, Cho, D.S. and Chu, W. (1998) 'Strategic supplier segmentation: the next "best practice" in supply chain management', *California Management Review*, **40**(2): 57.
19. *Financial Times*, March 6, 1997.
20. *The Economist* (1997) **344**(8034): 7.
21. *Fortune* (1998) **137**(2): 102.
22. *Financial Times*, March 6, 1997.
23. *Financial Times* (1998) 'Survey – Financial Times Auto', 3 December.
24. *Ward's Automotive Yearbook*, 1998.
25. Carbone, J. (1996) 'Honda pushes suppliers toward six-sigma level', *Purchasing*, **120**(1): 52–54.
26. These details came from Honda of America. Excellent insight into Honda of America's phenomenal achievement is provided in Nelson, D., Mayo, R. and Moody, P. (1999) *Powered by Honda*. John Wiley & Sons, New York.
27. *The Economist*, October 5, 1996.
28. Bessant, J. (1993) 'The Lessons of Failure: Learning to Manage New Manufacturing Technology', *International Journal of Technology Management*, **8**(2/3/4): 197–215.

7

Managing human resources

Introduction

A vital ingredient to ensuring that strategic resonance takes place is human resources. This chapter looks at the specific involvement of human resources in manufacturing, and asks the key questions:

- Are human resources seen as part of the core competence of the plant?
- How are human resources viewed within the plants – in particular, how are they managed in the present era of chaos?
- Are human resource capabilities seen as replaceable by technology and how does this affect attitudes toward downsizing?
- What role does training play?
- What role does learning play?

The chapter discusses how plants manage these key areas of human resources in the present manufacturing era. Undoubtedly, human resources can play a vital pivotal role in enlightened approaches to manufacturing. A number of studies have attempted to demonstrate the importance of human resources on subsequent performance within the firm,[1] but as *The Economist* has pointed out, human resources are important for both national as well as individual firms:

> The rich economies are coming to depend increasingly on the creation, distribution and use of information and knowledge involving both technology and human capital. The most distinctive feature of the knowledge-based economy is not that it churns out lots of information for consumers though it does that too but that it uses knowledge pervasively as both an input and an output throughout the economy.[2]

In 1978, the prominent management writer, Peter Drucker, wrote prophetically:

> To make knowledge work productive will be the great management task of this century, just as to make manual work productive was the great management task of the last century.[3]

Firms are becomingly increasingly dependent on their human resource capabilities. This is because much of the tacit, as well as coded, formal or documented knowledge that a firm possesses centres around human resources. This knowledge and general know-how related to processes can be accumulated by a firm's manufacturing plants over time. A motivated, highly trained workforce must form the backbone of any would-be world-class manufacturer. As Grindley observes:

> The skills base is one of the firm's main assets. It is hard for competitors to imitate ... this calls for an attitude to encourage learning and to reward efforts which add to the firm's knowledge. Skills go out of date and need constant replenishment. In the long term what is most important may not be the particular skills, but the ability to keep learning new ones.[4]

GE's Jack Welch mentioned how 'We spend all our time on people . . . The day we screw up the people thing, this company is over.'[5]

Despite being over-simplified, this statement shows how CEOs will often go on record to state the importance of their staff. *Fortune* stated how Gerstner has changed life at IBM:

> When Lou Gerstner parachuted in to fix the shambles John Akers had left of IBM ... he focused on execution, decisiveness, simplifying the organisation for speed, and breaking the gridlock. Many expected heads to roll, yet initially Gerstner changed only the CFO, the HR chief, and three key line executives – and he has multiplied the stock's tenfold.[6]

What *Fortune* omitted to say, though, was that Gerstner did fire staff at IBM – over 100,000 of them in fact. In an earlier article, *Fortune* said:

> ... Gerstner became CEO of IBM in 1993 ... Within 90 days, he made fundamental decisions about the company's future course, completing the reduction of its workforce from 406,000 to 219,000 ...[7]

No doubt the strategy has worked in terms of making IBM prosperous again but it has fundamentally changed the culture of IBM for ever. IBM, once the firm that prided itself on never firing anybody, is now capable of downsizing like other firms. For sure, IBM's culture had to change. IBM had become a victim of its own success in the mid-1980s when extraordinary profits deflected attention from a new breed of aggressive entrants into the PC industry whose operations capabilities were superior to IBM. Part of the problem too was with not confronting issues:

> Our culture was very congenial, so congenial you never knew where you stood . . .
> Meetings would always go fine. You'd go in, and everything would be very proper and
> well-dressed, and a bunch of people would sit around and have a nice chat. The
> results might be good, and people would say, 'Thank you very much.' Or the results
> might be awful, and it would still be, 'Thank you very much; we know you tried your
> best.'[8]

Many firms seem to confuse reconfiguring the organizational structure with firing. Radical downsizing does not always need to happen. There are many alternatives to firing, including seeking out areas where good employees can be of value by being employed elsewhere within the organization. The number of employees does not necessarily have to do with levels of hierarchy or reorganization. For example, Wal-Mart, the number one retailer in the USA, had far more employees at the end of the 1990s than Sears ever did. The difference is that at one time Sears had numerous levels within its hierarchy, whereas Wal-Mart has always been a flat company.

What is remarkable when firms fire people is the speed with which CEOs themselves can be fired. Take the following example:

> . . . a single spotlight beats down on Michael H. Spindler, the new CEO of beleaguered
> Apple Computer inc. . . . 'I didn't have to be CEO,' says the 51-year old executive.
> Suddenly, his eyes tear up. His voice wavers, and he delivers a last sentence, his fist
> raised to the roof, 'The reason why I made this . . . decision is: We can win this.'[9]

This is all good, dramatic stuff and certainly the sort of speech that the business press likes, but just a few short months after this night of drama, Spindler was fired. Presumably either he was not up to the job, or Apple made a bad appointment. But Apple seemed to repeat the decision with Spindler's successor, Gil Amelio. Amelio was in the post only between 1996 and 1997. More to the point, perhaps the turnaround at Apple did not take place within the time required for the nanosecond, bottom-line culture that determines the fate of CEOs.

The good news . . . and the bad news

Firms can be full of highly intelligent, qualified men and women, who are capable of inventing, creating and producing ideas and products on an ongoing basis. Such an atmosphere can result in high-quality, innovative ideas, and other important traits that are central to enlightened manufacturing. Firms are also full of people who, as we will see in this chapter, are, on occasions, capable of doing remarkably stupid things. Interesting examples include:

- There was the case of a worker being given a raise in salary in the morning and was then told in the afternoon that he was one of those who would be downsized.

- The plant manager who, having seen the managing director with me in the plant, thought that he would impress the MD. He pointed at a worker, clicked his fingers and shouted, for all to hear: 'Oi-you-office-now!' What a sad indication of the way in which a plant manager thought he would impress his MD with his authority over his staff. What he actually showed was remarkable incompetence.

- I saw a newly installed CEO in the USA making his opening address to 400 managers, informing them that within 12 months, only 40 of them would be left – and this in a middle of a crisis period for the firm when it was depending on its human inventiveness for new innovations.

- I saw plants that had committed to TQM and BPR, and then the workforce were told that they had done so well that they had 'done themselves out of a job' and that downsizing would now take place.

I have looked into the eyes of these employees and seen the utter hurt – and sometimes hatred – because they are now being downsized through no fault of their own. Some of these had been fully committed to the firm but now saw their sometimes herculean efforts rewarded with being fired.

It should be self-evident: the things that make business worthwhile include passion, guts, commitment and dedication. All of these come from humans, not machines. Yet the reality is that far from being viewed as a key asset within the firm, human resources are often treated as the least important, and most easily disposable, of all assets. In high-volume manufacturing, labour costs will account for less than 10% of production costs. But human resources are the first target under threat when costs reductions are to be made. Why? The answer must be because it's the easy, instant solution approach to management. Firing people takes little or no skill. Sure, there are 'downsizing' specialists but their role, in reality, is merely to smooth over the impact of downsizing and somehow to ensure that life within the firm goes on as before with minimum disruption. However, enormous damage can be done to the firm when it reduces staff. Part of the brain of the firm can suffer a corporate lobotomy and entire firms, or specific plants within firms, can forget how to perform to world-class standards. There will be occasions when a firm has to reduce numbers: it must avoid becoming bloated, particularly in terms of hierarchy. But it is the rationale behind, and motives for, downsizing – together with how it is handled – that provide clues to how firms manage their most important asset, human resources. If firms wish to have rapid innovation and high quality, they need to adhere to Deming's famous command:[10] *Drive out fear from the workplace.* But some firms almost seem to enjoy the sometimes harsh means by which reductions in headcount takes place. As a result, the strategic importance of human resources in achieving world-class, excellent, enlightened approaches to manufacturing can be lost.

The importance of human resources in all areas of manufacturing

As we saw in Chapter 1, forming and implementing strategy in recent times is dependent upon the firm's capabilities. A key element is human resources as exemplified in the following:

> In fact, numerous researchers have recently noted that people may be the ultimate source of sustained competitive advantage since traditional sources related to markets, financial capital, and scale economies have been weakened by globalization and other environmental changes . . . firms wishing to succeed in today's global business environment must make appropriate HR investments to acquire and build employees who possess better skills and capabilities than their competitors.[11]

The problem is that industries are littered with firms who paid lip service to such sentiments and then, with their attention drawn to quick-fix approaches, simply downsized at will. In doing so, firms have often taken very little time to do any sort of skills audits that might be needed. Alternatives to this approach are rare but a success story of the importance of human resources is described in Box 7.1.

The Nucor story is almost textbook in terms of what can be done. But there aren't many firms who have such policies in place. The core issue is that human resources are profoundly important to enlightened, world-class manufacturing.

Human resources have had major implications for all of the preceding chapters for at least the following reasons:

- Human resources management concerns itself with the actual skills and capabilities of senior managers, together with the means by which these senior managers work together at the highest levels of the firm in order to devise, implement and monitor strategies.[12]

- Human resource inputs are vital for both the initial ideas and the extent to which implementation and management of process and product technologies will be successful.[13]

- Quality is dependent, to a large degree, on the capabilities and motivation of human resources within the firm – which is why Deming stated that fear should be driven out from the workplace.

Box 7.1

The strategic importance of human resources at Nucor: the views of CEO Ken Iverson[14]

I get calls from students at prestigious business schools all the time . . . The first thing they ask is, 'May I have a copy of your mission statement?' And I say, 'We don't have a mission statement.' Then they ask, 'Well, can we have a copy of your job descriptions?' And I say, 'We don't have any job descriptions . . .' If there is a Nucor success formula, the primary ingredients include:

- Maintaining a lean management structure – the corporate headquarters office in Charlotte has a staff of just 25 people, and there are just four management layers between the CEO and front-line workers.
- Pushing decision making down to the lowest possible level – which means that the firm's business unit managers have a high degree of autonomy, and production workers are involved extensively in devising methods to improve operations.
- Encouraging experimentation and risk-taking – Nucor accepts that roughly half of its investments in new ideas and new technologies 'will yield no usable results,' Iverson says.
- A performance-based bonus system – one that rewards managers and other employees for improving return on assets and production crews for increasing productivity. (Last year, the company generated a record $623,000 in sales per employee.)
- A commitment to fostering two-way loyalty – by cultivating a sense of 'shared purpose' among managers and workers. Not only do employees at all levels share in the financial success of their work groups or business units, but a 'share the pain' philosophy dictates that everyone bears part of the burden during difficult times. (Although it has gone to reduced workweeks in slow periods, Nucor has never laid off an employee or shut down a facility for lack of work.)
- Cultivation of an egalitarian atmosphere – with few, if any, of the management perks common at many other firms. Everyone, including senior executives, flies coach on business trips. And there are no company cars, no reserved parking spaces, and no executive dining rooms.

- Successful inventory management owes much to the human resources skills in forming alliances with other partners and is not just dependent upon the sophistication of computerized monitoring and controlling systems.[15]

Although the abilities of a highly trained, motivated and skilled workforce will be most evident at operational levels, decisions on the nature and direction of human resources will be made at the policy/strategic levels of the firm. For example, in 1992 Rover agreed a deal with its workforce called 'Rover tomorrow – the new deal'. The deal centred around:

- Continuous improvement is a requirement for everyone.
- Associates are expected to be flexible.
- There will be maximum devolution of authority and accountability.
- Communication will be honest, open and two-way.
- There will be no compulsory redundancies.

All well and good but the problem is that in 1994 Rover was sold to BMW. With that sale came the distinct possibility that the new deal might become null and void. In other words, change of ownership, which is of strategic import- ance (and which is becoming increasingly important in the car industry) may well nullify attempts to become strategic in human resource management. For many months at the end of the 1990s, there was ongoing confusion and con- cern over the future of the Rover plants. The problem is that strategic decisions and subsequent operational capabilities are interwoven. As one of Rover's managers said, when asked about how this confusion might result in Rover's employees forgetting all the expertise gained with Rover's links with Honda: 'We learned world-class practices over a number of years [from Honda]; it would take a total of about five days to forget them all!' In March 2000 Rover was broken up by BMW, and with that came the end of the new deal.

 ## The changed role of human resources management

How human resources are managed in the current era of manufacturing presents a major challenge to many manufacturing firms in the West.[16] In the past, manufacturing has often had an association with repetitive, lowly motivated tasks. But this has changed to some degree. This change is largely due to learning about Japanese manufacturing practices both within Japan itself and in the Japanese transplants in the West. Workers are far more involved in the management of production/operations – both within Japan itself and in Japanese transplants in the West – which is in contrast to the more traditional Western approaches. Part of the reason behind the Japanese plants' accumulation of skills is due to the ongoing investment in training; another factor is learning gained within teamwork approaches:[17]

Japanese compensation strategy for high technology firms has historically been more team oriented than most American systems.

Another Japanese human resource strategy implemented in high technological firms is the consultative decision-making process called *nemawashi* . . . The process involves the accommodation of employee input in middle-down-up collaborative style.

The Nissan plant in Smyrna, Tennessee, provides vital insight into the important contributions of humans in manufacturing. In 1997, for the fourth year in succession, the plant was named the most productive in North America. Perhaps not surprisingly, other Japanese transplants excelled too with Honda's Marysville, Ohio, plant coming second, followed by the NUMMI plant in Fremont, California, and then Toyota's plant in Georgetown, Kentucky. Nissan in Smyrna uses only 2.23 workers to build its vehicles. This is in contrast to the three, four or sometimes more workers per vehicle at typical unionized auto plants operated by the Big Three auto makers. But Nissan's workers do not work harder; just more efficiently than their US counterparts:

There is little evidence to support UAW's contention that Smyrna employees work harder than their counterparts at less-productive plants . . . [Nissan] doesn't run shifts longer than nine hours, and it rarely asks employees to work more than one Saturday per month. Many unionized – and less productive – plants work longer shifts and far more weekends.[18]

The key difference seems to be in ongoing investment in developing skills and encouraging learning, which are central features of the enlightened plants' approach. The problem for many firms is that they have not kept pace with the changes in manufacturing eras. This is true not only in how firms form strategy, but in how firms struggle to manage staff in a way that is needed for the current era. Put simply, many firms have remained stuck in the mass-production era. Let us have a quick look at how human resources have changed in manufacturing over time.

The change of manufacturing eras and their impact upon human resources

As we have seen in previous chapters, manufacturing has evolved along three major eras; this evolution has helped to shape the way in which human resources have been managed in manufacturing firms.

Craft manufacturing

In craft manufacturing, which was European in origin, workers were generally highly skilled; the same people who performed the operations were sometimes owners of their own small enterprises. The skills and knowledge of a particular trade would often be passed from one generation to the next within the family. There was a development process from apprenticeship to journeyman to master, which led to the creation of guilds of skilled people. These small enterprises would be in the business of producing small volumes of customer-specific products in, essentially, 'job shop/very-low-volume batch' production.

Mass manufacturing

In the transition from craft to mass production, major changes took place. First, workers were largely de-skilled and work itself became narrow in scope, repetitive and specialized. During this era, the Taylorist approach to manufacturing – based upon scientific management – was in place and a large amount of job specialization occurred. With this specialization, workers became locked into a narrow range of activities, and inherent in this was a lack of flexibility. Workers were incapable of transfer from one type of operation to another. It must be said, though, that Taylor had a largely uneducated and unskilled workforce and what he did was to make the best use of these limited skills. At the beginning of the twentieth century, there were advantages of specialization and, to some degree, it was appropriate. Over a period of time, however, this over-specialization became a major source of unrest – strikes, high labour turnover, and general mistrust between workers and managers pervaded in much of industry in the West in the 1960s and 1970s.

A major feature of mass manufacturing was the emphasis upon manufacturing efficiencies gained by greater dependence upon machinery to transform inputs into outputs. In essence, machines replaced human skills.

The current era: post-mass-production

The current era, which demands agile, lean and world-class capabilities, is very dependent upon human resources. The term 'strategic manufacturing' is a preferred term to describe the current era, which includes at least the following traits:

- A greater customer-driven approach from the firm, rather than the former, product-offered, or resource-driven mentality of the mass-production era.

- An emphasis on quality, which in turn demands much greater human resource commitment than did mass production.

- A greater reliance upon human resources as a central means of achieving innovation and flexibility and other customer requirements.

The differences are illustrated in Figure 7.1.

Undoubtedly there are those people who see little or no difference between mass production and strategic or enlightened manufacturing when

Figure 7.1   The changing role of human resources in manufacturing

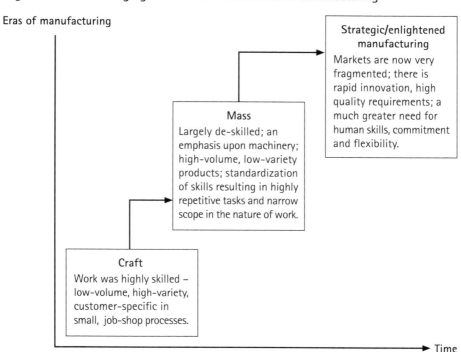

Source: Adapted from Brown, S. (1996) *Strategic Manufacturing for Competitive Advantage*.

it comes to the role of production workers; some have described the current approaches of empowerment, teamwork and so on as a 'democratic version of Taylorism'.[19] But the main problem is that some firms continue to manage human resources in a way more suited to mass production than to strategic, enlightened manufacturing. And it is too easy to dismiss all forms of strategic manufacturing as disguised or clever exploitation of workers by managers. Instead, what is now possible is a highly developed, mutually beneficial approach to work, far in advance of any worker–manager divide, which was a feature of the mass production system. The new approach has at its core a highly trained teamwork approach and a return to self-management in operations, which was a feature of the craft era. Self-management, often in teams, makes the practice of close supervision by managers a redundant requirement:

> One of the main factors that distinguished the Toyota Production System from Fordism was the amount of responsibility and individual control given to workers. In the West the assembly-line worker was a cog in a large machine . . . At Toyota . . . each worker was trained for a variety of jobs which they performed in teams. They were expected to think about how the tasks, parts, or equipment could be improved.[20]

This sort of approach is known to all by now. However, it's one that many firms fail to replicate in their own plants.

The downsizing factor

This discussion sounds great for workers – each worker can expect training, empowerment, teamworking and so on. However, the reality necessitates a balanced discussion to this overly simplistic scenario. The reality is that often, human resources will be the first target in cost-cutting; this was clearly evident in the epidemic levels of downsizing that took place in the early 1990s. As Hamel and Prahalad wrote:

> In 1993, large US firms announced nearly 600,000 layoffs – 25% more than had been announced in a similar period in 1992 and nearly 10% above the levels of 1991, which was technically the bottom of the recession in the United States.[21]

At the same time *Business Week* put the situation in a more dramatic fashion:

> The sight of so many bodies on the corporate scrap heap is sparking a corporate debate – about profits and loyalty, and about the benefits and unforeseen consequences of layoffs. Critics . . . believe massive downsizing has become a fad, a bone to throw Wall Street when investors begin baying for cost-cuts.[22]

IBM slimmed itself down from 406,000 employees in 1987 to 202,000 in 1995, one of the most dramatic workforce reductions ever. Other developments were disturbing. For example, after only 15 months after opening its plant in Tyneside in the north of England, Siemens of Germany closed the plant at a cost of around DM1 billion ($564 million).

In 1995, AT&T's announced that it was sacking 40,000 people – AT&T shed 140,000 in the ten years after the deregulation of 1984. But the announcement in 1995 was painful for AT&T's employees because it came at the very time when the company was prospering. What made matters worse was that at the time of the downsizing announcement, AT&T's CEO, Bob Allen, saw his salary increase to $5 million a year (although he was ousted from AT&T in 1997). Just to complete the picture, Wall Street responded to the dismal news of AT&T's downsizing by boosting the company's shares. Other headlines in the mid-1990s were equally alarming: 50,000 reductions at Sears, 10,000 at Xerox, 18,000 at Delta, 16,800 at Eastman Kodak, and a further 35,000 at IBM. The downsizing trend had not finished by the end of the decade either. In 1998, Motorola announced that it would lay off 15,000 staff and consolidate its manufacturing. The reason? Second-quarter earnings were expected to fall 'well below expectations'. More alarming, Motorola did not say more specifically where the staff cuts and facilities consolidations would take place and uncertainty was rife. At the time of writing, it remains to be seen what impact such an announcement will have on Motorola's world-class quality performance where six sigma quality has been touted as the norm within its plants.

In 1998, General Motors announced it would close a number of domestic factories, shed jobs and eliminate models in an effort to become more competitive. GM's North American sales and marketing operations would be reduced to a single division, thereby reducing bureaucracy, costs and jobs.

The problem with downsizing

Fortune provided interesting insight into how many US firms have simply downsized and outsourced much of its human resources:

> The standard history of modern American manufacturing reads like a Rocky script. Pummeled by foreign competitors, out-of-shape American manufacturers rehabilitated themselves with massive job sacrifices and clever technology. Today (cue the triumphant music), American factories are lean (with 12% fewer employees than at the 1979 peak), strong (producing 51% more stuff), and fast (increasing productivity at a torrid 3.5% annual rate). Dramatic, yes. If only it were true. Sure, American factories have cut costs and are making more widgets with fewer hands. But the manufacturing job out-look is nowhere near as grim – and productivity growth isn't quite as marvelous – as is generally believed. How could this be? Simple. Many factory layoffs have really been 'outsourcings' in which workers returned as (not always cheaper) vendors or contractors. And many newly resurgent factories, loath to increase permanent payrolls, are paying temp agencies instead.[23]

The concern is that not only does it make a nonsense of workforce figures but that these firms then have dependence upon those very people who have been downsized and outsourced. The only difference can be that these ex-staff then have little or no loyalty towards the firms that have just fired them. But it's the way that firms were downsizing that was the main cause for concern:

> The (final) thing the American experience has taught is that there are good ways of getting rid of people and bad ones. Apple . . . regularly announces that a certain number of people will be laid off in a few weeks' time, leaving its workers to wonder whose neck is for the axe. Some companies tell the victims by sending anonymous messages via e-mail or voice-mail. Others deliver the news simply by putting rubbish bags on the desks of those doomed to leave. This is not only brutal, but foolish. Workers waste their time worrying about the future. The survivors of each downsizing may spend less time working and more time in building their family life. Few have the energy or the commitment to engage in creative thinking.[24]

How can firms possibly hope to harness the creativity and abilities of their human resources when these sorts of approaches are in place? The simple answer is that they cannot. As we saw in Chapter 5, the essence of business process re-engineering (BPR) was sound enough. The intention of BPR was to focus on core areas on which the firm could excel and to outsource the rest. The reality, however, is that activities are often so interwoven that it is very difficult to cut out areas without doing damage to the core or heart of the firm. About 85% of BPR projects have failed[25] and the horrific effects of BPR on the morale and motivation of the survivors are often ignored.

But it's not just BPR downsizing that results in problems for both employer and employee – any downsizing can cause major problems. Managing downsizing – among a range of other problems connected to human resources – has been an ongoing problem for GM. Insight is gained into the reaction to the closure of GM's plant in Tarrytown, New York, at the beginning of the 1990s:

> When Bob Stempel announced in early 1992 that Tarrytown would be among the plants scheduled for closing, there was stunned disbelief among the workers, followed by outrage. It was as least the fourth time in GM's recent history that a particularly motivated group of workers tried to save their jobs by doing exactly what management asked, only to see the company fail them.[26]

GM continues to battle with its workforce. In 1994, after GM had shed many thousands of jobs – and by which time GM's previous purchasing director, Lopez, had annihilated good relationships with suppliers in the name of becoming lean – *Fortune*[27] raved about the '$11 Billion Turnaround at GM'. *Fortune* enthused how GM's finances were stronger, costs were coming down, engineering efforts were better focused, and global expansion was under way. The reality was all of this was a facade and that Wall Street, and other short-term indicators, were rewarding GM for the wrong things. In particular, the short-term draconian measures against suppliers resulted in a backlash that came to fruition in the late 1990s – GM struggled to launch new models because its suppliers were, understandably, loath to be involved in early conceptual stages of the development process. The supplier problem is mentioned here again because supplier relationships are relevant to human resources for a number of reasons including:

- managing suppliers is a relationship, in the same way that the firm has relationships with its own staff;
- this relationship is dependent upon personal skills in order to develop and nurture it; and
- the level of trust in the workplace is often reflected in the levels and types of trust that the firm has with suppliers.

As we saw in Chapter 6, a committed involvement from suppliers remains a crucial element in successful, and timely, innovations. GM remained the world's largest company at the end of the 1990s (number 1 in the Global 500 with $178 billion in revenues), but it under-performed in a range of operations standards against competitors in the USA. GM's difficult relationship with its workforce undoubtedly had dramatic impact on its financial performance. In 1998, GM was involved in a devastating strike, the longest for many years. The impact of the strike was summarized by *The Economist*:

> . . . Detroit is not the home of the Big Three but of the Big Two – the American car industry and the United Auto Workers' union. These two 'firms' are in direct competition, with the former trying to cut costs and increase profits, and the latter trying to cut lay-offs and increase salaries. It is impossible for both to win - so both keep losing. Ford and Chrysler can claim to have escaped this vicious circle: neither has had a serious dispute since signing their last round of national agreements with the UAW in 1996. General Motors, by contrast, has had more than a dozen strikes at different factories. Now the world's biggest car maker has reached the end of its most damaging strike for a generation – a two-month shutdown that began at a stamping factory in Flint but managed to bring the whole of GM's North American production to a halt. And it is still not clear what, if anything, the car company has won.[28]

During this strike, about 175,000 workers were idle and 26 of GM's 29 North American assembly plants were closed. In 1998, GM reported that its second-quarter profits were $389 million, a fifth of what they had been a year earlier. The strike had cost GM $2.5 billion and had cut its vehicle sales in America by 38%. In June, 1999, the United Auto Workers union stated its principal aim in negotiations with GM, Ford and Chrysler as: 'Job security is the number one issue . . . We can negotiate the best wage and benefits package but it won't mean anything if we don't have the jobs.'[29] It was clear, then, that the past damage of downsizing was the main concern of the United Auto Workers union in the negotiations.

Reorganizing human resources

On occasions, firms have to entirely reinvent and reconfigure themselves. Such change often comes about by necessity rather than choice and, as we saw earlier with IBM, such reconfigurations can be dramatic, including a large amount of downsizing. However, this does not always have to be so. For example, before its merger with Daimler, Chrysler underwent change that was fundamental and company-wide. Chrysler embarked on a dramatic cultural change from a traditional, bureaucratic, vertically structured organization to one organized into four nimble, cross-functional platform teams: small cars, large cars, minivans, and Jeep vehicles and trucks. Team work was the pivotal issue here, and at Chrysler, everyone focuses not just on pieces of the car, but on the total vehicle. Communication flows are simultaneous and two-way – not sequential and one-way. As we saw in Chapter 3, this change enabled Chrysler to be very innovative. Between 1992 and 1995, Chrysler introduced more models than it had done in the previous 20 years. The reorganization resulted in development times that matched that of the Japanese.

One of the major areas of learning from Japanese styles of organization is in the lack of levels of hierarchy within Japanese firms:

> In contrast with their Japanese competitors, American firms have several extra layers of hierarchy arranged as an organizational tree. To communicate with one another, people working in different departments often have to go up the tree to their lowest-level common superior and then back down. In Japanese firms the hierarchy has fewer levels and it is layered rather than strictly treelike: people in one layer generally know and can easily communicate with people in the next-higher and next-lower layers, regardless of departmental boundaries.[30]

At one time, General Motors had 22 layers of management, and Ford had 17, in contrast to Toyota, which had only seven layers. A number of Western firms have undoubtedly recognized the importance of reducing levels of hierarchy and to promote cross-functional teamwork, but in the traditional plants, this has been linked essentially with downsizing, rather than re-organizing, existing numbers.

At NUMMI, the GM/Toyota joint venture, there are only four job classifications and workers enjoy frequent job rotation. Production is based largely on teamwork and other organizational initiatives that GM has learned from the Toyota production system. There have been no forced redundancies at NUMMI. Workers are called 'associates' and regular meetings take place in order to review production processes and to make improvements. Staffing and materials-sourcing decisions are made by teams, rather than by a personnel or purchasing function. There are indications that progress is being made at other GM plants, though not as impressively as at the NUMMI plants: GM's Cadillac division has reduced job classifications from 18 to seven, each with its own payscale, and teams of workers are evident throughout the plant, responsible for their own training.

But reorganization can be more fundamental than reductions of management levels, important as this is. A number of companies told me how they had sold off divisions and areas that were non-core to the business in order to further focus resources and efforts within the plant. We saw in Chapter 1 how vital it is for firms to be focused at a strategic level. For example, Chrysler sold its stake in Mitsubishi, Lamborghini, and a number of component companies and 'The result of such policies has been a progressive climb in sales and earnings.'[31] Although equating success of strategies with short-term, financial criteria can be misleading, it is fair to say that the firm that has to continually invest in non-core areas, in which it may have little or no expertise, is likely to suffer financial hardships. More telling than these financial criteria has been Chrysler's increased ability in key operations capabilities – able to innovate new products faster than both GM and Ford and to exceed the speed of some of their Japanese competitors.

In the 1990s, many firms focused by organizing around specific product or market groups. This means of organizing was central to the enlightened plants. Indeed, during a three-year period of the research for this book, several plants in the computing industry had changed from functional to product-based divisions. This meant that a division, rather than corporate headquarters, now became more responsible for managing products within the overall firm. This change to greater divisional responsibility also enabled the division to be flexible, highly responsive and rapid in its approach to new product developments. The enlightened firm, including its plants, moves away from the need to own unrelated assets to concentrate instead on its core competence. A requirement for doing so, of course, is much stronger linkages with other firms, both vertically and horizontally.

Ford has undergone major change. Ford *had* to change in order to compete. The company's Ford 2000 approach linked together the company's European business with its North American one. This almost amounts to a merger since Ford has separate management structures, products, factories and processes in the USA and Europe. The reorganization was necessary because:

> The Japanese owed some of their success to their legendary leanness. Toyota makes 37 cars a year per worker, compared with Ford's 20. But the Japanese firms had also stretched economies of scale around the globe. Ford sells 500,000 of its biggest-selling car, the Taurus, every year; Toyota sells 1.4 million Corollas . . . having different models in North America and Europe means that Ford's engineering costs are as much as three times higher than Toyota's. And the Japanese seemed determined to extend their global advantage. As well as opening ever more plants in the United States, they were preparing to do so in Asia and Latin America. This would be likely to allow them to reduce production costs still further.[32]

Ford's Mondeo in Europe and the Contour/Mystique in North America, had cost $6 billion to bring to market, which was six times more than Chrysler's models. The revised version of the Ford Taurus took five years to achieve, whereas Japanese companies could launch new products in less than two. Not surprisingly, the reorganization involved massive disruption: around 25,000 managers were repositioned in a six-month period from January 1995. The role of leadership from Ford's former CEO, Alex Trotman, was key:

> Addressing an audience of 2,000 of Ford's most senior managers, Mr Trotman pulled out all the stops. Ford 2000 was not just a re-drawing of an organization chart, he said,

but a whole new way of working. And the aim was not just to cut costs and increase efficiency, but to produce cars that would surprise and delight the punters. After this rousing call to action, Mr Trotman led his audience to sign up for the new Ford 2000 project on a 'wall of commitment' . . . A video of Mr Trotman's speech has since been shown to all Ford's 320,000 employees around the world.[33]

The profound impact of the Ford 2000 reorganization extends to external suppliers as well as all internal employees. For example, Ford aims to have 250 suppliers who will account for 80% of its purchases worldwide. Ford also aims to reduce the time it takes to develop a new product from 36 months to less than 24, and to shorten its order-to-delivery cycle to less than 15 days. By 2005, Ford aims to have cut the number of basic vehicle platforms it makes in half, at the same time increasing the number of models built on them by 50%. These are dramatic targets, the achievement of which will depend to a large extent upon the commitment, skills and inventiveness of Ford's staff.

 ## Training and learning

Unfortunately, training is often the first casualty of any financial cutbacks within the firm. For some it's simply a question of 'show me the return I'll get for every dollar I spend on training.' This should be changed to: 'Show me the cost if I *don't* spend money on training,' because, like the problem of the lack of investment in process technology that we saw in Chapter 4, the biggest cost will ultimately be in not investing. Training at all levels within the firm has been one of the fundamental differences between Japanese and Western manufacturing. For example, back in the late 1980s in the UK, a number of studies were undertaken of British managers. One of these by Charles Handy found that less than 25% of British managers had either a degree or professional qualifications. Moreover, management training was generally poor, with many managers receiving no training during their career. However, since then, there has been a major upsurge in business education in the UK. The number of MBA courses offered increased from a handful to more than a hundred in the space of a decade. Business studies became very popular and many new business schools were established.[34]

The ownership of degrees and professional qualifications is not, by itself, sufficient. Tom Peters[35] pointed out that the increase in the number of business-school graduates, MBA qualifications and business-school publications in the USA happened at exactly the same time as the decline in the performance of many of its industries. Simply throwing money at education, training and management development, therefore, cannot be the answer. Spending on corporate education grew by 5% a year during the 1990s. In the mid-1990s, companies spent $50 billion a year on education and training, and accounted for about half of America's total spending on higher education.[36]

But this increase in spending is linked to the changes that have taken place in the employer–employee relationship. An interesting and profoundly important development has come into play in recent years: the notion that a firm can offer a job for life has now gone for good. In its place is a new psychological contract between employer and employee, whereby the employer undertakes to make the employee more employable as a result of working for a particular firm. This approach was exemplified in the following:

> A highly skilled computer programmer interviews at a major technology company and insists on receiving a package of benefits he'll be able to take with him when he moves on. A meeting planner is reluctant to come on board until she's promised help in gaining advanced certification. Managers might find such demands unnerving, but qualified candidates like these are becoming the norm. Call them the new American worker, the nontraditional employee, or the entrepreneurial independent.[37]

This approach was endorsed, interestingly, by Intel's' CEO Andrew Grove who, in language that offers optimism – and a little threat – stated:

> No matter where you work, you are not an employee ... You are in a business with one employer – yourself – in competition with millions of similar businesses worldwide ... Nobody owes you a career – you own it as a sole proprietor. And the key to survival is to learn to add more value every day.[38]

The key factor in training is the ability to learn. This applies to individuals as well as firms, and learning is something that an organization may or may not do. Harvard's David Garvin suggests:

> A learning organization is an organization skilled at creating, acquiring, and transferring knowledge, and at modifying its behavior to reflect new knowledge and insights.[39]

He continues by saying that learning organizations are adept at five activities:

1. problem solving;
2. experimentation with new approaches;
3. learning from their own experience and past history;
4. learning from others; and
5. efficiently (and speedily) transferring this knowledge throughout the organization.

Learning gained from the firm's own experience and learning from others demand that organizations make time to reflect on this learning in order to reinforce and confirm what has been learned. Learning in all of the ways cited above is a feature of world-class manufacturing firms. These firms learn quickly and effectively; these outstanding firms also learn quickly from mistakes and failures and then utilize the intellectual capability from their trained workforces to rectify the situation. Such learning then manifests itself in competitive areas such as lower cost, enhanced delivery speed and reliability, higher levels of process quality, and speedier new product development. But the alarming thing is that in the quick-fix management culture, not enough firms take time to learn as Garvin observes:

> . . . few companies . . . have established processes that require their managers to periodically think about the past and learn . . . There must be time for reflection and analysis, to think about strategic plans . . . Only if top management explicitly frees up employees' time for the purpose does learning occur with any frequency.[40]

Learning is an invaluable ingredient: it includes forgetting bad practice as well as embracing new ideas. Learning undoubtedly impacts upon key areas in manufacturing processes. It would seem, therefore, very sensible for firms to set aside time for learning rather than having an ongoing pursuit of being busy – often in the wrong things.

Data from the plants

The above sets the tone for the information gained from the plants. I examined a range of issues including:

- The degree of single status within the plant.
- Average percentage of revenue spent on training over a four-year period.
- Average percentage of the number of staff trained over a four-year period.
- Average levels of absenteeism over a four-year period.
- Percentage of compulsory downsizing of staff over a four-year period.

Again, the distinctions between enlightened and traditional plants were considerable (*see* Figures 7.2, 7.3 and 7.4). All enlightened plants have single status; only one of the traditional plants has single status. All of the traditional plants engaged in telling distinctions between 'staff' and 'workers', including different eating areas, toilet facilities, and car park allocations. Major differences are also noticeable in training and absenteeism – the revenue spent on training within the enlightened plants is 4–5.8%; in the

Figure 7.2   Contrasting enlightened and traditional plants: percentages of staff who received training

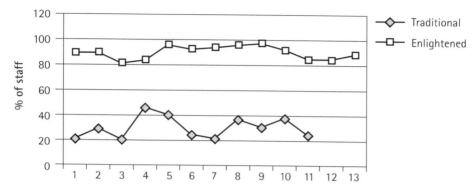

Figure 7.3   Contrasting enlightened and traditional plants: absenteeism rates

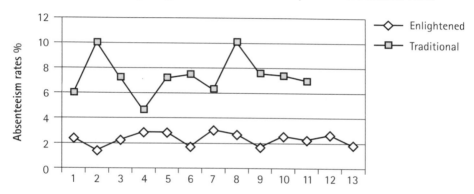

Figure 7.4   Contrasting enlightened and traditional plants: revenue spent on training

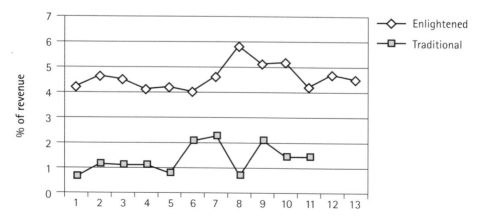

traditional plants this dropped to 0.6–2.3%. Absenteeism ranged from 1.4% to 2.9% in the enlightened plants, and between 4.7% and 10.1% in the traditional plants. Lastly, no enforced downsizing took place within any of the enlightened plants, while in the traditional plants, where the range of downsizing was between 10% and 30%.

However, we also need to get behind the numbers in order to see the main differences between the traditional and enlightened plants. Better insight is gained by looking at the previous discussions on basic differences of attitudes to human resources within the plants: the extent to which they are seen as a core competence; the role and importance of training; and the extent to which learning became part of the ongoing development within the plants. The data above is really an expression of the differences, rather than the cause. What causes the major difference between the two groups are the less tangible, but powerful, factors such as the basic attitudes toward the workforce which then manifests itself in commitment to areas such as training and worker involvement.

Further findings within the plants

A number of areas arose in providing insight into human resources within the plants.

The general importance given to human resources within the plant

There were a number of underpinning attitudes that distinguished traditional from enlightened plants. One of these distinctions was in how the plants perceived the specific contribution that human resources might have in manufacturing. The specific areas included worker participation and involvement, organizational focus, training and learning. We have seen in previous chapters that one of the distinguishing features between traditional and enlightened plants has been in the holistic approach of the enlightened plants who embrace this approach and apply it to at least the following areas:

- formulating business strategies;
- choosing and implementing process technology;
- new product development; and
- developing master production schedules that provide data for suppliers.

For the enlightened plants, these were seen as areas of skill within human resources, and human resources became a source of strategic stretch[41] – a source that would enable technology and market opportunities to be exploited by the plant. Enlightened plants saw a range of capabilities in flexibility, quality and innovation as very dependent upon human resources.

The use of teams and the empowerment of manufacturing personnel

While teamwork was evident in some of the traditional plants, we can make a distinction in terms of degree, if not kind. In the enlightened plants, teamwork was essential and central to manufacturing efforts. We saw in Chapter 5 how important this was to quality. In traditional plants, teamwork, if it existed at all, was not pervasive throughout the plant. In the enlightened plants, teamwork and empowerment were linked closely. For example, one of the enlightened manufacturing managers stated:

> The work is fulfilling because we empower the employees. Plant employees work in teams of about eight members each. Teams have the responsibility for guaranteeing the quality of their own work. And they have the authority to modify their work procedures as necessary to make the work flow more smoothly, to prevent problems, or to enhance the working environment.

A manufacturing director of another enlightened transplant stated:

> People are involved in their work in every sense. Focus groups, IMPACT teams, shop floor management, work group activities – each one offers opportunities for people to contribute their talents and ideas . . .

Another transplant manager said:

> A key point in the production system is that team members are treated with consideration, respect and as professionals. As such the system is designed to allow team members to take responsibility for their work. They are expected to be multi-functional and work toward the goal of using their talents to solve problems and make decisions within their group or team.

This approach is also explicit in some of the Western plants, and the distinction is not so much between Western and Japanese practices as it is between traditional and enlightened approaches. For example, one enlightened plant has around 5,000 employees organized into groups of 6–15 workers. Each group is a collection of small, self-directed business units that manage everything from scheduling and inventory control to recruitment and firing, without direct supervision from top management. This added responsibility seems to have made workers more accountable. This is most telling in absenteeism rates where averages of 2.5% compared with 10–14% at other plants within the same company. Workers spend at least 5% of their work time in further training, which again is higher than their sister plants. Sometimes these groups have responsibilities for a range of activities, which formerly came under the control of a personnel department. Several enlightened plants had taken the personnel department out of the decision-making loop by empowering line managers to take responsible action on human resource issues. This is summarized in the following:

> The intent is to provide an atmosphere where everyone feels that the company does not just belong to management, but that the company belongs to each and every team member. The philosophy is carried out to the extent that traditional management benefits such as an executive cafeteria, reserved parking and offices are not used. These items are viewed as barriers between management and labor.

The use of human resources alongside technology

We saw in Chapter 4 that the enlightened plants did not seek to replace human resources by purchasing technology. Indeed, they saw a strong skills base as a necessary precursor to process technological investment. In addition, other chapters have shown that in enlightened plants, workers at all levels were seen as a key input for new ideas on process and product development and quality improvements. Such a view was lacking in the traditional plants, who saw human resources as the most volatile and difficult area to manage. For these plants, human resources were an input, which, to a large degree, could be replaced by technology. Human resources in the traditional plants did not form part of the perceived core competence. In the enlightened plants, human resources were seen as a central means by which innovation and flexibility – two major required tenets of the current manufacturing era – could be met.

Chapter 4 showed how traditional plants struggled in their use of technology, as a means of coming to terms with the current era. In the same way, these plants, governed by a short-term mentality, tend to view human resources as a cost-cutting device, where downsizing can easily occur, rather than as a key source of transformation within the plant. For the Western enlightened plants, their approach matches the mentality of Japanese world-class practice.

The importance of senior manufacturing personnel in human resources

What became clear was that senior manufacturing personnel were central in helping to ensure close collaboration between workers and managers within the plants. There was far more openness and commitment in these enlightened plants than in their traditional counterparts; this manifested itself in areas such as the number of suggestions by employees, brought about by involvement in teamworking. Manufacturing strategy also played an important role here because areas such as training, skills audits and learning became the responsibility of senior manufacturing personnel both in terms of identifying needs and then creating operational plans to meet specific criteria contained within the manufacturing strategy.

Enlightened plants had senior manufacturing personnel in place, helping to guide the business and not just the technical aspects of the plant. One of their major inputs was in helping to choose strategic partners. This often involved contact and agreement with corporate levels of the firm but, in contrast to the traditional plants, manufacturing personnel were seen as a key input in helping to choose the right strategic partners – both vertical and horizontal.

The perceived importance of training

Traditional plants did spend money on training. The distinction between traditional and enlightened plants must therefore be seen in terms of degree, rather than kind, which was also the case in the use of teamwork. All of the Japanese transplants were clearly committed to training. One of the most striking insights into the importance of training within Japanese transplants was provided by a manufacturing manager who had formerly worked for one of the Big Three car makers in the USA:

> I used to work in Detroit . . . here [a different city] you would not think you were in the same country! I mean they spent millions of dollars on training before we even made the first car . . . $20,000 of training for every person before we made a car – that's something else, eh?

However, this enlightened plant did not see training as a one-off payment, but as an ongoing approach – an average of 4.1% of sales was spent each year. Part of this was to do with teamwork:

> We focus on the benefits of teamwork and provide employees with opportunities and resources that encourage team building . . . through the use of extensive internal training . . . we remain an organization that is continually learning and evolving.

Training takes place for all personnel at every rank within this enlightened plant.

There seem to be two major distinctions between traditional and enlightened approaches when it comes to training:

- *Seeing training as a cost (traditional), rather than an investment (enlightened)* – simply, Japanese companies, including Japanese transplants in the West, see training at all levels as an investment and not just cost, which has tended to be the Western approach.

- *Failure to train at all levels* – enlightened approaches see the need for company-wide training at all levels, including senior executives. On this point, one of the most startling of surveys on training undertaken by the Institute of Directors in the UK in 1994 revealed that more than 90% of UK directors had not been involved in any training or development activity since their appointment at director level.

The role of learning

The important feature of learning in the enlightened plants is that they took time to learn. Learning in the enlightened plants took place in at least the following areas:

- At senior levels in terms of the integrated approach, including manufacturing personnel, who together would make strategic, business decisions.

- In new product development where the traditional, sequential, function-to-function approach was replaced by the enlightened, cross-functional development process.

- Quality where learning by doing is central to continuous improvement in process and product quality – one of the key roles for quality circles is that what has been learned in one area is then transferred into other appropriate areas.

- In materials management where JIT management has been transferred to enlightened Western plants.

- In technological scanning in order to see what process and product developments could be exploited within the plant.

- In competitive analysis and benchmarking to learn from competitors' capabilities and determining if such capabilities would provide customer satisfaction and competitive advantage for the plant.

Conclusions

While it is too simplistic to be prescriptive about a 'one, best way' for human resources to be managed,[42] it is clear that Japanese human resources management in manufacturing has been seen as a benchmark for many firms in the West. Therefore, there is much that may form part of organizational learning for manufacturing firms in the West:

> If organizational principles and management are the root cause of competitiveness, then Japanese success is replicable. In fact various elements . . . such as TQC, JIT production and teamwork have been introduced outside Japan, either in transplants of

Japanese companies or by non-Japanese firms. Successful application . . . outside Japan tends to silence those who emphasize the cultural uniqueness behind Japanese production. The purely cultural view cannot explain the apparent success of Japanese subsidiaries in the United Kingdom and elsewhere.[43]

It is clear from seeing the enlightened plants that Japanese, world-class practice has been emulated in Western plants. But the temptation is to simply look at the evidence and data without paying attention to the background or supporting factors. What became clear was that the role of senior manufacturing personnel was vital; so, too, was manufacturing strategy, which saw human resources as an important factor. These two factors are absent from many publications on human resource management which, myopically, often concentrate on human resources without looking at the big picture.

The major differences between enlightened and traditional plants in managing human resources included the following:

- In enlightened plants, senior management involved themselves in determining the skills requirements of the plant which would be needed alongside, and in addition to, any investment in technology.

- Manufacturing strategies included action plans to ensure that ongoing training took place.

- Human resources in enlightened plants were seen as part of the plants' core competence – a competence that would need to be continuously updated and nurtured.

The transfer of Japanese practices to Western plants can only be realized if a strategic view of human resources is in place. This change of view is one of the greatest, and perhaps hardest, learning opportunities for many manufacturing firms. One of the lessons for firms is that the role of senior manufacturing personnel can be crucial in the transfer from Japanese practices to Western plants. Key issues include teamwork, worker empowerment, ongoing training and learning. These are the expression of a deeper, more imbedded mindset, however. Underpinning this is the belief that human resources are a major contributor to the core competence for the organization and human resources input are equally important as technology in managing the current era of chaos. For the enlightened plants, senior manufacturing were central in managing this change and commitment to training, learning and other issues discussed in this chapter were part of their managerial role.

This chapter has shown that the role of senior manufacturing personnel and the contribution of manufacturing strategies – which, among other areas, focused on training needs – were the major telling distinctions between enlightened and traditional approaches to human resource management within the plants.

NOTES AND REFERENCES

1. There is a large number of articles on this. See, for example: Prahalad, C.K. (1983) 'Developing strategic capability: An agenda for top management', *Human Resource Management*, **22**; Pfeffer, J. (1994) *Competitive Advantage Through People*. Harvard Business School Press, Boston, USA; Wright, P.M., McMahan, G.C. and McWilliams, A. (1994) 'Human resources and sustained competitive advantage: A resource-based perspective', *International Journal of Human Resources Management*, **5**: 301–326; Arthur, J.B. (1994) 'Effects of human resource systems on manufacturing performance and turnover', *Academy of Management Journal*, **37**: 670–687; MacDuffie, J.P. (1995) 'Human resource bundles and manufacturing performance: Organizational logic and flexible production systems in the world auto industry', *Industrial and Labor Relations Review*, **48**: 197–221; Youndt, M., Snell, S., Dean, J. and Lepak, D. (1996) 'Human resource management, manufacturing strategy, and firm performance', *Academy of Management Journal*, **39**(4): 836.

2. *The Economist*, September 28, 1996.

3. Drucker, P.F. (1978) *The Age of Discontinuity*. Harper & Row, New York.

4. Grindley, P. (1991) 'Turning Technology Into Competitive Advantage', *Business Strategy Review*, Spring: 35–47.

5. *Fortune*, June 21, 1999.

6. Ibid.

7. *Fortune*, April 14, 1997, **135**(7): 68.

8. Ibid.

9. *Business Week*, October 3, 1994, p. 66.

10. Deming, W. (1986) *Out of the Crisis*. MIT Center for Advanced Engineering, Cambridge, MA, USA.

11. Scott, A., Snell, M., Dean, J.W. Jr. and Lepak, D.P. 'Human Resource Management, Manufacturing Strategy, And Firm Performance', Special Research Forum: *Human Resource Management and Organizational Performance*.

12. See, for example, Argenti, J. (1980) *Practical Corporate Planning*. Unwin, London; Adair, J. (1983) *Effective Leadership*. Pan Books, London; Quinn, J.B. (1980) 'Managing Strategic Change', *Sloan Management Review*, Summer: 3–20.

13. See, for example, Wheelwright, S. and Clark, K. (1992) *Revolutionizing Product Development*. Free Press, New York.

14. *Industry Week*, June 8, 1998, **247**(11): 22.

15. See, for example: Lamming, R. (1993) *Beyond Partnership*. Prentice Hall, Hemel Hempstead, UK.

16. Examples of excellent insight into how human resources are affected by change include: Kanter, R. (1989) *When Giants Learn to Dance*. Touchstone – Simon & Schuster, New York; Kanter, R. (1989) 'Swimming in New Streams: Mastering Innovation Dilemmas', *California Management Review*, Summer: 45–69; Kenney, M. and Florida, R. (1993) *Beyond Mass Production*. Oxford University Press, New York.

17. Gowen, C. and Pecenka, J. (1992) 'Impact of Technological Leadership on American and Japanese Turnaround Strategies', *The Journal of High Technology Management Research*, **3**(2): 263–287.

18. *Ward's Automotive Yearbook*, July 1999.

19. Adler, P. (1993) 'Time and Motion Regained', *Harvard Business Review*, January–February.

20. Keller, M. (1993) *Collision*. Currency Doubleday, New York.

21. Hamel, G. and Prahalad, C. (1994) *Competing For The Future*. Harvard Business School Press, Boston, USA.

22. *Business Week*, May 9, 1994.

23. *Fortune*, November 10, 1997, **136**(9): 28.
24. *The Economist*, December 21, 1996.
25. *The Economist*, July 2, 1994.
26. Keller, M. (1993) *Collision*. Currency Doubleday, New York.
27. *Fortune*, October 17, 1994.
28. *The Economist*, August 1, 1998.
29. *Financial Times*, June 14, 1999.
30. Dertouzos, M., Lester, R. and Solow, R. (1989) *Made In America*. MIT Press, Cambridge, USA. See also Leonard, R. (1996) 'Reengineering: the missing links', *Human Resource Planning*, **19**(4): 40.
31. *Financial Times*, April 13, 1995.
32. *The Economist*, March 30, 1996.
33. Ibid.
34. Scarbrough, H. (1998) 'The unmaking of management? Change and continuity of British management in the 1990s', *Human Relations*, **51**(6): 691.
35. Peters, T. (1986) 'The World Turned Upside Down', *The Business of Excellence*, Thames TV, London.
36. *The Economist*, October 28, 1995.
37. Greco, J. (1998) 'America's changing workforce', *Journal of Business Strategy*, **19**(2): 43.
38. *Industry Week*, August 17, 1998.
39. Garvin, D. (1993) 'Building a Learning Organization', *Harvard Business Review*, July–August: 78–91.
40. Ibid.
41. A discussion on the meaning and application of strategic stretch is given in Hamel, G. and Prahalad, C. (1994) *Competing For The Future*. Harvard Business School Press, Boston, USA.
42. I am not trying to describe a one-best way on how to manage human resources; what I am doing is reporting on how enlightened plants managed human resources in comparison to their traditional counterparts. There is interesting recent material on human resource management, including the following: Blyton, P. and Turnbull, P. (1992) *Reassessing Human Resource Management*; Thompson, P. and Warhurst, C. (1998) *Workplaces of the Future*, Macmillan. Basingstoke; Felstead, A. and Jewson, N. (1999) *Global Trends in Flexible Labour*. Macmillan, Basingstoke.
43. Sengenberger, W. (1993) 'Lean Production – The Way of Working and Producing in the Future?' in *Lean Production and Beyond*, International Labour Office, Geneva.

8

Becoming enlightened – creating and sustaining strategic resonance

Introduction

Plants do not fail to become enlightened because they are stupid or totally inept. They fail because they are stuck and cannot move or progress. They are stuck, essentially, in the past approach of mass production, which although totally appropriate, and hugely successful, for its time is now a casualty of global competition – with its array of world-class manufacturing firms. The key issue with plants – and indeed whole firms – is that the strategy-making process is stuck in an old, top-down hierarchical approach which, as we saw in Chapter 1, is almost designed to fail.

This book has shown how enlightened plants outperformed their traditional rivals in a range of operations capabilities. The information for the book was gained deliberately from large manufacturing firms in the auto and computer industries (the reasons for choosing these industries were given in Chapter 2). But the motive for this book was not simply to report on these industries only. This chapter will show that *any* firm – large or small – can become enlightened. More to the point, all manufacturing plants – including plants within large firms, strategic business units (SBUs), containing manufacturing plants, and small manufacturing firms – will have to become enlightened if they are to stand any chance of competing against other manufacturers who are also becoming enlightened. The need to become an enlightened plant within a large firm, or in the case of small companies an enlightened enterprise, is vital for all manufacturing firms, in any industry, who want to compete successfully in the future. The key issue is that in order to perform to the level of enlightened plants, the firm must first radically change its approach to forming and operationalizing strategy. It has to do this in order to create strategic resonance. Although it is naïve to say that there is no difference between large multi-national manufacturing giants and small enterprises, there are at least similarities. Both large and small firms often suffer from an inability to create and sustain strategic resonance. This is due to the fact that even in a small firm, the operational capabilities (and incapabilities) may be ignored or – even worse – not known. The person who founded an SME may now be out of touch with how operations are performing within the firm and may be concentrating, instead, on financial aspects of the company. Thus the conflict between financial and operational goals are as evident in a small owner-managed firm as they are in a large company – in which managers will be given financial targets, including profitability and returns for shareholders. The very things that stifle traditional plants, and the factors that enable enlightened plants to perform to such exceptional levels, are found not only within large multi-national firms but also in small manufacturing enterprises. The key to becoming enlightened is in the inability to create and sustain strategic resonance, and small firms will encounter difficulties in doing this just as large firms do. CEOs of the future will be judged on their ability to create and sustain strategic resonance within their firms. This calls for the very best managerial skills because strategic resonance includes a range of both internal and external requirements. The CEO has to ensure that, internally, business goals and operations capabilities (or competences) resonate; at the same time, the CEO has to ensure that the firm's internal alignment and consistency between business goals and operations capabilities are in line, and resonate, with market requirements.

So this chapter will describe how a plant can become enlightened. First, let us remind ourselves of the characteristics and competencies of the enlightened plants.

Characteristics of enlightened plants

All enlightened plants have manufacturing personnel in place at senior levels of management. Some traditional plants also have senior-level manufacturing personnel (though the majority do not), so we can say that this senior-level presence is a necessary, but not sufficient, condition to becoming enlightened. This senior-level presence is vital, but is missing in many firms who then struggle to translate business goals into customer-focused capabilities within their operations.

The role of these senior manufacturing personnel distinguishes enlightened from the traditional plants. In the enlightened plants, senior manufacturing personnel are actively involved in the business strategy planning process, and are not employed purely as technical specialists – as was the case in the traditional plants. Enlightened plants have plant-specific manufacturing strategies that support the business. The scope and range of content in the manufacturing strategy is vital and must include at least the following:

- **Human resources** – to ensure that the workforce knows what customer requirements are. The workforce is skilled, trained and motivated, often enhanced by introducing remuneration packages that reward quality of output, not just hours spent at work. Seeing human resources as a major, strategic contributor is vital. As we saw in Chapter 7, enlightened plants have this view whereas traditional plants tend to see human resources as 'disposable' – for them human resources can be downsized, and training will often be the first casualty of any cutbacks in budgets.

- **Technology management** – to acquire and understand process technology that will provide vital leverage for the plant; to avoid excessive purchase of technology for its own sake (the technophilia problem that we saw in Chapter 4); and to make sure that the workforce understands and utilizes the process technology.

- **Quality** – implementing quality standards so that process and product quality are understood by all. Training is critical in ensuring that tools such as SPC, Ishikawa (cause and effect) diagrams, and ongoing commitment to improvement takes place. The temptation – which traditional plants fell into – was to associate quality with accreditation to ISO 9000 only. For enlightened plants, quality went way beyond such accreditation to an ongoing pursuit of satisfying customers, as part of seeking and maintaining strategic resonance.

- **Flexibility** – this means that the workforce can create a range of volumes and variety for customers. Process technology underpins this but human resources complement this investment. Layout, cell manufacture and excellent systems are necessary requirements here.

- **Innovation** – this becomes part of the everyday kaizen developments in processes, as well as in breakthrough design. In other words, innovation becomes a way of life.

- **Inventory** – this includes forming and sustaining strategic partnerships with suppliers, and ensuring that in-house inventory systems are in place to expertly monitor and control inventory.

These manufacturing strategies feed into, and form part of, the overall business strategy and, just as important, there is cohesion in timing between manufacturing and business strategies.

A major distinction between enlightened and traditional plants is in the process of formulating strategies: in the enlightened plants, a collaborative, holistic, cross-functional approach took place at senior levels. The process was much more fluid and dynamic in the enlightened plants than in the traditional divisions, where an elitist group tended to dominate the strategy process and where the approach was much more top-down than collaborative in style.

The planning approach in enlightened plants was much more strategic in intent and scope than in their traditional counterparts. By this, we mean that immediate cost-cutting dominated in traditional plants and became the rationale behind, and justification for, areas that might be seen as strategic – in particular investment in technology. Thus for traditional plants, quality was seen as a means of cost-cutting in processes, and JIT was seen as a means to cut costs in inventory. In the enlightened plants, cost was one of a range of competitive variables. Flexibility, quality (in terms of meeting customer needs) and innovation were vital areas for the enlightened plants, and these were seen as long-term, ongoing commitments – in fact part of the culture of the enlightened plant.

Competencies of enlightened plants

Thus far, we have looked at the characteristics of the enlightened plants in terms of the strategic process. The key question of this book, however, was to ask if being enlightened made any difference to subsequent manufacturing performance. As we have seen in previous chapters, being enlightened in the way of forming strategy *does* make a difference to subsequent operations performance. As well as the actual individual performance indicators given in the previous chapters, there are several major points concerning the enlightened plants to note. First, the abilities of the enlightened plants are accumulative. Having learned expertise in one area of operations, this becomes part of the overall capability alongside other manufacturing capabilities within a particular plant. Enlightened plants excelled over traditional plants in the following areas:

- They had better process and product quality.
- They innovated more quickly and more successfully in new product introductions.

197

- They successfully managed process technology – which is a notoriously difficult area to manage. They did so without being technologically myopic; in particular, they recognized that technology was not simply a replacement for human resources. Process technology was adopted to meet market requirements.

- Their expertise in inventory management resulted in fewer hours of bought-in components, work-in-process and finished stock levels; just as important was that they managed the relationships with suppliers as a mutually beneficial strategic partnership. Suppliers in enlightened plants were instrumental in the design and development process of new products; traditional plants struggled with this because suppliers were constantly faced with costs pressures from traditional plants and this made them reluctant to be involved in new product developments.

Second, enlightened plants perform these abilities simultaneously – there was no notion of trade-offs for enlightened plants: all of the enlightened plants scored better than their traditional rivals in all areas. Once these abilities have been accumulated in the first place they become part of a set of simultaneous capabilities. Enlightened plants simultaneously provided low cost, delivery speed and reliability of existing products as well as rapid innovation of new products.

Becoming enlightened

Enlightened means that an entire firm (or a plant within a firm in the case of large enterprises) creates strategic resonance. We saw in Chapter 1 that a firm needs to avoid strategic dissonance. Strategic dissonance comes from an imbalance between market requirements and in-house capabilities. There is a danger in that the firm will chase after markets in which it has no chance of winning business (an imbalance pursuing a market-driven strategy). On the other hand, a firm might be resource-driven, believing that it has core competencies – and the danger with this is that it can excel in the wrong things.

The strategic, focused, holistic approach

The underpinning feature to strategic resonance is the strategic, focused, holistic approach. We saw how important this is in Chapter 1. It is vitally important and we need to remind ourselves of its pivotal contribution here. This underpinning approach to becoming enlightened is that the strategic, focused, and holistic stance is at the very centre of, and drives, the firm's strategic-making process, as shown in Figure 8.1.

Figure 8.1   The strategic, focused and holistic model

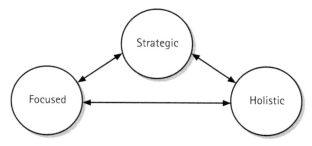

This three-pronged approach is designed to ensure balance. First, the firm really does need to be strategic in its intent, which means it makes decisions that are:

- Made by cross-functional (rather than functionally myopically biased) senior level staff.

- Aimed at creating and maintaining competitive advantage.

- Simultaneously long term and short term in impact. Strategic decisions are long term, but they also need to have a sense of urgency for implementation. Enlightened firms are those that see strategic planning and implementation as simultaneously long term in vision and short term in application and implementation.

The firm needs to be focusing constantly. By this we mean that the firm's business focus process:

- Decides those business activities in which the firm will, and will not, be involved. The temptation for manufacturing firms is to abuse the strategic power of business focus. They do so by hurriedly selling off manufacturing activities to others in the name of focus and 'core competences'. In doing so, though, the firm will often rob itself of key linkages between innovation and volume production. Moreover, powerful, tacit knowledge can be lost within the firm. Also, these divestment decisions are almost impossible to reverse: it is easy to sell off manufacturing divisions; it is almost impossible to buy back the know-how and expertise which has been sold.

- Focuses operations activities in terms of products, processes, and types of customers. In doing so, the plant becomes both focused and flexble. It is a vast change from the past approaches of mass production. Focus is one of the major strengths of enlightened plants.

The holistic approach is vital in ensuring:

- That the firm looks at complete markets – this will help when deciding which segments are attractive and which the firm should not be competing in. Deciding not to compete in a particular segment is not a weakness; instead it is a necessary linkage to business focus and will prevent the firm from competing in segments in which it cannot satisfy market requirements.

- That the firm engages in strategic partnerships and manages the relationship with these other partners. In doing so, the firm will see itself as part of a strategic architecture.[1]

The strategic, focused and holistic model is a powerful approach in ensuring that a balanced strategy process is in place. Once this approach is at the core of the firm's strategy process, the enlightened approach begins to take shape. The next, vital factor is in ensuring that internal and external resonance comes into play, as we shall now see.

Internal and external resonance

The first – and sometimes most difficult – stage in becoming enlightened is to create internal resonance. This is often a major challenge because it demands an integrated approach across all functions. This is difficult in both small and large firms, where men and women will seek to safeguard their territories or specific functions within the firm. Getting cross-functional agreement is made extremely difficult in those firms that are arranged by functional groupings – e.g. where the sales division is located many miles away from the manufacturing division. Sometimes a firm will need to reconfigure itself into multi-functional units. We have seen how giants like IBM and Hewlett-Packard have had to do this; many other firms have done so in order to avoid functional myopia within their firms.

Many functional clashes and problems can come to light but the typical conflict is between marketing and operations staff – and trying to get them to agree on a common agenda can be problematic. What can drive this, though, is for both functions to focus on the business and not just their functional involvement within the business. A common dialogue needs to take place so that manufacturing and marketing strategies can resonate, as illustrated in Figure 8.2.

The process of strategic resonance

Although we can think of the process of creating strategic resonance developing over stages, these stages are not mutually exclusive and can take

Figure 8.2   Creating dialogue within manufacturing and marketing strategies

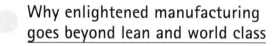

place simultaneously. In fact the stages will, over time, feed into each other. These stages are illustrated in Figure 8.3.

Why enlightened manufacturing goes beyond lean and world class

In the introduction to this book, I stated that it is not the book's intention to score points over those who advocate lean or world-class approaches to manufacturing. It is clear that the operations capabilities within enlightened plants are similar to those in lean and world-class firms. Wanting to be faster, leaner and more responsive in all operations – which are traits of lean and world-class aspirations – are perfectly good and valid aims. The problem, though, for any would-be world-class or lean plant is that there are often no strategic, underpinning factors in place. For example, I have seen numerous cases of plants that had no manufacturing strategies in place to enable the plant to be lean or world class. Executives think that it is a good idea for the plant to be lean, agile, world-class and flexible – and a whole host of other terms. But often these executives have no idea how these capabilities will be put in place. In other words, they have no real grasp of manufacturing strategy – its scope, purpose and content. Lean is not, by itself, a manufacturing strategy – lean is the ability to achieve a range of capabilities, which can be measured against other, non-lean plants. These measurements will include space utilization, process times, inventory usage etc. The essence of lean is to attack waste in all forms, and waste includes all operations that do not add value. A similar approach has

Figure 8.3 The process of creating strategic resonance

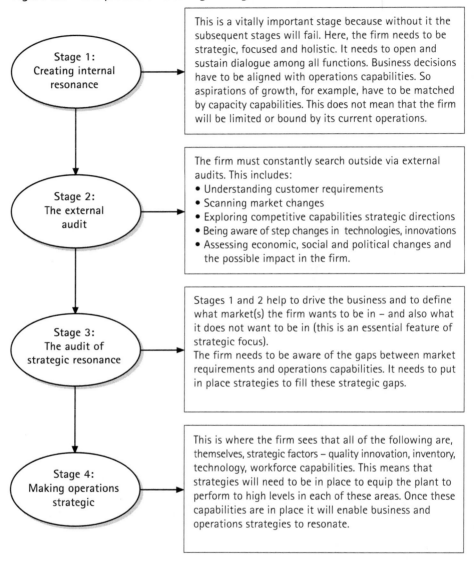

been stated by Richard Schonberger in his important book, *World Class Manufacturing*.[2] 'Lean' includes all of the following:

- Integrated production, with low inventories throughout, using JIT management.

- Emphasis on prevention, rather than detection in quality.

- Production is pulled in response to customers, rather than pushed to suit machine loading or other in-house ideas of scheduling.

- Work is organized in teams, using multi-skilled workforce problem solving to eliminate all non-added value.

- Close vertical relationships, integrating the complete supply chain from raw material to customer.

These are vital requirements, and are included in enlightened manufacturing, but I have seen numerous cases of plants within firms struggling to become lean because they do not have strategies in place which underpin enlightened approaches. These strategies are:

- Senior-level manufacturing personnel who are involved in helping to shape the business of the firm, and are not employed purely for their technical expertise.

- Plant-specific manufacturing strategies that focus on key operations – quality, cost, innovation, inventory, delivery speed and reliability, process technology, and a range of capabilities in human resources.

The original book on lean, *The Machine That Changed the World* [3] published in 1990, boldly asserted that lean production would pervade all types of manufacturing:

> . . . the adoption of lean production, as it inevitably spreads beyond the auto industry, will change everything in almost every industry – choices for consumers, the nature of work, the fortune of companies, and, ultimately, the fate of nations.

But a decade later this prophecy has not been fulfilled. That is not to say that companies should not aspire to become lean. But the point is they often do not have the strategic factors in place that will enable them to do so. Being lean in terms of manufacturing processes may be necessary in many ways, if a firm wants to compete in global markets but it is not sufficient. While there have been a plethora of excellent publications on lean manufacturing they all still fail to address the key points that need to be in place if strategic resonance is to be in place. Firms need to think *beyond lean* – the operational capabilities of enlightened plants described in this book owe everything to a completely different, strategically minded approach which is alien to many Western plants.

The contribution of the manufacturing function to business strategy

The explicit role of the manufacturing function is largely ignored in terms of its contribution (at any stage) to corporate or business planning. For the enlightened plants, this involvement was critical and contributed to the subsequent manufacturing performance – a sense of ownership of strategy was felt within enlightened plants.

Manufacturing strategy

Many publications on lean assume that lean is a manufacturing strategy – it is not. Plants need a plant-specific – and comprehensive – manufacturing strategy – in the enlightened plants this was vital.

Senior-level manufacturing personnel

Lean and world-class publications forget a critical component of Japanese manufacturing firms. These firms have senior-level manufacturing personnel who help set the agenda for both internal and external strategic factors such as:

- the nature, scope and extent of horizontal strategic alliances;
- strategic partnerships with suppliers;
- commitment to training; and
- quality capability.

We must ask a major question, though: 'Why is the role of senior manufacturing personnel so important?' The answer to this is at least three-fold. First, manufacturing personnel are charged with the responsibility of managing the greatest amount of assets within the plant, including machinery (fixed assets) and materials (current assets). In terms of costs alone, therefore, the task is daunting and the weight of responsibility is considerable.

Second, more important than management of assets is the contribution that senior-level manufacturing personnel can bring to the overall business. In that sense, inventory, machinery and technology are far more than financial assets – they are, instead, major features of the firm's or plant's competitive capability.

Third, senior manufacturing's involvement in the running of the business, rather than just technology, is important because:

- there is a sense of ownership and commitment from senior manufacturing personnel who will be charged with meeting requirements of quality, delivery speed and reliability and flexibility; and
- this involvement helps to focus the broader business overview (in which senior manufacturing personnel have input) into time-specific action plans at operational levels.

This also creates a sense of urgency for implementation. Manufacturing strategies become the key means of bridging the gap between business and operational plans enabling strategy to be realized and implemented at plant level. An example comes, not surprisingly perhaps, from Toyota. When, in 1998, Toyota opened two, all-new manufacturing sites in Buffalo, West Virginia, and Princeton, Indiana, enabling the firm to produce over 960,000 vehicles in North America, it did so with senior-level manufacturing personnel being central in the process. The business strategy – growth – was matched by an element of manufacturing strategy-capacity. In other words, strategic resonance has occurred within Toyota.

A final note on strategic partnerships

In Chapter 1, we saw that the idea of strategy includes forming alliances with other players. This will continue to be the case as globalization becomes more prominent because no firm can afford to go it alone. Being enlightened will be a requirement to be considered as a would-be partner in many industries in the future. But the ability to form and sustain alliances is vital. There have been a number of examples – of which the Rover–Honda alliance is a prime example – where a firm claims to be lean (and might even be so), but because of the lack of strategic importance given to the alliance, the relationship between partners then becomes irretrievably damaged. In March 2000, BMW announced it would sell off Rover. As a result, all of the learning that Rover gained from its former alliance with Honda came to nothing. Rover's claim to be a lean player was not enough. The strategic intent of the parent company destroyed any possible hope of strategic resonance with Rover cars. What lay before Rover was the prospect of thousands of job losses within its plants as well as the destruction of any strategic buyer–supplier relationships that Rover had formed with its suppliers.

Conclusions

In Chapter 1, we stated that 'strategy matters'. It is mentioned again here deliberately: the fact is that strategy does matter. And how it is formed and implemented is a key distinguishing factor between enlightened and traditional approaches. For the traditional plants, strategic planning, if it exists at all, concerns itself with survival by reducing costs, both in-house and in how it manages its external businesses, especially suppliers. For the enlightened plants, a radically different approach is apparent: a longer-term view pervades here and strategic efforts are made to ensure that the plant at least deals with intense competition, rapid change and continuous innovation.

It is important to note again that the term 'enlightened' is not a substitute for either 'lean' or 'world class' manufacturing. The former has been critiqued in this chapter because it deals with operational capabilities without addressing the reasons behind these capabilities and fails to deal with other strategic issues that I have mentioned. It is important to note that world class no longer means being better than a competitor; it means just being able to compete in global markets, as Harvard's Hayes and Pisano ask, 'How can a company expect to achieve any sort of competitive advantage if its only goal is to be "as good as" its toughest competitors?'[4]

Enlightened plants greatly out-perform their traditional rivals in all areas of manufacturing. This ability depends on having senior manufacturing involvement in business decisions, allied to explicit manufacturing strategies – the key areas explored throughout this book. In 1996, I wrote:

> Changing this approach is perhaps the biggest challenge for many manufacturing firms. It is clear from the decline in performance of many Western manufacturing firms that a massive change has to take place in terms of both philosophy and practice. The outcome of this challenge may yet determine the future prosperity of entire nations.[5]

The need to become enlightened through creating and sustaining strategic resonance is greater now than it was even a few years ago. Such is the rate of competitive change – it is one in which enlightened plants and entire firms will flourish, and also one in which traditional ones will not.

NOTES AND REFERENCES

1. This term is used in slightly different ways by Kay, J. (1993) *Foundations of Corporate Success*. Oxford University Press, Oxford, and Hamel, G. and Prahalad, C. (1994) *Competing For The Future*, Harvard Business School Press, Boston, USA.
2. Schonberger, R. (1986) *World Class Manufacturing*. Free Press, New York.
3. Womack, J., Jones, D. and Roos, D. (1990) *The Machine That Changed the World*. Rawson Associates, New York. A more recent treatment on lean manufacturing is given in Henderson, B. and Larco, J.L. (1999) *Lean Transformation*. Oaklee Press, Virginia.
4. Hayes, R. and Pisano, G. (1994) 'Beyond World-Class: The New Manufacturing Strategy', *Harvard Business Review*, January–February: 77–86.
5. Brown, S. (1996) *Strategic Manufacturing for Competitive Advantage*. Prentice Hall, Hemel Hempstead, UK.

Index